THE
DYING GAME

Melanie King studied at the Universities of Sussex and Oxford, and is now a full-time writer. She lives in Oxford, England with her husband, the writer Ross King.

'Who knew reading about death could be so much fun? From corpse medicines to ancient forensic science and Buddhist monks who embalm themselves, Melanie King offers a feast of fresh insights into the fascinating, gruesome, and ingenious ways that humans have dealt with death throughout history.'

Beth Conklin, author of *Consuming Grief:*
Compassionate Cannibalism in an Amazonian Society

'Melanie King has succeeded in making a grim subject a very good read.'

Ann Granger, bestselling crime author.

'It's all here, from plastinated bodies in museums to desperate grabs at immortality, and all told with the kind of dry champagne wit that such a topic needs but seldom finds. What I consider most impressive is King's ability to remain very much in charge of such a compelling, outrageous narrative.'

Michael Sims, author of *Adam's Navel:*
A Natural and Cultural History of the Human Body and *Apollo's Fire:*
A Day on Earth in Nature and Imagination

THE DYING GAME

A Curious History of Death

Melanie King

ONEWORLD

OXFORD

A Oneworld Paperback Original

Published by Oneworld Publications 2008

Copyright © Melanie King 2008

ISBN 978–1–85168–592–9

Typeset by Jayvee, Trivandrum, India
Cover design by James Nunn
Printed and bound in Great Britain by
TJ International Ltd, Padstow

Oneworld Publications
185 Banbury Road
Oxford OX2 7AR
England
www.oneworld-publications.com

Learn more about Oneworld. Join our mailing list to
find out about our latest titles and special offers at:

www.oneworld-publications.com

CONTENTS

ACKNOWLEDGEMENTS

So many people offered me information or assistance. All deserve a thank you, but the following people in particular warrant a special mention: my agent Heather Holden-Brown and her team, James Pryor and Elly James, for their faith in this project. A special thanks also goes to my editor, Kate Kirkpatrick, for her enthusiastic support, and to Juliet Mabey and Fiona Slater.

I would like to thank my dear friend Sue Adams for reading through the first draft and offering useful suggestions, and Len Kehoe for always being at the end of the phone when my computer threw a wobbly. For their help, I am also grateful to the following people: Dr David McFadyen, Steve Bradshaw, Dr Josephine Reynell, Hazel Hobbs, Neil Gregson, Russell Ash, Julian Atkinson, Ella Poppitt, Philip Pullman, Kerry Sharpe, Dan Leon, Peter Mitchell and Sally Woodcock.

I would also like to thank my husband Ross for his continuous love and support, without which *The Dying Game* would never have come to life.

INTRODUCTION

Alternative Endings

In the middle of the seventeenth century a German named Johann Schroeder published a book giving the recipe for a medicine. His recipe called for: ' the cadaver of a reddish man . . . whole, fresh, without blemish, of around twenty-four years of age, dead of a violent death (not of illness), exposed to the moon's rays for one day and night, but with a clear sky. Cut the muscular flesh of this man and sprinkle it with powder of myrrh and at least a little bit of aloe, then soak it, making it tender, finally hanging the pieces in a very dry and shady place until they dry out. Then it comes to resemble smoke-cured meat, without any stench.'[1]

Schroeder was no ordinary cannibal: a respectable pharmacologist, he was the first man to recognize that arsenic was an element. There is no evidence that he himself actually tested out his recipe for 'cadaver of a reddish man', but many Europeans of his day regularly consumed medicines made from human body parts: powdered human skull was seen as particularly effective in cases of epilepsy, and ground-up Egyptian mummies were eaten in their thousands as remedies against numerous ailments, from skin diseases to liver complaints. Even a sceptic who deplored this 'barbarous inhumanity', the great French surgeon Ambroise Paré (1510–90), admitted that he had tried mummy 'an hundred times'.[2]

The fate experienced by these mummies or proposed by Schroeder for any ruddy-complexioned twenty-four-year-old who had died a violent death indicates how dead bodies can end up serving the most unusual purposes. The Bible is adamant about what becomes of the body after death: 'The death of man and of beasts is one, and the condition of them both is equal: as man dieth, so they also die . . . And all things go to one place: of earth they were made, and into earth they return together' (Ecclesiastes 3:19–20). But it is not always ashes to ashes and dust to dust as far as the dead body is concerned. There are in fact many other alternatives, from the self-embalmed Japanese monks who have become objects of intense religious veneration, to the preserved corpses of notorious outlaws and Native Americans that went on tour as nineteenth-century side-show exhibits or found their way into the collections of famous museums, to the Amazonian tribesmen whose bodies were consumed out of respect by their grieving in-laws.

Mark Twain famously described death as 'a great Leveler',[3] but death is no democrat, and not everyone experiences it in the same way. Our deaths are in fact as unique – and as dependent on our personalities and cultures – as our lives. We have certain brute, biological matters in common, such as the way our outer shells destroy themselves with the help of microbes, bacteria and insects (though even that, as Chapter 9 shows, is dependent on any number of variables). Beyond that, however, a rich and diverse set of practices emerges. Death is only the beginning of a series of biological events, cultural practices, legal opinions and, increasingly, high-tech scientific investigations. Even the definition of death is dependent on cultural and medical attitudes. Since the 1960s, death has been 'reinvented' as the success of resuscitation techniques such as cardiopulmonary resuscitation (CPR) and defibrillation raised the question of when a body was truly dead and forced the legal and medical authorities to revise their definitions of what exactly constituted a dead body.

Death is deeply embedded in our culture, lending itself, as we shall see, to dozens of fears and superstitions. In previous centuries, those contemplating the fate of their mortal remains expected or feared – often with good reason – such unpleasant eventualities as premature burial, body-snatching or the unwelcome attentions of the anatomist's scalpel. Even in an age of advanced technology, robust laws and supposedly strong ethical views, these anxieties and obsessions are still very much with us. Scare stories of premature burials still exist to the extent that today some people will stipulate that they must be buried with a fully-charged mobile phone in order to make that all-important call should they wake up while six feet under. Nor are we free from fears of bodysnatchers: newspaper exposés have catalogued the cases of the modern-day bodysnatchers – medical researchers, employees of biomedical tissue companies, avant-garde artists and sexual deviants – who have taken or used bodies or body parts without the consent of the owners.

These stolen corpses are the black market in what has become a large and flourishing death industry. The funeral business alone is worth more than £1 billion annually in the UK, where 600,000 people die each year.[4] In the United States, where the yearly death toll is 2.4 million, the industry employs more than 100,000 individuals and generates $11 billion a year in revenue.[5] Upon our bodily extinction depend not only casketmakers, florists, manufacturers of embalming fluid, cemetery associations, insurance agencies, grief counsellors and crematoria – of which there are some two hundred in England and almost two thousand in the United States – but also things such as charter boats that ferry cremated remains out to sea for scattering by relatives and biomed companies that harvest body parts for the multibillion-dollar human tissue industry. Over the years the industry has drawn in such creative stars as Frank Lloyd Wright, who designed the Blue Sky Mausoleum in Buffalo, New York, and Britain's Poet Laureate, Andrew Motion, who in 2003 produced a booklet entitled *Well Chosen Words: How to Write a Eulogy.*

Death is often called the 'last taboo', but far from being a prohibited subject, it is actually one of our greatest obsessions. The media show an appetite for gruesome facts collected by scientists for criminal evidence, as well as for the ethical issues involved in euthanasia, organ donation and 'transhumanism' – the prospect of conquering death and (as Chapter 10 discusses) creating, by means of nanotechnology and genetic engineering, a race of immortal 'posthumans'. People may feed their morbid curiosity about this 'taboo' subject by means of numerous websites, such as deadoraliveinfo.com, findadeath.com and findagrave.com, the latter of which is visited by more than 100,000 people each day. The death certificates of everyone from Ruth Ellis – the last woman hanged in Britain – to John F. Kennedy, Jr, can now be viewed on-line, and the whereabouts of the ashes of dead celebrities discovered. Death also features on many tourist trails. Cemeteries in London such as Kensal Green and Highgate have regular open days, offering guided tours of their catacombs and graves, and companies in Los Angeles, such as 'Dearly Departed Tours', ferry rubbernecking and camera-clutching tourists past the sites of famous Hollywood murders, suicides and drug overdoses: the modern equivalents of pilgrimages to the shrines of venerated saints.

On his deathbed, Somerset Maugham told his nephew: 'Dying is a very dull, dreary affair. And my advice to you is to have nothing whatever to do with it.'[6] Death may be difficult to avoid; but it is not always dull and dreary. As we shall see, it negotiates the realms of ethics, economics, religion, the law, entertainment and technology. Dying, like living, can often prove quite an adventure.

CHAPTER 1

An Early Grave

Premature Burial and Its Prevention

In the summer of 2005, an 'art-technology-philosophy group' called Monochrom – an avant-garde Austrian collective that once manufactured and ate a black pudding made from their own blood – offered the people of San Francisco an unnerving experience: that of being buried alive. 'The people present,' the group's website excitedly proclaimed, 'will have an opportunity to be buried alive in a coffin for fifteen minutes.'

This announcement proved to be no hoax. Members of the group arranged for a lorry to deposit a skip filled with ten tons of soil on the kerb outside an art gallery in downtown San Francisco. A pit was then excavated in the dirt and, to the astonishment of onlookers, a pine coffin partially interred. Intrepid members of the public (of whom there seems to have been no shortage) were then given the opportunity of clambering into the coffin and having its lid screwed down – though not before signing a waiver that explained how they were to be covered with two feet of dirt in a wooden box with no ventilation and 'no easy means of escape'. The dirt was duly shovelled over the coffin by the black-clad, dark sunglasses-wearing *artistes*, who then planted a wooden cross at its head. After the regulation fifteen minutes, the participants were exhumed and presented – amid much snapping of cameras and whirring of camcorders – with certificates vouching for their ordeals.

'The fear of being buried alive is one of our most primal fears,' Monochrom's website states. 'The mere thought gives us the creeps and makes our heart beat faster. We find reports about people awaking on their alleged deathbed even in classical antiquity. There's more than one text testifying that some poor fellow came back to life right on their cremation table and could not be spared the gruesome fate of being burnt alive.'[7]

Live burials are indeed the stuff of legend. If we believe many of the bloodcurdling tales, taphephobia (the fear of being buried alive) was, in earlier centuries at least, not an entirely unreasonable condition. Cases among the ancient Romans were recorded by Pliny the Elder in his *Natural History*, written in 77 CE, and Shakespeare even used a premature burial at sea as a plot device in *Pericles: Prince of Tyre*. However, it was in the eighteenth and – especially – the nineteenth century that taphephobia truly came into its own. The new science of statistics, the Victorian cult of death, sensationalizing newspapers hoping to shift copies, the difficulty of making accurate diagnoses of death, a short story by Edgar Allan Poe entitled 'The Premature Burial' – all conspired to frighten the public witless in both Europe and America.

Certainly the statistics were not reassuring to those contemplating their fate in the family vault. The Revd J.G. Ouseley in his 1895 pamphlet *Earth to Earth Burial* estimated that at least 2,700 persons in England and Wales 'are yearly consigned to a living death, the most horrible conceivable'. These alarming statistics were reiterated in the same year by an American, Colonel Edward P. Vollum, along with William Tebb, an English activist against premature burial. In their book, matter-of-factly entitled *Premature Burial and How It Can Be Prevented*, they listed 161 cases of premature burial in the UK, as well as – equally disconcerting – 219 narrow escapes, ten premature dissections and two embalmings that commenced before consciousness unexpectedly returned to the body on the table. As a member of the Medical Department of the United States Army, Colonel Vollum was so concerned about premature burial that he recommended all American soldiers who fell in battle be buried with some chloroform so if they were to awaken they could hastily despatch themselves. He went on to estimate that one person in every thousand is buried alive.

On the other side of the pond, it was a Bavarian immigrant named Franz Hartmann who tapped into the American public's fear of premature burial. As with Europe, by the late nineteenth century the American newspapers were full of so-called 'true' stories of people being buried alive. In his book *Buried Alive*, also published in 1895, Hartmann enumerated over seven hundred such cases. One of his more amusing tales was that of an unnamed Frenchman who died in Nantes and was given a superb funeral, complete with a priest who prayed incessantly for his soul. However, just before being lowered into the ground, the man miraculously revived, only to be presented with a bill for expenses from both the clergy and the undertakers. Naturally the man refused, on the quite reasonable grounds that he had not requested their services. Despite Hartmann's medical pedigree, he was taken even less seriously than Tebb and Vollum as his stance on premature burial was heavily influenced – some would say undermined – by his belief in the occult and theosophy.

One of modern Europe's first documented cases of premature burial is that of Madam Blunden, a woman from Basingstoke whose unhappy fate was recorded in a pamphlet entitled *News from Basing-stoak*, published in 1674. Feeling ill one day, Madam Blunden drank some poppy water to ease her cramps. Sadly, she overdid it and passed out, never to regain consciousness – or so it seemed. Her husband, William Blunden, a wealthy brewer, was in London at the time of her apparent demise and sent word not to bury her until he returned. However, Madam Blunden was beginning to smell so pungently that her relatives insisted on burying her immediately. She was duly laid to rest in the grounds of the Chapel of the Holy Ghost, which was adjacent, as luck would have it, to a school for boys. Soon after the funeral, two young students playing near Madam Blunden's grave claimed to have heard groans coming from beneath the ground. The words 'take me out of my grave' – so the boys maintained – issued agonizingly from the freshly turned earth. Petrified, the boys ran to find a schoolmaster. Naturally they were not believed and received a beating instead. Boys being boys, however, they decided the following day to make another visit to the grave: noises were still emanating from Madam Blunden's grave.

This time the schoolmaster believed the pupils and rushed off to find the verger so the grave could be opened. Unfortunately, they needed to get permission from the churchwarden, who could not be found. Hours ticked away; a crowd gathered. Finally, the schoolmaster was given permission and the grave was opened. Madam Blunden appeared to be dead, but her body was covered, to the horror of the bystanders, in what looked like self-inflicted bruises. For a second time she was pronounced dead, with the witnesses slinking off home with the uneasy feeling that their neighbour had been buried alive.[8]

Laments from the grave to alert bystanders were a common theme of buried alive stories, as were other scarifying details such as young pregnant women giving birth in their coffins after their untimely interment. And exhumed bodies, the newspapers chillingly informed their readers, nearly always displayed the tell-tale sign of a struggle. Stories of bodies found in contorted positions or with fingers and arms gnawed to the bone were repeated in drawing rooms all over Europe and America. By the nineteenth century such tales reached a fever pitch, making the fear of waking up in a coffin widespread. Editorials in reputable magazines further fuelled these fears. The 14 September 1895 issue of the *Spectator* ghoulishly assured its readers that 'burning, drowning, even the most hideous mutilation under a railway train, is as nothing compared with burial alive'. Premature burial truly was, it seems, a fate worse than death.

Luckily, help was at hand. By this time, many people had become so spooked by grisly reports of premature burial that they added special instructions to their wills in order to forestall the possibility of waking up six feet underground. It was not uncommon for wills to stipulate that a person not be buried until six days had passed, or until a key artery had been severed. The Victorian novelist and Member of Parliament Edward Bulwer-Lytton, for instance, left instructions that his heart should be punctured by his doctor before he was laid in his coffin. There is no evidence that his wishes were acted upon, but the prospect of such a procedure must no doubt have reassured the author who penned the immortal phrases 'It was a dark and stormy night' and 'The pen is mightier than the sword.'

Bulwer-Lytton was not alone. People were still instructing medics to mutilate their corpses well into the twentieth century. An obituary in the

3 August 1915 issue of *The Times* reported that Miss Emily Harriet, a resident of Bayswater, issued £20 – the equivalent of £2,500 in today's money – to a Dr Stanley Bousfield on the condition he slit her throat from ear to ear on confirmation of her death. A few years later, Miss Lucy Soulsby, educational reformer and former headmistress of the famous Oxford High School for Girls, made a similar request in her will: 'I desire that at my death the doctor shall cut my carotid artery, and if by some mistake this be omitted, I desire that my body be exhumed and this be done.' Miss Soulsby died in May 1927, at which point, presumably, the doctor wielded his scalpel before she was laid to rest. Still, it remains unclear whether, even for financial rewards, doctors were willing to carry out such requests. If by chance the body was still alive when a doctor undertook his macabre obligation, he could have found himself in the dock for murder.

Others took even more ingenious precautions. Inventors came up with various ways for the prematurely interred to escape their incarceration. For example in 1868, Franz Vester of Newark, New Jersey, invented the 'burial case'. This contraption included a ladder by which the victim of a premature burial could ascend to the surface as well as a bell to summon assistance from the land of the living. Then there was the electric alarm that an Austrian, Carl Redl, invented in 1887: the victim could ring the bell by pulling a cord, while plates opened automatically to admit fresh air, thanks to a battery connected to the bell. A few years later, in 1891, William H. White of Topeka, Kansas, came up with the idea of attaching a wire to a ring on the body. Pulling the wire would trigger an 'enunciator', admitting air into the coffin through a flue. If after a period of time no signal was heard the flue could be sealed. Adalbert Kwiatkowski, a Prussian, came up with a particularly cumbersome apparatus in 1893: a girdle that was strapped around the body with an attached thread passing through a tube to the surface. Any movement in the coffin would be visible on the surface as the thread twitched frantically. A few years later, George H. Wilems of Roanoke, Illinois, received a patent for a system of mirrors strategically placed in the coffin such that vigilant passersby – or the ghoulishly prurient, perhaps – could in effect peer into the coffin to see either a peacefully reposing corpse or a frantically gesticulating victim.[9]

A century later, inventors are still perfecting fail-safe coffins to reassure twenty-first-century taphephobics. In the mid-1990s in Italy a clockmaker, goldsmith and designer of costume jewellery named Fabrizio Caselli became so disturbed by reports of premature burial that he turned his hand to the invention of what he patented as the *bara salvavita,* or 'lifesaver coffin'. This high-tech contrivance seems to have more in common with an ICU (intensive-care unit) bed or the cockpit of an aeroplane than a conventional pine box. It comes equipped with a computer, closed-circuit TV cameras, an alarm, microphones, motion sensors and also monitors to detect a heartbeat. Casselli advertises his product with the alarming slogan: 'Cases of apparent death are much more common than you think!'[10]

HOUSES OF THE DEAD

Almost a century earlier in Germany, a few other campaigners against premature burial had thought on a larger scale than simply an ingeniously rigged coffin. 'Waiting mortuaries' – what the Germans called *Leichenhaüsers* – were advertised as a way of preventing 'a living death'. They worked on the principle that a body would not be interred until it had begun to rot – the only sure sign that a body was dead. Corpses would be laid out in a sort of antechamber to the grave, a halfway house, so to speak, between the hospital or mortuary and the tomb. A sentinel would sit in this Limbo and watch . . . and wait.

Waiting mortuaries were conceived in 1788 by the Austrian Johann Peter Frank, who originally called his invention a *Totenhaus* ('house of the dead'). But it was Christoph Wilhelm Hufeland, a physician-cum-philanthropist who in 1791 was to build the first one in his hometown of Weimar in Germany. Renamed a *Leichenhaüser*, it consisted of a 'corpse chamber' with eight beds for the deceased and an attendant who watched through a window for signs of putrefaction in his charges. A fire was kept constantly alight in the kitchen, while steam from boiling water was fed through underground pipes to the corpse chamber in order to heat the room. This heat was not for the comfort of the inmates: it was to aid their decomposition.

Between 1795 and 1828 *Leichenhaüsers* were built in cities all over Germany, eventually becoming ever more sophisticated. In the later versions, separate chambers for males and females were common, as if to ensure propriety and privacy among the dead. The *Leichenhaüser* built in Munich in 1808 even had separate sections for its wealthy and poor cadavers: social distinctions were important, apparently, even after death. Rather disturbingly, the later *Leichenhaüsers* charged punters a small fee for the dubious privilege of wandering around the corpse chambers to look at the decaying corpses. Vast arrangements of scented flowers were positioned strategically around the beds to disguise the pungent smell that announced the bodies were ready for burial.

All of the *Leichenhaüsers* were large enough to cope with epidemics or disasters, and they featured kitchens, hot baths and resuscitation equipment as well as porters who lived on the premises. Bodies brought to the *Leichenhaüser* were fitted with bells, and wires were attached to their feet and hands so the porters could be hastily summoned by a reviving 'corpse'. Spare a thought for the *Leichenhaüsers'* porters: lonely midnight vigils waiting for the stink of putrefaction or the startling tinkle of a bell. One of the drawbacks of this alarm system was that decaying corpses had a habit of expanding and moving as putrefaction ran its course and so the bells were unwittingly set to jingling by the bloating cadavers. It was the task of the attendant to clear up the mess since dealing with exploding corpses was, it seems, part of the job description. Unsurprisingly, keeping staff was difficult. The stench of putrefying corpses was unbearable and the attendants were expected to clean the corpses' beds on an hourly basis; in return they were not even allowed to leave the premises for five minutes without written permission from the director. It must have been an unenvied profession even during the days of the 'dark Satanic mills' of the Industrial Revolution.

By the middle of the nineteenth century the popularity of *Leichenhaüsers* began to wane in Germany, although in Lisbon in 1840 there were riots in the streets as concerned citizens demanded that the government provide them with their own 'houses of the dead'. However, in Germany large sections of the general population refused to give up their dead to the *Leichenhaüser* as they feared their beloved would end up instead on the anatomist's table. Nonetheless, *Leichenhaüsers* were still being built as late as 1875, and the last one, in Speyer, Germany, was still intact, though not in use, in 1959. Interestingly, out of the thousands of cadavers that spent their last days above ground reposing on a bed in a *Leichenhaüser*, there was not one recorded case of an inmate waking up and ringing the bell to alert the porter.

'THE PERSON YOU'VE CALLED KNOWS YOU ARE WAITING . . .'

William Tebb was a leading light in the London Society for the Prevention of Premature Burial, formed in 1896 – the year after his and Colonel Vollum's book was published – by a spiritualist and eccentric named Arthur Lovell. No stranger to good causes, Tebb, who was born in Manchester in 1830, had previously been involved in demonstrating against the Corn Laws and fiscal protectionism before moving to America and becoming an Abolitionist. Returning to England after the American Civil War he next protested against vaccinations, proclaiming those against smallpox evil and unnecessary: cleanliness and Godliness were, in his opinion, the keys to human health. Tebb no doubt did much harm to the advancement of health care in the UK.

If he did little service to the living, Tebb was, however, more helpful to the dead. In *Premature Burial and How It Can Be Prevented*, he and Vollum made several recommendations. It was customary in Britain for death certificates to be issued without a doctor ever being summoned, so they proposed that no death certificate should be supplied unless a doctor had seen the body. In addition, they argued that doctors should be given medical instruction on the state of trance, catalepsy and other forms of suspended animation that were the prime suspects – albeit only imperfectly understood – in victims going to their early graves. Moreover, no one should be buried, they argued, until the first signs of putrefaction were evident, and every district in the UK should provide *Leichenhaüsers* like those in Germany. Yet despite frequent publicity surrounding their book and its aims, only one of their recommendations was taken forward: thanks to their efforts, a doctor must examine a corpse before signing a death certificate, a provision which still exists today.

The London Society for the Prevention of Premature Burial, like most of William Tebb's campaigns, proved to be short lived. After gaining much publicity at the turn of the twentieth century, it fell into terminal decline by 1910, as medical knowledge was advancing, until it finally dissolved through lack of interest in 1936. By this time Tebb had been dead for eighteen years and Vollum for thirty-four.

Yet live burials are not – if we are to believe some testimony – a claustro-phobic experience that ended on the stroke of the twentieth century. In the 1950s, a French engineer named Dr Louis-Claude Vincent was asked to carry out checks on water supplies needed to maintain American war cemeteries in France, Holland, Belgium and Luxembourg. While working at the cemetery in Saint-Laurent-sur-Mer he came across a team of American officials exhuming graves. Behind the privacy of closed doors, the bodies – all 150,000 of them – were placed in brand new coffins and then reburied. Dr Vincent claimed that this top secret operation was actually meant to determine how many American servicemen had been buried alive. Evidence emerged – through disturbing discoveries such as wrists that had been gnawed and skeletons in contorted positions – that six thousand of these, or four per cent, had been buried alive.[11] Another investigation at the end of the Vietnam War claimed that some two thousand American ser-vicemen were possibly victims of premature burial.[12] Alas, these soldiers had not been issued – as Colonel Vollum once advocated – with chloroform.

These days over fourteen thousand sites pop up on an internet search engine if you type in the word 'taphephobia'. Many of these websites offer help and advice – for a fee – to overcome this fear; the advertised remedies include hypnotherapy and a rather ambiguous 'energy psychology solution'. Furthermore, according to an Irish undertaker, Keith Massey, the fear of being buried alive has recently prompted many people to request that their mobile phones be buried with them.[13] He explains that relatives are encouraged to switch off the phone during the funeral service: a 'Crazy Frog' ringtone sounding in the coffin during the homily could be rather unnerving. Many people request that their phones be switched off after interment so that if they do wake up there will be battery power for that vital call. As yet, however, no one has tested whether a mobile phone can pick up a signal when buried at the regulation three feet below the surface.

Or, at least, no one has yet received a telephone call or text message from beyond the grave.

There is no doubt premature burial did occur, especially since – as we shall see in Chapter 2 – diagnosing death was (and still is) fraught with problems. However, it is debatable whether live burials occurred as frequently as the eighteenth- and nineteenth-century scaremongers predicted. Peter Mitchell, director of an exhumation company based in Kent, and one of the directors of the Institute of Cemetery and Crematorium Management, claims never to have come across evidence of a premature burial despite having exhumed and reburied hundreds of human remains each year.[14] And even the corpses that do seem to show signs of premature burial – such as those of the American servicemen – may have other explanations. Exhumed skeletons found in contorted positions may be explained by the fact that the cadaver moved inside the coffin as it was transported for burial or else during the burial itself. More than likely it is the decomposition process that causes limbs to move into awkward positions that make the skeleton look as if it is trying to escape its confinement. Fingers and arms thought to have been gnawed by a frantic victim desperate to escape a living death can in some instances be explained as the work of rats and other vermin. Indeed, in 1859, a Dr Von Rösser in an experiment buried live rats and mice in a coffin underground. Two days later he exhumed it and discovered that some of the animals survived by eating each other while others gnawed their way out of the coffin and escaped to the surface.[15] The implication is that if a rat can escape from a coffin, then it can likewise get in.

Noises from the grave such as those heard by the two boys playing near Madam Blunden's recently interred body can be explained as the work of the *Totenlaut* – the build up of intestinal gas inside the corpse (a natural part of the decomposition process) that emerges from the throat and voicebox, producing a moaning noise. Jan Bondeson, author of *Buried Alive: The Terrifying History of Our Most Primal Fear* (2002) and himself a doctor, suggests that the author of *News from Basing-stoak* fabricated the story that the boys heard Madam Blunden lamenting 'take me out of my grave' simply to scare his readers.[16]

Indeed, it seems that making up stories of premature burial was extremely common as newspaper editors soon learnt that terrifying stories would sell more copies. The French doctor Eugène Bouchut, winner of a scientific award, the Prix Manni, in 1846, wrote to mayors and town clerks throughout France in the 1850s to get verification of the buried alive stories that were circulating. Not one case was validated. In 1862 a Dutch physician named Alexander van Hasselt reported that in twenty-four years as a doctor in Utrecht he had never come across a single premature burial. He claimed they were, at best, an extremely rare occurrence.[17] And a Frenchman, Professor Paul Brouardet, likewise spent twenty years at the end of the nineteenth century investigating premature burial stories. In his book *Death and Sudden Death,* published in 1902, he was unable to verify a single case and concluded that journalists had invented the stories to sell copy.

And if all this evidence is not reassuring enough, then worried Victorians could take heart from the studies of the German physiologist Ernst Hebenstreit. From calculations he made in 1862, Hebenstreit claimed there would not be enough air in an average airtight coffin to sustain a person for more than sixty minutes.[18] Dr Von Rösser was to verify this by enclosing a dog in an airtight coffin with a glass lid: the dog died within three hours. So, taking into account the difference sizes of a human and dog, he concurred with Hebenstreit's findings. Therefore, any victim of premature burial would soon be put out of his misery: he would suffocate to death within the hour.

CHAPTER 2

Dead or Alive?

The Problem of Diagnosing Death

THE SIGNS OF DEATH

How can we tell when, and even if, a body is really dead? 'The boundaries which divide life from death,' muses Edgar Allan Poe's narrator in 'The Premature Burial', 'are at best shadowy and vague. Who shall say where the one ends, and the other begins? We know that there are diseases in which occur total cessations of all the apparent functions of vitality, and yet in which these cessations are merely suspensions . . .'

The fear of premature burial stems – as Poe shows in his short story – in large part from the difficulty of accurately diagnosing death. Diseases such as plague, cholera, typhoid and typhus – all common maladies in Europe until modern medicine was developed to treat them effectively – were known to produce coma and lower the heart rate as well as the body temperature, mimicking the symptoms of death and confusing even the most diligent of physicians.

Cholera, one of the greatest culprits, was first recorded in Bengal, India, in 1817. Caused by a microbe, the disease was spread by contaminated water or food. Abdominal pain, vomiting, diarrhoea and the loss of body fluid were followed by muscle cramps, weakness and collapse. At this stage, the pulse would be extremely low and the body very cold; it may have looked as though death had already occurred.

Typhus, on the other hand, is an acute viral infection spread from person to person by body lice. It first appeared in England in 1643, flourishing in crowded, dirty and unhygienic conditions such as those common in gaols, asylums and slave ships. Indeed, for this reason it was often called 'gaol fever'. It claimed the life of Anne Frank, the Dutch girl famous for her diary recording daily life while hiding from the Germans in an attic during the Second World War. Sufferers experience a rise in temperature, followed by fever, a rash on the chest, abdomen and wrists, weakness and delirium. The pulse becomes faint as a death-like coma follows. In 'The Premature Burial', Poe tells the story of a London attorney named Edward Stapleton who fell ill with typhus and, to all appearances, died – only to startle the anatomists, as they began slicing him up for their studies, by climbing off the slab and starting to speak.

Typhoid, a disease not related to typhus but also highly infectious and caused by a bacillus transmitted by contaminated food and water, could likewise trigger coma. Interestingly, one of the many theories into the death at the age of thirty-two of Alexander the Great in 323 BCE, put forward by David Oldach, a professor of pathology at the University of Maryland, was that Alexander was not poisoned, as is commonly thought, but had contracted typhoid. Dr Oldach and his colleagues studied historical accounts of Alexander's symptoms – chills, sweats, exhaustion, fever and a severe abdominal pain that caused him to cry out in agony. This latter symptom, according to Dr Oldach, might have been the result of a perforation of the bowel caused by untreated typhoid fever. Furthermore, historical accounts recorded that Alexander did not begin decomposing for days after his alleged death. Typhoid fever paralyzes its victims, which suggests that it was the embalmers who actually killed this great warrior, not the disease.[19]

A fourth condition that frequently mimicked death – and, according to legend, led to premature burials – was catalepsy. This condition was characterized by a loss of consciousness and a rigidity of the limbs that could last for days or even weeks on end, and that, to unwary physicians, suspiciously resembled death. This is the 'singular disorder' periodically suffered by the anxious narrator of 'The Premature Burial'. Therefore, to forestall the possibility suggested in the title, he made sure the family vault was well stocked with food and water as well as adequate ventilation and a handy means of escape. Intriguingly, it was stories of cataleptics being buried alive that prompted Fabrizio Caselli, 150 years after Poe, to create his 'Lifesaver Coffin'.

Not everyone, however, believed that ingenious bells-and-whistles coffins, or leaving the dead to reside in *Leichanhaüsers* until putrefaction began, were the best means of avoiding premature burial. Solving the problem of premature burial lay instead, they proposed, in inventing reliable tools to ascertain whether or not death had actually occurred.

BLOWING SMOKE

Over the centuries many tests were devised in an attempt both to diagnose death and to resuscitate a victim whose symptoms mimicked those of death. Before returning victims of crucifixion to their families, Roman centurions kindly ensured they were indeed dead by goring them with spears. This was not done as a kindness to prevent premature burial but because the centurions knew that Jewish women administered sponges soaked in mandrake wine (later commonly known as morion or 'death wine') to their dying husbands or sons during crucifixion. Not only did this concoction dull the pain and put the victims to sleep, it also gave them the appearance of death. There were supposedly cases of a few lucky victims coming back to life after the effects of the death wine had worn off. [20]

Other methods used by the Romans, such as vigorously washing the corpse, were less invasive. Washing the corpse was an important ritual in many cultures. The Ancient Greeks and Romans scrubbed a dead body rigorously, perfumed it and then wrapped it in white robes. For eight days a group of Roman women known as a *praeficae* would sing, lament and howl around the body at regular intervals – a performance, known as the *conclamatio*, from which we take the word 'clamour'. The rigorous washing and loud clamour were aimed at waking a body that might be mimicking death. On the ninth day, if there were no visible signs of life, the body would be sent for cremation or burial. There was a solid scientific basis behind the *conclamatio*: it is now known that physical stimulation such as massaging and washing a supposedly dead body can stimulate the heart and blood circulation, awakening the victim. In Muslim cultures today, vigorous washing of the body is still practised – an important ritual as most bodies are buried within twenty-four hours.

By the seventeenth century, methods of diagnosing death had only moderately improved in their sophistication. A Dane named Jacob Winsløw (1669–1760) invented numerous techniques. Having studied medicine in Paris, Winsløw was personally motivated in his investigations after he had narrowly escaped the ordeal of being buried alive on two separate occasions. Once as a child and then again in early adulthood he had lapsed into a coma, exhibiting the outward symptoms of death before reviving in the nick of time. 'Death is certain, since it is inevitable,' he once said, 'but also uncertain, since the diagnosis is sometimes fallible.'[21] Therefore, to detect the absence of life, he suggested putting the corpse through a series of somewhat bizarre tests: balancing a glass of water on the chest; irritating the nostrils with salts, stimulating liquors, onions, garlic or horseradish; or tickling the nose with a feather. He also suggested whipping the skin with nettles and violently pulling the limbs; but perhaps his strangest prescription was pouring warm urine (he did not stipulate whose) into the corpse's mouth. Other of Winsløw's methods seemingly had more to do with the torture chamber than the mortuary, since he recommended thrusting long needles under the toenails and pouring boiling Spanish wax over the head. It's hard to say which would be less preferable: being buried alive or finding yourself subjected to a battery of tests on Winsløw's slab.

Others made their own suggestions as to how to make sure a body was truly dead, including a French clergyman who advocated a particularly eye-watering technique: thrusting a red-hot poker up the back passage.[22] Indeed, bottoms played an important role for some eighteenth-century physicians in their attempts to confirm a death. Antoine Louis in 1752 proposed blowing tobacco smoke into the victim's anus with a contraption that looked remarkably like a bellows with pipes attached.[23] Another physician from Belgium, P.- J.- B. Prévinaire, improved Louis's version of the bellows in 1784, calling it *Der Doppelblässer*. Tobacco enemas were regularly used on corpses by physicians in nineteenth-century Holland, an indoor sport which cannot have been any more pleasant for the administrator than the victim. There is no evidence, however, that this rather extraordinary practice was ever successful in resuscitating a corpse.

The nipples rather than the bottom held the clue to death for a later doctor, a Frenchman named Jules-Antoine Josat, who in 1854 invented a sadistic-looking device called the *pince-mamelon*, or 'Nipple Pincher'. These pinchers resembled a huge pair of tweezers and squeezed the nipples very hard with the aim of shocking the victim out of its slumber. No statistics are available on the heart attacks it caused on arousal.[24]

Less offensive methods of diagnosing death were also used. Napoleon Bonaparte's physician, one Dr Larry, reputedly took a small mirror with him on campaigns, not for admiring his appearance but for positioning in front of the mouth of a dead soldier. If the glass did not mist up, the soldier, Larry decreed, could be pronounced dead. Less traumatic than a *Doppelblässer* or Nipple Pincher, the mirror was not, however, an infallible tool for diagnosing death, as some conditions that are known to mimic death do not produce enough breath to mist a glass.

A more reliable device was the stethoscope. Invented by René Laënnec in 1816, it enabled sounds in the chest to be heard, particularly in patients with pneumonia. Ironically, Laënnec died at the age of thirty-eight from tuberculosis. But it was another Frenchman, the physician named Eugène Bouchut, who was first to use the stethoscope to listen for a heartbeat – or rather the lack of it. Bouchut stated that if no heartbeat was heard for two minutes, the patient could reliably be declared dead. He experimented on animals to prove his point, winning his 1846 Prix Manni for this solution. The stethoscope in Bouchut's day was very primitive; made of wood and with only one 'ear', it was not sophisticated enough to hear a faint heartbeat due, perhaps, to illness or the use of narcotics. Incidentally, Bouchut was an opponent of 'waiting mortuaries' and vehemently argued that reports of premature burial were exaggerated.

According to Hippocrates (460–370 BCE), a diagnosis of death could be made if there was a pallid face, sunken eyes, caved-in cheeks and rigidity of the body. These rather vague indicators of death were still used during the nineteenth century. However, they were by no means infallible. In 1851 the *Gazette Médicale* cited the case of Dr Girbal, head of the Faculty of Clinical

Medicine in Montpellier, France, who examined a woman who was believed to have died. Though she displayed all of Hippocrates's indicators, Dr Girbal insisted on double-checking by means of several tests: he waved smelling salts under her nose, rubbed alcohol into her wounds and applied a mustard poultice to her heart. An hour later she sneezed. No one had realized that she had simply become extremely dehydrated due to dysentery. The woman had been bled, as was custom of the day, to release 'bad humours', and this procedure had induced coma.[25]

Perhaps one of the most novel ways of determining death is the Icard test, also known as the florescin test, which was devised and patented in 1905 by a French doctor named Séverin Icard. Dr Icard began researching reliable ways of diagnosing death after he injected a needle into a woman's heart to detect if she was still alive: she had indeed been alive, but the needle, unsurprisingly, finished her off. Escaping the wrath of her family, Icard went on to invent a harmless coloured fluorescent solution that was injected into a vein in the arm: if blood still circulated, the entire skin would turn yellow and the eyes an emerald green; if the body was dead, these fluorescent transformations did not occur. Fortunately the 'canary look' and devil eyes faded after a few hours. A modern equivalent is the radionuclide cerebral angiography (nuclide or radioisotope scanning), one of the tests used in determining brain death. In this procedure, a harmless radioactive dye is injected into the patient's brainstem. If circulation below the base of the brain does not occur, showing no evidence of fluid draining away, the patient is declared brain dead.

It is apparent, therefore, that determining death has always been something less than straightforward. Indeed, decapitation or decomposition might seem to be the only sure ways of diagnosing death. However, even decapitation offers no absolutes, since there have been reported cases, particularly during the French Revolution, of heads blinking and making facial expressions for several minutes after their disembodiment. One such victim was Antoine Lavoisier, the famous chemist, who asked friends to observe him after his beheading. They reported that he blinked for at least fifteen seconds after the blade of the guillotine severed his head. [26]

Even in modern times, diagnosing death is not always clear cut, as eighty-six-year-old Mildred Clarke found in 1994. After the emergency services discovered Mildred collapsed in a heap on the floor of her house in upstate New York, her doctor could detect no pulse when he examined her so declared her dead. Zipped up in the heavy-duty plastic body bag, she was sent to the morgue at the Albany Medical Center Hospital. But dead Mrs Clarke most certainly was not. One of the porters noticed that the bag lying on the slab was breathing, and the fortunate woman was rushed to intensive care.

A year later in rural Cambridgeshire, England, Australian-born Daphne Banks was to suffer the same fate. At sixty-one years old Daphne, who had been married to her husband for forty years, began suffering from depression. Battling with epilepsy and struggling with the loneliness of living on a remote farm, she attempted to commit suicide on the evening of 31 December 1995. She swallowed her epilepsy and sleeping pills, along with anti-depressants, sure that this would end her misery. When her husband discovered her, he rang for the doctor, who, after checking for vital signs, pronounced her dead in the early hours of New Year's Day. Mrs Banks was subsequently taken to the local mortuary. One of the undertakers, as it happened, was a friend of Mrs Banks, and in the course of preparing her body – she was due for cremation – spotted a vein twitch in her right leg. Fortunately for Mrs Banks, she too was rushed to intensive care, where she was carefully nursed back to health.

The over-hasty diagnosis of death could have been attributed to the fact that Mrs Banks was heavily sedated by narcotics, some of which affect the brainstem, which controls the heartbeat and breathing, thereby triggering coma. Apart from the misuse of drugs, coma can also be caused by head injuries, bacterial infections and cerebral strokes, all of which send the victim into the no-man's-land between life and death.

On her release from hospital, Mrs Banks and her husband decided to sell up and move to the local town, where she was able to make a full recovery – and, no doubt, dine out on stories about her near miss with the crematorium.[27]

UNQUIET SPIRITS

In 1890 the Académie des Sciences in France awarded the Prix Dusgate to a doctor named Maze, who argued (like the supporters of *Leichenhaüsers*) that the most reliable way of diagnosing death was simply by observing whether putrefaction had started.[28] Only the nose knows, he argued.

Putrefaction is the last in a series of transformations that the body experiences after life. Before putrefaction begins, the body usually undergoes certain physical changes which were also used as signals that death had occurred. By the mid-nineteenth century, one of the ways European pathologists determined death was by checking the three stages that a body would go through. The first stage, *rigor mortis*, is manifested in the gradual stiffening of the body muscles in the initial hours after death. However, this was not always a foolproof sign since certain conditions such as catalepsy could mimic the stiffening of limbs to make it look as though death has occurred.

The second indication that death has occurred is *algor mortis* – the slow cooling of a warm-blooded corpse as it equilibrates with the surrounding temperature. However, *algor mortis* is likewise not infallible. Bodies can still be alive despite seeming unusually cold. To confuse the matter further, Dr Harry Rainy, Regius Professor of Forensic Medicine at the University of Glasgow, found in 1860, when researching body temperature of cadavers, that temperatures could actually rise after death. How can this happen? The body, when alive, requires oxygen, of which twenty-five per cent is used by the brain. When the body dies and the oxygen flow ceases, the cells fall back on anaerobic energy production or fermentation. However, the inefficient fermentation process depletes any stores of blood sugar, starch and fat so the cell begins cannibalizing its own enzymes and membranes. Without a fresh supply of oxygen, the end products of fermentation are converted into lactic acid. The acid inside the cell starts corroding outwards and the body, though dead, generates warmth. In addition, the temperature of a dead body can be affected by factors such as body weight, fat distribution, muscles, clothing material, and whether these are wet or dry, or whether they totally or partially cover the corpse. The list is a long one and can often confuse forensic experts when they attempt to diagnose time of death. A victim struggling with an attacker just before dying could also elevate his temperature by several degrees as the 'fight or flight' response kicks in. Likewise, certain drugs, such as cocaine, can cause a raised body temperature after death.

The third stage of death is *livor mortis*, which occurs when the red-purple stain of lividity appears, a state caused by the gradual settling of blood as blood pressure drops to zero. This leads into the most reliable stages of death, autolysis – the breaking down of tissues by the body's own internal chemicals and enzymes – and putrefaction, the breakdown of tissues by bacteria. Both are necessary for the decomposition of the dead body, and once these processes start a body is very definitely dead.

Putrefaction brings an end to both rigor and lividity by turning muscle into mush. The first signs of putrefaction are a subtle flush of green over the right lower abdomen between twenty-four and forty-eight hours after death. The body then starts to bloat. Sir Francis Bacon in the fifteenth century wrote that this bloating was the work of 'unquiet spirits' fighting to break free of the mortal remains. However, in fact it is the work of bacterial fauna that live in the cecum – a small sac that sits at the head of the large intestine containing warm liquid faeces. When we are alive, this bacterial fauna is controlled by the white cells in our immune system. Two to three days after death, however, these white cells also die, so the bacterial population runs riot until it breaks free, multiplying and bursting through the intestinal wall. In its bid for freedom it spills into the abdomen and moves along the passive circulatory system. The gases produced by the moving bacteria react with the deoxygenated blood, producing feathery wisps of green and black that run along the old blood vessels. By the fourth or fifth day these wisps broaden to black smears, first on the face, then moving along the torso and limbs. Bacterial gases inflate the trunk of the body, causing the tongue and eyes to protrude, the lips to swell and the breasts and genitals to balloon. A body in this state is not a pretty sight – but at least it is clear to everyone that funeral plans can now safely be made.

British television viewers may well have the opportunity to witness these phenomena in action. In November 2004, Channel 4 advertised for a terminally ill patient willing to be filmed after death – decomposing. It was reported in January 2006 that several suitable candidates had been found. Mediawatch-UK (an organization founded in 1965 by Mary Whitehouse) was outraged, lamenting that this was the worst kind of voyeurism. Indeed, the project does smack, on one level, of the questionable commercialization that induced owners of *Leichenhaüsers* to throw open their doors to a paying public determined to satisfy its ghoulish curiosity. But *Dust to Dust* is meant to be a serious scientific programme overseen by pathologist Dr Richard Shepherd, president of the British Association in Forensic Medicine, in conjunction with the Science Museum. Hamish Mykura, head of history, science and religion at Channel 4, hopes the taboos about death will be challenged and overcome. Whatever its virtues or demerits, however, this is clearly not a telly programme to watch as you eat your dinner.

CHAPTER 3

Waking the Dead

Resurrections and Exhumations

Good friend, for Iesus sake forbeare
To digge the dust enclose heare.
Bleste be ye man [that] spares these bones
And curste be he [that] moves my bones

William Shakespeare's epitaph,
Holy Trinity Church, Stratford-upon-Avon

'Who builds stronger than a mason, a shipwright or a carpenter?' asks one of the gravediggers in *Hamlet*. The answer is, of course, a gravedigger, because 'the houses he makes last till doomsday'. Indeed, when the lid is screwed into place and the coffin lowered six feet into the ground, we assume the body will repose for all eternity, or at least until the Resurrection. Christian principle holds that the burial of a body or its ashes is to mark a person's final resting place on earth.

Yet the dead are not always allowed to lie undisturbed, and often their resting place is far from their last. Criminal activities, cultural practices, political events, legal judgements and superstitions about vampires can lead to a body being raised – if not from the dead – then from its 'final' resting place. Juan Perón, for example, is on his third grave, having been dug up twice, while Abraham Lincoln has suffered no fewer than seventeen posthumous relocations. The famous are not the only ones, since in the UK the Church of England regularly receives 'exhumation petitions' from families who, after moving house, wish to dig up their loved ones and transplant them to a churchyard more convenient to their new home. The Church of England grants such requests only in the most unusual circumstances. But many other posthumous peregrinations have taken place, in England and elsewhere, often with little better justification.

'HUMAN JAM'

In Britain, the Church of England informs those who petition to have their loved ones exhumed that the deceased's remains 'are laid to rest in the care of the Church and should not be disturbed'.[29] Historically, however, the Church has been a rather fickle landlord for its legions of tenants. Overpopulation in the churchyard meant it was routine for the bones of the dead to be removed from their graves and then relocated to charnel houses or ossuaries. Medieval churchyards were so overcrowded that it was difficult for a sexton to dig one grave without disturbing another. No sooner has the gravedigger in *Hamlet* told his riddle about the work of a 'grave-maker' lasting until doomsday than, ironically, his spade turns up a skull, that of Yorick the jester.

The charnel houses to which remains were moved were often located in the crypts of churches, and prayers were regularly said over the bones. But even the promiscuous jumble of the charnel house was not the end for many bones. Most charnel houses were eventually cleared in the sixteenth and seventeenth centuries, after the Reformation. A few charnel houses still remain, however, notably in Rothwell, Northamptonshire, and at Hythe in Kent. In 1999, archaeological excavations in the basement of the law firm Allen & Overy, in Tower Hamlets, London, unearthed a charnel house originally constructed in the cemetery of St Mary Spital. After the Dissolution of the Monasteries in 1625, the building above it was converted into a house – not the most desirable residence, surely, for anyone of a nervous or superstitious temperament. The archaeologists unearthed more than ten thousand human remains, which have since been transferred to the collection of the Museum of London.

Sometimes the dead are moved to make way not for more dead, but for the living. Cemeteries often sit on very valuable land. Unfortunately, human remains that get in the way of progress are not always accorded a great deal of respect. During the 1860s, the Midland Railway line was designed to cut though St Pancras Cemetery in London. Thousands of human remains, many only recently interred, needed to make way for Victorian commuters. Exhumation speedily commenced, to the dismay of bystanders, who claimed to have witnessed fresh corpses with glossy hair being ejected from their graves; the headstones, meanwhile, were recycled for use on paths and porches. Responding to this outrage, the Bishop of London commissioned the architect Arthur Bloomfield to supervise over forty thousand exhumations, ensuring the bodies were removed with care and respect. Bloomfield passed the task on to his young assistant, Thomas Hardy, later to become famous as a novelist. In 1882 Hardy wrote a poem entitled 'The Levelled Churchyards', in which he remarked dourly on the fate of the bodies dispossessed of their graves:

We late-lamented, resting here
Are mixed to human jam,
And each exclaims in fear,
I know not which I am!

One hundred and fifty years later, in the Camley Street Cemetery, just around the corner from St Pancras, history has repeated itself. In 2002, officials of the Channel Tunnel Rail Link (CTRL) sent bulldozers in to scoop up soil and bones in order to clear the site quickly for the new Eurostar terminal at St Pancras. Archaeologists were allowed just three weeks in which to excavate the remains. CTRL had been permitted to remove the graves by a special Act of Parliament, despite protests by English Heritage, who claimed that the usual clause stating that all remains must have a 'respectful and dignified removal' was missing from the Act. Senior archaeologist David Miles told the *Evening Standard* in November 2002 that the government's decision to allow this clearance meant invaluable information about the population of London during the Industrial Revolution had been lost. Although it was later agreed by CTRL to extend archaeological involvement, only eighty-three detailed examinations were made out of the more than two thousand human remains removed by the bulldozers. When tourists catch their Eurostar from the gleaming new St Pancras International station to romantic European destinations they should pause to reflect on Hardy's poem, with its haunting evocation of the dead so rudely evicted from their last resting places.

RELOCATION, RELOCATION, RELOCATION

A less ignoble case of exhumation and relocation of human remains took place in the United States at almost the same time that the skeletons were being so rudely ejected from their graves at St Pancras. It involved the creation of a national cemetery for the dead, a twenty-acre site to venerate the victims of war.

It's hard to imagine what went through the minds of Samuel Weaver and his colleagues as they set off to work in the autumn of 1863. Though witness to terrible scenes of human misery during the Battle of Gettysburg several months earlier, Weaver, a photographer, could hardly have been prepared for the gruesome task that lay before him – retrieving the bodies of thousands of Union soldiers who had died in the three days of fighting at Gettysburg, Pennsylvania, at the peak of the American Civil War. The bodies were scattered over a large area of woodland, farmland and open scrub; most had merely been covered where they fell with a thin layer of top soil, and some had lain exposed for several days. To make matters worse, Pennsylvania experienced particularly heavy rains after the battle, and the makeshift graves of thousands of felled soldiers were washed away, exposing gruesomely decomposing bodies. Adding to the scene of death and desolation, hundreds of relatives had swarmed over the scene, searching for loved ones and, in the process, partially exhuming bodies before hastily and carelessly reburying them.

Appalled by reports of the bloated, rotting bodies, the Pennsylvania Governor Andrew Curtin successfully petitioned for state funds to build the Gettysburg National Cemetery (originally named the Soldiers'

National Cemetery). Weaver, who was one of the first official photographers to take pictures of the battle, was hired by David Wills, a Gettysburg judge, to retrieve the bodies of Union soldiers. 'There was not a grave permitted to be opened or a body searched unless I was present', Weaver wrote in his report to Wills, the agent for Curtin. This meant Weaver personally oversaw 3,512 exhumations, a process which began on 27 October and was not completed until the end of the following March. 'The bodies were found in various stages of decomposition', he laconically observed. Many of them, exposed to the heat as well as the rain, had turned to skeletons by the time Weaver and his team reached them.

Weaver's task was to exhume the Union Soldiers only. The Confederate dead were left rotting where they lay until 1871, eight years after the end of the battle, when the ladies' organizations in North and South Carolina, Georgia and Virginia raised funds to search for their soldiers. Their bodies were collected and reburied in Hollywood Cemetery in Richmond, Virginia.

Samuel Weaver died a dozen years after the battle. After a train accident in 1875, in which both his legs were severed, he was heard to mutter in shock, 'I am badly hurt.' Shortly after dying from blood loss, he was interred in the privately owned Evergreen Cemetery, a stone's throw from the gates of the National Cemetery in Gettysburg.

INVASION OF THE BODYSNATCHERS

'What's a Resurrection-Man?' young Jerry Cruncher asks his father in Charles Dickens's *A Tale of Two Cities*, to which his father replies: 'He's a tradesman.' Still confused, young Jerry inquires: 'What's his goods, father?' After thinking for a minute, Mr Cruncher replies that they are 'a branch of Scientific goods'.[30]

While many people in eighteenth- and nineteenth-century Britain and America were terrified of being buried alive, others had – often with better reason – quite a contrary phobia: that of being resurrected before their time. As medical science began to advance, a constant supply of dead bodies was needed for experimental purposes. Countries such as France, Germany, Austria, Italy and Holland were able to separate this scientific necessity from their Christian beliefs by passing laws to provide the anatomy schools with sufficient cadavers, usually the unclaimed bodies of ex-residents of poor houses or hospitals. But legislators in Britain and the United States resisted this expedient, thus inadvertently creating a macabre new profession – that of the resurrectionist or 'bodysnatcher'. So it was that Mr Cruncher, after witnessing by day a funeral at the old church of St Pancras, returned to the graveyard in the evening, equipped with a spade, a sack and a crowbar. First of all, though, he paid a visit to 'his medical adviser – a distinguished surgeon'.

The business of robbing graves for medical investigation was nothing new. It can be traced back to the fourteenth century, in Mondino, Italy, when four medical students were apprehended in 1319 and accused of exhuming a body and taking it to a medical school for dissection.[31] Indeed, bodies were not only dissected for medical science in medieval Italy: artists such as Michelangelo and Leonardo da Vinci cut up dead bodies to study muscle structure to ensure heightened realism in their paintings – though they acquired their bodies legally from hospital authorities. Luca Signorelli, a friend of Michelangelo, was, however, rumoured to wander around burial grounds in search of body parts from which to make his studies.

In Britain, it was Queen Elizabeth I who in 1565 granted the medical guild, the College of Physicians and Surgeons, an annual supply of four executed felons for anatomy; the number was later increased to six by Charles II in 1663. However, this number was by no means adequate for medical science. By the end of the eighteenth century there were two hundred medical students in London; a generation later, in 1823, there were more than a thousand, with another nine hundred in Edinburgh. It was compulsory for these students to pass a course in dissection, yet the qualification was almost impossible to obtain – legally, at least – given that only six bodies were officially made available each year. In Scotland, students were allowed to pay their tuition fees in corpses – a proviso that must have resulted in hard-up young medical students passing cemeteries that weren't on the way home.

The trade in dead bodies therefore became a lucrative one by the end of the eighteenth century. Medical men were forced to collude with gangs of graverobbers, paying them up to sixteen guineas per body (some £1,100 or $2,000 in today's money) in order to fine-tune their skills on a fresh corpse. The law was no real deterrent to this prosperous trade. Under English law in the seventeenth and eighteenth centuries, stealing a dead body was punishable only by a prison sentence and, rarely, by transportation to the colonies. Stealing a sheep, pig, calf or ox, on the other hand, could mean a death sentence. Ironically, until recently the law decreed that 'the only lawful possessor of the dead body is the earth' – so that a graverobber could be prosecuted only for stealing grave goods, such as a shroud or jewellery, not for removing the body itself.

The world of bodysnatching was a dangerous one for both the resurrectionists and the anatomists. Violent struggles could often be heard at the dead of night as fights broke out in graveyards where rival gangs competed for a freshly buried corpse. And if an anatomist procured a body from a gang other than his usual supplier, it was not unknown for a disgruntled resurrectionist to break into the dissecting room and mutilate the body, rendering it useless for anatomy. Alternatively, discontented bodysnatchers would sometimes anonymously tip off the police, sending a clear message to their paymasters that they should do business with no one but themselves. Anatomists also had reason to fear a discontented populace: in the United States, medical schools were attacked and destroyed by outraged mobs in New York and Baltimore, and at Yale University and in Ohio. The riot in New York in 1788 might have been avoided had the medical student who taunted passing children by waving a dismembered arm from an upper-storey window been more discreet.

The life of a resurrectionist was likewise a hard one. Joshua Napels recorded some of the occupational hazards in his 1812 *Diary of a Resurrectionist*. The hours of boredom waiting for the nod that a body had been buried, coupled with the fear of being caught, impelled many gang members to drink away their profits. If their nocturnal activities were discovered, feelings ran so high that there was no knowing what the general public might do. A year before Charles Darwin sailed off on the *Beagle* to explore the coasts of Australia and South America, he recorded in his diary an event that occurred in Cambridge in 1830. 'Two bodysnatchers had been arrested, and while being taken to prison had been torn from the constable by a crowd of the roughest men, who dragged them by their legs along the muddy and stony road', wrote Darwin. 'They were covered from head to foot with mud and their faces were bleeding either from having been kicked or from the stones; they looked like corpses.'[32]

Keeping their profession secret was therefore of the utmost importance to the graverobbers, while foiling them was foremost in the minds of everyone else. Many coffins had double rows of nails, making it impossible for a taphephobe to find a means of escape or a bodysnatcher to prize it open. Some people invested in metal coffins, which were on the market as early as 1781. The rich outwitted the bodysnatchers by burying their dead in vaults, mausoleums, private chapels, and in coffins with three layers of wood and lead. Graves were often booby-trapped or equipped with primitive landmines. Families also paid servants to guard the grave until putrefaction was sure to have started, thus rendering the body useless to the anatomists.

Sensing an opening in the market, a London tallow chandler named Edward Bridgman invented the 'Patent Coffin' in 1818 – a contraption that he boasted was guaranteed to keep out the resurrectionists. Made of cast or wrought iron, it prevented the levering of the lid from the outside by means of a series of concealed spring catches within the inner lid. Bridgman also cleverly patented designs that connected headstones to coffins or to cast iron vaults. But if special coffins or vaults proved too costly, 'Jankers' – heavy, coffin-shaped slabs of metal or stone – were placed on fresh graves to prevent tampering. There is no evidence why the word 'jankers' was used in this context, though during the British Raj in India the term was military slang for detention or punishment. Intriguingly, in the year that Bridgman invented his coffin, people in Britain were thrilled and horrified by a novel about a bodysnatcher. Anxieties about bodysnatching pervade Mary Shelley's 1818 novel *Frankenstein,* since Dr Victor Frankenstein's bold experiment is made possible only because he is able to gather body parts from charnel houses and what he calls the 'unhallowed damps of the grave'. Shelley's readers no doubt shuddered as much at the thought of Victor's nocturnal visits to the churchyard as they did at the prospect of a monster with electrodes in its head stumbling through the Swiss Alps.

The ingenious foils available to the rich meant the poor were extremely vulnerable to the bodysnatchers. They often acted in concert to protect graves, either by erecting watchhouses in churchyards or by paying for strategically placed lamps in cemeteries, thus making it difficult for bodysnatchers to work under the cover of darkness (rather in the way that our cars today are protected from thieves in car parks by lamps and CCTV). Indeed, in Ireland in 1819 the Humane Society of St John offered to fund a watch for the Hospital Fields burial ground in Dublin, a favourite haunt of the resurrectionists since it was home to the largest number of paupers' graves in the country. The Society's offer provoked a stiff letter of complaint to a Dublin newspaper from one Professor Macartney, teacher of anatomy at Trinity College, Dublin. Professor Macartney lamented that this watch would have a devastating effect on the medical school. 'I do not think,' he wrote, 'the upper and middle classes have understood the effects of their own conduct when they take part in impeding the process of dissection ... Very many of the upper ranks carry in their mouths,' he pointed out, 'teeth which have been buried in the Hospital Fields.'[33] This unpleasant reminder was no exaggeration: the resurrectionists would often remove teeth from bodies and sell them on to dentists before handing over the corpses to the anatomists. The poor of Dublin would remain inviolate, it seems, at the price of their social betters gumming their food.

In Scotland, those with the financial means used a 'mortsafe', an iron grid or cage that was either set in concrete above ground over the coffin or submerged with it. Several can still be seen today in Greyfriars churchyard in Edinburgh. The Scots were also partial to what they called 'dead houses'. These were similar to the German *Leichenhaüsers*, though the reasoning behind them was quite different: they were designed to render a corpse useless for dissection. A body left the dead house, in other words, only when it had truly gone off. Scottish parishes that embraced dead houses charged a fee for such a service, and those who could afford it were reassured that their loved ones would not end up on the anatomist's table. One such dead house is still standing in Crail, Fife, fifty-five miles north of Edinburgh. With thick walls and battlements, it looks like a miniature fortress – the ultimate foil to a resurrectionist.

'NATTOMY SOUP'

It was commonly felt by the lower orders that the government and doctors were hatching plans to appropriate their corpses if there was a shortage of

bodies for dissection. Unrest and riots periodically ensued in the workhouses throughout Britain. The inhabitants of the workhouse of St Paul's
at Shadwell, in Tower Hamlets, became particularly agitated when a new
inmate accused the workhouse master of dishing up a soup containing
human remains. The inmate found himself in front of a judge, and when
the workhouse master brought in some of his soup to show the court, the
gruel was quickly dubbed by the newspapers 'Nattomy Soup'. The accuser
was sentenced to twenty-one days in a house of correction – where he was
no doubt extremely wary of drinking the soup.

Despite anatomy riots in Aberdeen, Inveresk, Hereford, Greenwich and
Deptford, the Anatomy Act was passed by Parliament in 1832. It included
a clause to the effect that unclaimed bodies from workhouses could be sent
for dissection after forty-eight hours instead of seventy-eight, as originally
suggested. A proviso was made that allowed a person in a workhouse to
request in writing that his body not be used for dissection. Most people
were unaware of this clause, however, until William Roberts took up the
cause. Roberts, a London surgeon, came out against the Act, arguing that
the upper and middle classes, unlike the poor, were protected from having
their bodies dissected against their wishes. He campaigned in workhouses,
urging people to sign declarations refusing dissections, thus managing to
save large numbers from the knife. Interestingly, some parishes were of like
mind, refusing to give up dead bodies to the medical authorities. Between
1832 and 1842, the parish of St Giles offered 709 unclaimed bodies, while
the parish of Marylebone presented a paltry fifty-eight corpses and a neighbouring parish delivered only eighty-two.[34] However, it seems that Roberts
was right: between 1832 and 1932, out of fifty-seven thousand bodies dissected in London anatomy schools, only half a per cent came from any-
where other than poor houses. The London poor may not have ended up as
the main ingredient in 'Nattomy Soup', but they did wind up – voluntarily
or otherwise – donating their bodies to science.

The Anatomy Act brought an end to the careers of the resurrection
men. Despite this legal advance, however, bodies were still not guaranteed
an undisturbed repose. Resurrectionists working in furtherance of
medical science were not the only perils for a corpse once the last spade
of dirt was thrown. The flesh and bones could be worth a good deal of

money if the departed had either a celebrity value, wealthy relations, or both.

Alexander T. Stewart, known as the Merchant Prince, built the first department store in the United States and in 1846 founded the famous Garden City for working men on Long Island. By the time he died in 1876 he was one of the wealthiest men in America. Interred in the church of St Mark's-in-the-Bowery in Manhattan, his body was soon afterwards stolen by thieves and held for ransom. Mrs Stewart paid $20,000 (some $300,000 in today's money) for her husband's remains to be returned, whereupon he was reburied in a secure vault, fitted with a burglar alarm, at the Cathedral of the Incarnation in Garden City.

Protecting a corpse was important for those worried about the possibility of kidnapping for ransom. In 1901 Robert Todd Lincoln, son of Abraham Lincoln, came to the conclusion that strong measures were needed to protect his father's body. At least one attempt had already been made to steal Lincoln's body and hold it for ransom. Fortunately, the Secret Service foiled the plot, for which a ransom of $20,000 and the release of a convicted counterfeiter had been demanded. As a consequence, Robert arranged for his father's coffin to be housed in a renovated sarcophagus where it was encased in steel bars, sunk ten feet beneath the floor, and covered with tons of cement.

Lincoln's remains have had a particularly restless posterity. Soon after he was assassinated in Washington DC in 1865 he was embalmed and sent on a seventeen hundred-mile journey that allowed people to pay their respects in Baltimore, Philadelphia, New York, Albany, Buffalo, Cleveland, Columbus, Cincinnati, Indianapolis, Chicago and many other smaller towns as the body made its way back to Illinois for burial. Seven tiny pieces of his shattered skull, some bandages and the bloody cuff from one of the doctors that performed Lincoln's autopsy were sent to the National Museum of Health and Medicine in Washington DC in order to be preserved as a reminder of such a great man. The rest of Lincoln arrived at Oak Ridge Cemetery in Illinois and, although they never left the precincts of the cemetery, his remains have been moved or reburied no less than seventeen times in order to foil kidnapping threats while the mausoleum was built for him and later repaired. The coffin was actually opened five times between

1865 and 1901 for identification purposes. Let us hope he is safely ensconced for good in Oak Ridge Cemetery and can finally rest in peace.

A burglar alarm such as that on Alexander T. Stewart's tomb would probably not have saved Juan Perón, the former president of Argentina, who died in 1974. After Perón's body had been shipped to Moscow for embalming, it was buried in his grandfather's tomb in Buenos Aires. Every precaution was taken to ensure that Perón would rest undisturbed: the mausoleum was outfitted with twelve combination locks, bullet-proof glass and round-the-clock guards. Nonetheless, in 1987 thieves were able to break into the tomb and steal the ceremonial sword that had been buried with him; they also severed and removed his hands. They then threatened to pulverize the hands unless a ransom of $8 million was forthcoming. Despite strikes and mass rallies by the Perónistas, no ransom money was paid, and Perón's hands have never been seen since. Almost twenty years later, in October 2006, his body was disinterred and moved to a new, grander mausoleum in the countryside outside Buenos Aires. Costing more than $1 million, the tomb will present, like Lincoln's, a stiff challenge to the wiliest of bodysnatchers.

As with Perón's remains, not all relatives are prepared to part with huge amounts of ransom money. In 1978, shortly after Charlie Chaplin died, his remains were stolen from his grave in Switzerland and held for a ransom of £400,000. Chaplin's wife Oona refused to pay, claiming that her husband would think the sum ridiculous. The body was recovered eleven weeks later, and twenty-four-year-old Roman Wardas, a Pole, and thirty-eight-year-old Gantscho Ganev, a Bulgarian, were found guilty. Chaplin has been reburied in Corsier-sur-Vevey in Switzerland, this time in a theft-proof coffin.

The thought of being exhumed for ransom money is bad enough, but what if the motive is more sinister and depraved? On 5 September 2006, twenty-year-old Alexander Grunke, along with his twin brother Nicholas and friend Dustin Radke, loaded their vehicle with spades – tools of the res-urrectionist – and drove to St Charles Cemetery in Cassville, Wisconsin. First, however, as if on their way to a date, they stopped at a drugstore to purchase condoms. Alexander was later spotted acting suspiciously by his vehicle near the cemetery and admitted to the police officer who happened to be passing that he and the others were digging up a grave of a twenty-year-old woman who had recently died in a motorcycle accident. None of the men knew the woman, but they had seen her photograph in the local newspaper's obituary column. Nicholas, apparently, was smitten – and hence the shovels and condoms. Fortunately, they only managed to dig deep enough to reach the buried vault.[35] The disturbing case was not as isolated an incident as one might hope. A few weeks later, a North Carolina man called Garcia was sentenced to twenty years' imprisonment and ordered to register as a sex offender after he was caught attempting to dig up the grave of a twelve-year-old girl after he, too, saw her photograph in an obituary.[36]

POLITICAL PLOTS

Ideology as well as the interests of medical science and greed can likewise be responsible for the disinterment – and sometimes the desecration – of a corpse. Politics are fickle at the best of times, but not even a fortune teller like Peter of Albano, the respected astronomer and physician to Pope Honorius IV during the 1280s, could have foreseen how he would fall foul of the authorities after his death in 1317. His body was exhumed by the Inquisition shortly after he died due to his suggestion that Lazarus may have been in a trance, rather than dead, when Christ entered his tomb. It is ironic that Peter, like Lazarus, should have been raised from his tomb – though his disinterment, unlike that of Lazarus, was no joyous occasion: his bones were burnt on the orders of the Inquisition.

When political animosity is mixed with a dose of superstition there is little chance of a body reposing undisturbed. In 1478, a wealthy banker named Jacopo de' Pazzi, along with his nephew Rinato, attempted to assassinate Lorenzo the Magnificent, the ruler of Florence. Following the failure of their plot (Lorenzo survived, though his younger brother was killed), Jacopo and Rinato were hanged. Jacopo, one of the most powerful men in Florence, was interred in the tomb of his ancestors in the church of Santa Croce. However, supporters of Lorenzo soon spread a rumour that Jacopo had 'commended his soul to the devil' as he was dying, and, coincidentally, four days of heavy rains followed Jacopo's burial. Distraught people from the countryside poured into Florence in protest, lamenting that their crops were being ruined because of God's displeasure that a traitor to the faith had been buried in sacred ground. Fearful of a riot, the friars of Santa Croce exhumed Jacopo and reburied him in unconsecrated ground. The sun, it was reported, began to shine again; but all still was not well. Wailing noises (more than likely due to the *Totenlaut*) could be heard coming from the new burial site, and the locals feared that, due to its latest occupant, the ground had been turned into a place of demons.

Supporters of Lorenzo, enraged that the would-be assassin was causing so much trouble, exhumed his decomposing body and dragged it naked through the streets of Florence, even hauling it to his own palazzo, banging his skull on the front door and mockingly inquiring: 'Is there no one here to receive the master and his entourage?' Finally, after all this gruesome frivolity, Jacopo's body was cast into the waters of the Arno like a piece of rubbish. As Niccolò Machiavelli was later to comment on the sorry affair: 'A truly memorable instance of the instability of fortune, for a man to fall from such a position of wealth and prosperity, to such a depth of misfortune, ruin, and disgrace.'[37]

Such an observation could have been repeated two hundred years later in England, when Oliver Cromwell fell from political favour. On his death in 1658, Cromwell was embalmed, like the royalty he had deposed, given a huge state funeral, and buried in Westminster Abbey alongside past kings and queens. However, in 1661, following the Restoration of the monarchy, Cromwell was reviled as a regicide and for the years of puritanical fervour inflicted on the English people. He and two of his associates were exhumed, and their remains dragged through the streets of London to Tyburn, where common criminals were hanged. What was left of Cromwell's head (after several years in the grave, decomposition had well and truly set in) was finally slathered with pitch and fixed to a metal pole at Westminster Hall as a caution to other would-be regicides.

Recent events in England have shown that exhumation is still used as a weapon against political 'undesirables'. For over thirty years, Chris Hall and his brother, of Darley Oaks Farm, Newchurch, in Staffordshire, bred guinea pigs for medical research. The brothers were accused by animal rights activists of keeping the creatures in inhumane conditions, causing much distress, and then handing them over for grisly experiments and, inevitably, death. Their farm suffered years of protests and violent attacks, including the throwing of petrol bombs, the posting of excrement through letter boxes, and the daubing of cars with paint stripper. The campaign reached a horrifying nadir when, in October 2004, the remains of Mr Hall's mother-in-law, Gladys Hammond, were dug up and stolen by members of the Animal Rights Militia, an extreme arm of the demonstrators, in an attempt to have the farm closed down. The tactic produced the desired result. Ten months later, in August 2005, the Halls announced the closure of the guinea pig farm, but not until May 2006 were the four perpetrators arrested and the whereabouts of Mrs Hammond – who had been reburied by the activists in Cannock Chase, Staffordshire – finally disclosed.

NIGHT OF THE LIVING DEAD?

Possibly the most famous and evocative exhumations, in popular culture at least, are those of vampires. Sadly, those exhumations are not the exclusive domain of late-night double-feature picture shows.

Not for nothing did Count Dracula hail from Eastern Europe. After the Austrians annexed parts of Serbia and Wallachia early in the eighteenth century, officials became alarmed at a strange and disconcerting custom among the locals: that of digging up corpses and impaling them with sharpened wooden stakes. One notorious case of concern to the Austrian officials was that of a peasant named Peter Plogojowitz, who died in 1725 at the age of sixty-two. He was buried a few days later, as dictated by local custom in his village of Kisilova, in present-day Serbia. There are no suggestions that Plogojowitz was a contentious person in life, but in death he became truly unpopular. Suspicion fell on him after nine people in the village expired over the next few weeks, all of them claiming on their deathbeds that Plogojowitz had paid them a nocturnal visit, during which he attempted to throttle the life out of them. The villagers were anxious to check whether Plogojowitz showed telltale signs of vampirism. After voting unanimously to exhume him, they summoned the local priest as well as the Imperial Provisor, the government representative who incredulously reported to his superiors in Vienna all that transpired.

As the coffin was opened, the Provisor and the villagers were alarmed to discover that there was not the faintest whiff of what the Provisor called the 'odour that is otherwise characteristic of the dead'. Moreover, Plogojowitz's body, apart from his nose, was still intact; his hair, beard and nails were still growing; and his skin had begun to peel away, revealing what looked like a fresh growth. That wasn't all. He was also, apparently, sporting an impressive erection – a sure sign that he had turned into a vampire, since vampires, as everyone knew, were extremely sexual creatures. But the definitive proof was that he displayed fresh blood around his mouth, 'which, according to common observation, he had sucked from the people killed by him'. There was no doubt in the minds of the frantic villagers: Peter Plogojowitz was indeed a vampire. Drastic measures were called for.

What followed were scenes that anticipated the pitchfork-wielding mobs beloved of so many Hollywood B-films. A wooden stake was sharpened and, to vengeful cries from the crowd, plunged into Plogojowitz's chest. The result was yet more fresh blood from the mouth and ears. Warming to the task, the crowd began baying and braying as the body was dragged from the grave and burnt to ashes, which were then reburied – 'according to their usual practice', observed the Provisor – in unconsecrated ground. 'If a mistake was made in this matter,' the nervous bureaucrat informed his superiors, 'such is to be attributed not to me but to the rabble, who were beside themselves with fear.'[38]

The villagers needn't have been so fearful. Had they any knowledge of the decomposition process they would have realized that what they saw when their 'vampire' was excavated was simply the delayed onset of a natural series of events. Certain biological and environmental conditions, that is, and not the powers of the undead, were responsible for Plogojowitz's surprisingly radiant posthumous appearance, and even, indeed, his erection.

Any number of environmental conditions can hinder a swift decomposition. The rate of a corpse's decomposition depends on air, moisture, temperature, and the presence of micro-organisms and insects. Other factors include a body being buried in very cold temperatures, as Plogojowitz probably was. Coffins made from layers of wood and lead and then buried in clay soil can naturally preserve a body indefinitely, while corpses covered in lime (as opposed to quicklime) can do likewise. Plogojowitz's new growth of skin, moreover, need not have convicted him of vampirism either. The 'whitish' appearance of his old skin could easily have been due to adipocere, or 'grave wax'. Bodies buried in damp soil may develop this crumbly, white, waxy substance on the cheeks, breasts, abdomen and buttocks, caused by chemicals in the soil reacting with the body's proteins and fats. Decomposition is slowed in these cases where grave wax inhibits the bacteria that cause putrefaction.

Growing fingernails and the appearance of 'new' skin – other phenomena that screamed 'undead' to the villagers of Kisilova – are merely illusions created by shrinkage due to dehydration. The separation of the top layer of skin, normal in decomposition, exposes the fresh, reddish skin below. Likewise, old nails drop off and the skin shrinkage merely reveals the nail hitherto concealed below the surface. The Egyptians were familiar with this phenomenon and when embalming their relatives would either tie the nails to the fingers and toes or place metal thimbles over them.[39]

Evidence of fresh blood, either on the face of the corpse or after the body has been stabbed or pierced, can also be explained. Once blood is no longer circulating, its movement is determined by gravity, which gives it a tendency to pool. If, for example, a body is lying face down, the trachea is likely to fill with blood, which escapes through the nose or the mouth. There is no mention of Plogojowitz's position during exhumation, but it is likely that he was covered in a shroud and lying on his front. Blood can also migrate to the nose and mouth during the natural process of decomposition as the gases in the abdomen increase the pressure on the lungs, forcing them upwards and pushing blood with them. Peter Plogojowitz's tumescent member – further 'evidence' that he was a vampire – can also be explained because, as bacterial gases start to work, the genitals are inflated out of all proportion.

As with most vampire exhumations, things settled down in Peter Plogojowitz's village after he was staked and burnt. However, such scenes were not merely confined to the Slavic fringes of Europe during the eighteenth century. The last recorded case of a vampire exhumation is on the brink of the twentieth century, only 150 miles from New York City, in the unlikely location of Exeter, Rhode Island.

Mercy Brown was only nineteen years old when, in 1892, she died of consumption (pulmonary tuberculosis), a disease responsible for one out of four deaths in the nineteenth century. Mercy's mother and sister had both died of similar causes nine years previously, and her brother Edwin had been battling the disease for several years. Unlike Edwin, Mercy suffered from the galloping variety that killed her in a matter of months. Not long after Mercy's funeral, Edwin took a turn for the worse. George Brown, his father, was so frantic and deranged by grief that he started listening to rumours that a vampire was responsible for wiping out his family.

What transpired in Exeter was not unlike the scenes in Kisilova some 170 years earlier. A couple of months after Mercy had been temporarily interred in the crypt of the Chestnut Hill Cemetery (the ground was too frozen to bury her), George Brown went with some friends and exhumed his daughter's remains. Rumours of vampirism seemed to be confirmed when Mercy's body was found to be intact – thanks, no doubt, to conditions in the crypt – with no signs of decomposition. Brown then did what any father would do in the circumstances: he slit open her chest, took out her heart, burnt it, mixed the ashes with water, and fed the concoction to his son. Folklore brought by immigrants from Europe dictated that if the heart or liver still had liquid blood present – and Mercy's did – the offending organs were to be burnt and the ashes consumed by the ailing victim, in this case Edwin. Such culinary practices, it was believed, would bring the vampire's powers to an end. Edwin would therefore be saved. Unsurprisingly, the cannibalistic graveside horrors were in vain, since the young man died two months after eating his sister's ashes. Still, George Brown and the inhabitants of Exeter were satisfied that the vampire had been killed, since no one else succumbed to the same symptoms.

THE PLOT THICKENS

Suspected vampires were nearly always exhumed in order to satisfy a fearful populace, but thankfully there is little call these days for sharpened stakes or silver bullets. However, due to modern DNA testing techniques, death no longer guarantees that a body will rest in peace. Bodies are now being exhumed – often many years after burial – to confirm or deny that the resident is indeed the person described on the headstone.

Human nature abhors a mystery. There's hardly a dead hero, politician, outlaw or saint who hasn't been raised from the tomb and then subjected to the full CSI treatment – a barrage of X-rays, DNA testing, CAT scans and toxicological investigations – in order to satisfy our curiosity about how they might have died or who they might really have been. Not even US Presidents are spared these high-tech probes. In 1991 the body of Zachary Taylor, who died in office after only sixteen months, was exhumed and tested for poison. The results proved negative: 'Old Rough and Ready' had simply died of a gastrointestinal illness. Also in 1991, nine bodies were exhumed from shallow graves outside Yekaterinburg in Russia. Mitochondrial DNA sequencing indicated that the remains were those of the Romanovs – including Tsar Nicholas II – who were executed by the Bolsheviks in 1918.

In the largest and most ambitious of these forensic investigations, the business of exhuming the remains of forty-nine members of the Medici dynasty in Florence began in 2004. Cracking open the graves in the church of San Lorenzo in Florence was an international team of paleopathologists, anthropologists, archaeologists and historians. The bodies, including those of eight grand dukes, were to be subjected to various cutting-edge proce-dures to determine how they lived and died: researchers hoped to find out if some of them were poisoned, as legend has it, and if, as some have claimed, the family was originally Jewish. But problems arose as a number of interlopers – the remains of eight children – were discovered in the tombs. It also became apparent that, in some cases at least, the body in the coffin did not match the name inscribed on the tomb, as if the corpses had somehow gone walkabout and swapped places during their long centuries of repose. The experts now predict it may be several decades before any conclusions are reached.

Not even the holiest of saints are spared disinterment and the pitiless scrutiny of X-ray machines and DNA sequencing. In 1998 a body in Padua, said for centuries to be that of St Luke, was exhumed for examination. Thirty-nine sequences of mitochondrial DNA were obtained and com-pared to that of modern-day Greeks and Syrians (according to the Bible,

Luke originally came from Antioch in Syria). The body in Padua, as it turned out, did indeed come from Syria. More recently, late in 2006 Vatican archaeologists announced the discovery in Rome of a sarcophagus containing – so they claimed – the remains of St Paul. The remains were promptly X-rayed to confirm the saint's identity, though the tests failed because of the thick layers of concrete and plaster encasing the marble coffin. Plans are afoot, however, to prise open the sarcophagus and determine whether or not the bones are indeed those of the saint.

Few graves have been surrounded by as much mystery as that of the legendary outlaw Jesse James. After serving with the Confederate forces in the American Civil War, Jesse and his brother Frank formed the James-Younger band of outlaws that for sixteen years carried out bank and train robberies in Missouri, Minnesota and Tennessee. Jesse cheated death many times before being shot in the back of the head in 1882 by fellow gang member Robert Ford, who wanted to claim the $10,000 bounty placed on Jesse's head.

At the time of his death, Jesse was supposedly living with his wife and two children in St Joseph, Kansas, under the pseudonym of Thomas Howard. His remains were returned to his family's farm in Kearney, Missouri, and buried in the front yard, the site being chosen to prevent possible theft or desecration. Then, in June 1902, the remains were removed and reburied in the family plot at the Mount Olivet Cemetery in Kearney. The notorious outlaw was not, however, allowed to rest in peace.

Nearly fifty years later, in 1951, Sheriff Oran C. Baker was summoned to identify the body of a 103-year-old man from Granbury, Texas. The sheriff was in no doubt about the identity of the old man: he was looking, he believed, at the corpse of Jesse James. Frank Dalton, as the man was known, had consistently claimed to be Jesse James, and he even sported thirty-three scars on his body – the number of bullet wounds on the body of the real Jesse James. He also had burn marks on the soles of his feet, a punishment known to have been inflicted on James by the Yankees during the Civil War. Supporters of Dalton's claim argued that Robert Ford had actually gunned down another gang member, Charlie Bigelow, who not only looked similar to James but was, they claimed, living with the bank robber's wife. It was even suggested that James staged the shooting so he could live out his life incognito.

In 1995 the remains in the grave at the family plot at Mount Olivet Cemetery were exhumed for examination. The DNA of James's relatives showed a ninety-nine per cent match, confirming that the body was almost certainly that of the legendary outlaw. As for Frank Dalton, the man from Texas, he was exhumed in 2000, but since the body had only one arm, and since Dalton had possessed two, the remains may not have been those of the man whose name was on the headstone. In a strange irony, the man who spent so many years trying to convince people he was someone he was not, found himself, in death, the victim of a one-armed impostor. The unexpected discovery illustrates how exhumed bodies do not always tell us what we wish to know or behave in the ways we want them to. The story of a life does not always end when the name is chiselled onto the headstone. The dead can be as full of surprises as the living.

CHAPTER 4

Rest in Pieces

Body Bits and Their Uses

Jeremy Bentham was one person who did not fear the anatomist's scalpel. The English utilitarian philosopher – the man who coined the expression 'the greatest happiness of the greatest number' – wanted the bodies of the dead to be made useful to the living. To that end, he donated his body to his medical disciple, Thomas Southwood Smith, who, three days after Bentham's death in 1832, dissected the corpse before an assembly of twenty-four friends at the Webb Street School of Anatomy in London. Bentham's head was then mummified and his skeleton, clad in padded clothing and topped by a wax model of the philosopher's head, put on display in University College, London. Bentham hoped to become what he called an 'auto-icon' – a mummified commemoration of himself that would be more real and inspiring than a marble statue.

The dead had been of service to the living long before 1832, and not merely through anatomical dissection. In the Middle Ages a flourishing trade in 'corpse medicine' witnessed near-cannibalistic practices whereby the sick drank human blood, consumed powdered skulls, and caressed themselves with the lifeless fingers of executed criminals. Corpses not only made their way into artists' studios as anatomical models but also, strangely enough, as pigment. Today they are used as sources of spare parts, offering up organs and tissue for transplants and – on the black market at least, where a new generation of bodysnatchers has appeared – for beauty products such as collagen. In his utilitarian heaven, Bentham, a man who would definitely have carried a donor card in his wallet, must be highly pleased.

RELICS OF THE PAST

Life- and health-giving properties have long been attributed to dead bodies. One of the earliest examples comes from the Old Testament, where 2 Kings 13 describes a peculiar manner by which a dead man was brought back to life. The man was interred in the sepulchre of the Prophet Elisha, who had died a year earlier. During his lifetime Elisha had resuscitated a dead child by placing his mouth on the child's and apparently administering a primitive form of mouth-to-mouth resuscitation. These miraculous powers of healing continued even after his death, since the dead man revived after coming into contact with Elisha's bones: he 'came to life', the Bible reports, 'and stood upon his feet' (2 Kings 13:21).

There is no evidence that Elisha's bones (discovered in the 1970s in the Monastery of St Macarius, ninety-two kilometres from Cairo) afterwards became the site of pilgrimage by those seeking cures, but the bodies and body parts of many other religious figures have long served as health-bestowing relics. The word relic comes from the Latin *relinquere*, to relinquish or leave behind. The physical remains of saints and other holy men and women – including relics as small and seemingly insignificant as teeth or finger bones – have been venerated for many centuries in the Catholic Church. Catholics are encouraged to adore a saint's remains in order to help them keep the faith and attain their goal of salvation. As an added bonus, it was possible in many cases to cure physical ailments, since Church Fathers such as St Ambrose and St Augustine gave authority to the belief that bodily diseases could be healed by the relics of saints. Pilgrims to the Holy Land brought back thousands of relics, and by the Middle Ages there was hardly a cathedral or abbey in Europe that did not boast at least one set of healing relics. A dedicated pilgrim was thus able to make his way around Europe in a quest to cure every infirmity imaginable. In cases of toothache, he was advised to visit the shrine of St Gudule, the patron saint of Brussels. Those seeking a cure for blindness could make their way to the abbey at Ely to press their hands on the coffin of St Æthelthryth, the abbey's founder. The relics of St Junianus at the monastery of Nouaillé were said to have cured a woman of elephantiasis and many others of fever. In Palermo, the bones of St Rosalia were successful in warding off epidemics – miraculous powers that did not seem to wane even after they were shown by the geologist William Buckland to be those of a goat.[40]

In actual fact, relic worship had as much to do with the economic well-being of the Church as it did with the physical well-being of its parishioners. Possession of a saint's relics was a way of ensuring a steady flow of money into church coffers as worshipping pilgrims were expected to leave a payment on their way out. Having the holy relics of a saint was also good for the local economy, since it brought to town pilgrims who required refreshments and lodgings. That is why, in 1087, sixty-two Italian sailors hatched a plan to steal the bones of St Nicholas from the crypt of his church in Myra, Turkey.

St Nicholas, the prototype for Santa Claus, died on 6 December 326, and was made a saint on account of the many good deeds and miracles he performed during his lifetime. St Nicholas's metamorphosis from a pious Mediterranean saint into a jolly, tubby, white-bearded old man, dressed in a red jump suit and riding a sleigh pulled by a fleet of reindeer, began quite innocently in the twelfth century. A group of French nuns, inspired by the story of how he had saved three impoverished sisters from prostitution by tossing separate bags of gold through the family's window for the young women's dowries, began delivering stockings packed with oranges and nuts to the homes of the poor. St Nicholas was also renowned for numerous miracles. In one of the most spectacular, he revived three children from the dead after they had been butchered and then pickled. A famine in Myra had induced a depraved butcher to kill the three children and pickle their remains in a barrel, with the plan of selling them as ham. Nicholas, learning of the crime, brought the dead children back to life. Another version of the legend – which is thought to have inspired the story of Sweeney Todd – claims that the butcher murdered three men and then, at the suggestion of his wife, turned them into meat pies. Once again, Nicholas not only kept the victims from the dinner table but revived them from the dead.

St Nicholas's popularity with pilgrims meant transferring his bones to the small town of Bari, on the east coast of Italy, made good business sense. After stealing the bones in 1087, the sailors reburied them in a chapel in Bari, where today visitors still flock to pay their respects. However, in the 1950s, the crypt in Bari's Basilica di San Nicola, where St Nicholas is interred, was in dire need of repair, and despite the thousands of visitors to his shrine every year, his bones needed to be moved. At this point it became apparent that some of his bones were missing – which may explain why other churches claim to hold fragments of this venerated saint: Toulouse has a fingerbone; Rimini a humerus (the upper arm); Corbie, in France, a tooth; while various fingers are scattered around Germany. During reno-vation of the tomb, the bones were carefully placed in an urn that was then laid on top of a linen cloth. The bones were seen to 'perspire' a clear liquid that left the linen cloth soaking wet. The devout interpreted this substance as 'manna', the divine food miraculously produced for the Israelites and mentioned in the Book of Exodus. Since 1980, about 50ml of this manna has been collected each 9 May (the feast of translation) and then distrib-uted to the faithful. Taken internally or applied externally to ailing parts of the body, it is believed to have miraculous properties. Sadly, St Nicholas's bones are deteriorating, and this deterioration is probably due to the moisture in the 'manna' – the very substance that confirms to his followers that he is divine.

Relics are almost as popular today as they were in the Middle Ages. In the summer of 2001 some three million people in Ireland – seventy-five per cent of the entire population – turned out to see the bones of St Thérèse of Lisieux, known as the 'Little Flower', who died of tuberculosis in 1887 at the age of twenty-four. Numerous other relics were exposed for veneration in the year 2006 alone. The miraculously preserved heart of St John Vianney, the patron saint of parish priests, was viewed by thousands of worshippers in New York and Boston after being brought over from France, and several months earlier, in March 2006, some two thousand relics from the 233 martyrs from Valencia, killed during the Spanish Civil War in 1936, were distributed for worship in churches, religious communities and even private homes in more than thirty countries. According to the Catholic News Agency, most of these relics consist of 'small bone fragments' of the martyrs.[41]

If, in the Middle Ages, relics were bought from people such as Chaucer's Pardoner, today they may be acquired on eBay. Offered for auction in the month of June 2007 was a single strand of hair from St Bernadette of Lourdes ($300) and a sterling silver locket containing what was described as 'extremely rare and substantial relics of Our Lord Jesus Christ'. This latter collection, which attracted bids of close to £1,000, included fragments of the True Cross, the Crown of Thorns and the Holy Knife of Circumcision. More relics would presumably appear on eBay if the company did not have a policy of banning the sale of human remains.

SPARE PARTS

If the London poor of the nineteenth century had good reason to fear a posthumous rendezvous with the anatomist, so too is there cause for concern, in the twenty-first century, that a dead body might be dissected – and even sold for a handsome profit – against the wishes of its late owner. A new generation of bodysnatchers has hit the headlines.

The list of perils that await a dead body – bodysnatchers, anatomists, misguided vampire hunters – must now include, in some cases, the mortician. Legends abound of undertakers prising fillings from the teeth or rings from the fingers of the corpses who pass through their mortuaries. This sort of unprincipled undertaker provides the plot for Umberto Lenzi's 1988 slasher movie *Ghosthouse*, in which a mortuary worker steals a clown doll from the coffin of a little girl and gives it to his own daughter, who then embarks on a gory killing spree. Some undertakers, though, have been tempted by more than just a piece of bling or a sentimental keepsake.

There's an old saying that your doctor and your undertaker should never be the same person. The adage might now need amending: never let your undertaker double as the owner of a biomedical tissue company that harvests organs and other body parts for transplantation and for medical research. Michael Brown, from Murrieta, California, sixty-five miles northeast of San Diego, wore both hats. In October 2003, the funeral home proprietor pleaded guilty to sixty-six counts of mutilation of human remains and embezzlement. Between February 2000 and March 2001, he had scavenged the bones and torsos of at least three hundred corpses placed in his care, stored them in six large meat freezers, and then sold them through a biotech company that he also owned. In the process he netted some $400,000.

Two years later, this illegal trade in body parts made emphatic headlines. In 2005 the New York police discovered that the legs of the recently deceased broadcaster Alistair Cooke, host of PBS's *Masterpiece Theater*, had been sawn off without consent from the family and the bones sold for profit to two transplant companies. In March 2006, four men, including a dentist and an embalmer, were charged with stealing skin, bones, heart valves and other tissue from 1,077 corpses, Cooke's included, for use in surgery. Corpses, often left unrefrigerated, were plundered of their most lucrative parts by a team of 'cutters' working out of the funeral home. To fool relatives the cutters replaced the bones of the deceased, as in the case of Cooke, with PVC tubing; and to fool the biomedical companies they forged consent forms and faked blood tests. The cause of death was often falsified, and at least one of the victims turned out to have tested positive for both HIV and hepatitis C.[42]

As Michael Brown's ill-gotten fortune indicates, the trade is a lucrative one. Surgically removed bones and a forged consent form can easily earn an unscrupulous undertaker a quick $7,000 (£4,000). Skin, which aids in wound healing, can fetch up to $1,000 (£600) a square foot; heart valves are worth up to $7,000 (£4,000); while a brain is a snip at $600 (£350). Even the fingernails (used in the cosmetics industry) can be scavenged. A whole body can be worth up to $150,000 (£85,000) – meaning that, on the black market at least, many people are worth more dead then alive. Between 1987 and 2006, over 16,800 American families have been represented by legal firms in their claims that the body parts of loved ones have been illegally harvested.[43] In the United States alone, the black market in body parts is estimated to have earned profits of $6 million (£3 million).

A large market exists for body parts. Each year, more than a million people undergo operations that use tissue or organs from deceased human donors – the vast majority safely and legally. Organ transplants are governed by strict laws, with each stage carefully monitored so that recipients can track exactly where their organs came from. Organs as well as tissue such as skin and bone used for human transplants must be screened for specific communicable diseases. In the United States, the organization responsible for the organs must register with the Food and Drug Administration (FDA) and follow strict guidelines. However, tissue banks are not required to register with the FDA, and therefore they are not subject to strict screening and testing regulations. As a buyer from a medical research company or educational establishment does not by law have to see a consent form or know where the tissue or body parts has come from, it is relatively easy for stolen body parts to enter the system. Due to short supply, there is often not much incentive for buyers to ask too many awkward questions. As there is no legal requirement for the buyer to do further testing to ensure their 'product' is disease-free, tests for communicable diseases are not always performed. Implanting unscreened body parts into another human body is, besides unethical, extremely risky. One fear for patients who have received unscreened tissue is that they could develop the same illnesses that the donor might have succumbed to. According to the FDA, diseases such as HIV, hepatitis and syphilis can all be contracted by transplants, although the risk is small. The FDA has recommended that doctors inform patients if they have received tissue or body parts from Biomedical Tissue Services, the company that stole and sold the bones of Alistair Cooke, but they are not legally obliged to. The ninety-five-year-old Cooke had died of bone cancer, rendering his body useless for any intended recipient.

The dangers of implanting organs of unknown origin have been highlighted by a number of tragedies, such as that of Brian Lykins, a twenty-three-year-old student from Minnesota who was given cartilage from a cadaver during elective knee surgery in 2001. The cartilage does not seem to have been illegally harvested, but since the donor's corpse had been left unrefrigerated for nineteen hours, and since the cartilage had not been properly cleaned and disinfected, Lykins died four days later from a bacterial infection. This needless fatality prompted a Republican Congressman, John Kline of Minnesota, to sponsor the Brian Lykins Human Tissue Transplant Safety Act. Introduced in 2005, the Act was aimed at amending the Public Health Service Act to authorize the Commissioner of Food and

Drugs to oversee organizations and individuals involved in the recovery, storage and processing of human tissue. The Act never became law, however, and in May 2006 tragedy repeated itself as Ken Alesescu, a fifty-five-year-old chiropractor from San Luis Obispo, California, died several years after being given a heart valve infected with a fungus.

The story of illegally harvested body parts features an even more appalling sidebar. In August 2006 the *St Louis Post-Dispatch* reported that vital organs such as livers and hearts – costing respectively $130,000 and $160,000 – were being made available in China for transplant into foreigners. The donors, according to *Post-Dispatch* reporter Deborah L. Shelton, were executed prisoners whose crime was to have followed the spiritual movement Falun Gong. A month earlier, in July 2006, an international investigation led by the former Canadian politician David Gilgour and the human rights lawyer David Matas concluded that large-scale seizures of organs from unwilling Falun Gong practitioners were taking place. The report for the Coalition to Investigate the Persecution of the Falun Gong in China (CIPFG) alleged that as many as 41,500 organs transplanted in China between 2000 and 2005 could have come from executed prisoners, including followers of Falun Gong. The Chinese government admitted in 2005 that it does harvest and sell the organs of executed prisoners, though it claims the practice never happens without the consent of the prisoners or their families. Kilgour disagrees, alleging that the Chinese torture prisoners to get their consent.[44]

Just as, in the nineteenth century, Professor James Macartney pointed out in a Dublin newspaper that the health and happiness of the middle classes came at the expense of Dublin paupers dissected on anatomists' tables, so too the health and happiness of some twentieth-first-century patients desperately awaiting organ transplants appears to depend on stick-at-nothing undertakers and ruthless Chinese executioners.

PUCKERING UP

Bits of human corpses are not just being used for replacing dodgy heart valves or damaged ligaments. They are also being used – unbelievable as it might seem – to make us more beautiful.

According to the popular magazine, *New Woman*, in her lifetime the average British woman spends £182,528 on beauty products and treatments (a figure that excludes dentistry and cosmetic surgery). The five hundred women who answered the magazine's questionnaire claimed that about £600 of this is spent annually on facials and anti-aging treatments. Collagen injections to plump up lips or reduce worry lines are no longer affordable only by the rich: a lip enhancement can cost as little as £250 – a small price to pay, it may seem, for a luscious, strawberry-lipped pucker. Or is it?

Collagen is a structural protein found in skin, bones, tendons and other connective tissue. For many years, scientists used animal collagen – that from cows and pigs – in surgical sutures; then in 1976 a group of Stanford University biochemists and physicians discovered a way of purifying animal collagen so it could be used to replace lost tissue. Plastic surgeons subsequently began using injections of collagen for cosmetic purposes, filling acne scars, smoothing wrinkles, and giving their patients gorgeous pouting lips. Many Hollywood actresses over the age of thirty-five – if you are to believe the gossip columns – are inflating their lips and decreasing their brows with injections of cow or pig collagen. However, about three per cent of all collagen users have a bad reaction to these bovine injections, which are unsuitable for those who are allergic to meat products or suffer from asthma or hayfever. That leaves the seekers of eternal youth with another alternative: collagen extracted from deceased human donors.

Some might find it more than a little distasteful to think that their beloved's lips contain dead men's stem cells, but they may perhaps reassure themselves that the materials were willingly donated and are medically safe. Yet not every collagen-enhanced pout has come about with both medical safety and consent of the donor. In September 2005, the *Guardian* reported that collagen harvested from executed Chinese prisoners and aborted foetuses was being used in beauty products exported to Europe and America.[45] The newspaper reported that Chinese prisoners were being skinned after they were shot, with the skin then used by a China-based biotech company to manufacture anti-aging treatments and lip-enhancing injections. Apart from the obvious ethical questions involved, collagen collected from such donors poses, like unscrupulously harvested organs, serious health risks. As no health checks are made on the donors, there is a serious possibility of the recipient being infected with hepatitis or new variant CJD. As of 2007, there are no European regulations governing cosmetic treatments, and therefore there is no way of knowing the origin of a particular batch of collagen. As if that were not disturbing enough, some physicians have reported a rise in autoimmune diseases – rheumatoid arthritis, systemic lupus erythematosus, dermatomyositis and polymyositis (the latter two involving the destruction of muscle tissue) – following collagen injections.[46] Such risk factors seem a high price to pay for even the most voluptuous pout.

CORPSE MEDICINE

The trade in body parts – and the use of the dead to preserve the living – is nothing new. Throughout history, the pieces and by-products of the human body have been used in all sorts of ways to cure all manner of ailments. Robert James in his *Pharmacopoeia Universalis*, printed in 1747, reported that human bodies were the source of raw materials for numerous medicines. Virtually anything the human body produced or excreted found its way into the cabinets of seventeenth- and eighteenth-century apothecaries. Every imaginable discharge was pressed into service, from earwax (a cure for colic) and sweat (for tuberculosis) to dried menstrual blood (for both gout and epilepsy). Even urine was consumed, since women suffering difficult labours were advised to drink some of their husband's number one – a prescription that gives a whole new meaning to the expression 'taking the piss'. Those afflicted with tonsillitis (known as quinsy) experienced an even worse fate: they were encouraged to consume human dung.[47]

If these particular remedies came from living donors, it was a short step for apothecaries to create their medicines from the bodies of dead ones. Indeed, the dead have long been exploited to cure the ailments and prolong the lives of the living. According to the Ebers Papyrus – an Egyptian medical text which dates from about 1550 BCE, and which was discovered between the legs of a mummy – human brains could be cut up and used to cure eye ailments (the papyrus also suggested that breast milk could be used as an alternative). In *De Medicina*, the ancient Roman philosopher

Celsus wrote that epileptics could be cured if they drank the blood of a slain gladiator. In many other cultures, parts of a dead body were used as medicinal cures. For example, a traditional cure in England for ulcers, goitre, scrofula and cysts was touching a dead man's hand, preferably one who had died an untimely death. People flocked to a public execution and paid the hangman handsomely to let them rub the hand of the still-warm victim as he dangled from the rope. In 1785 James Boswell recorded witnessing people rubbing themselves with 'the sweaty hands of malefactors in the agonies of death'. In the Fens of East Anglia, dead men's hands were thought to act as a contraceptive. It was widely believed that a woman would not become pregnant for two years if for two minutes she held the hand of a recently deceased man. The executioner at Newgate Prison in London capitalized on the belief that the touch of a dead man's hand could cure diseases such as the King's Evil – scrofula – by chopping off the hands of his victims and selling them for as much as ten guineas a piece.

The belief in the curative powers of human blood persisted into the seventeenth and eighteenth centuries. Drinking blood was, it seems, not just for vampires. At public hangings in Denmark, people waited with cups to catch fresh blood from the corpse in the hope it would cure their epilepsy. In the late seventeenth century a New England minister named Edward Taylor claimed that human blood, drunk 'warm and new', was a cure for 'falling sickness' – that is, epilepsy – and English doctors were likewise prescribing a draught of 'recent and hot' human blood as late as the middle of the eighteenth century. Those suffering from rheumatism would go not to the doctor but – in seventeenth-century Paris, at least – to the hangman. One of the perks of the hangman's job was that he was allowed to harvest the body fat of his victims: he would mix it with aromatic herbs to produce his remedy. Epileptics were prescribed powdered human hearts and distilled brains. Bone was used as well as flesh and blood. In the 1680s, human skulls were sold in London for as little as eight shillings apiece. A famous potion named 'Spirit of the Skull' was believed to cure epilepsy and various other ailments, and as late as 1721 the *Dispensatory of the Royal College of Physicians* was recommending 'three drams of human skull' in cases of epilepsy. Skulls and bones were obtained for these medicines through the efforts of men such as an eighteenth-century doctor named Toope, from

Marlborough in Wiltshire, who excavated old burial grounds in the Marlborough Downs and then turned Bronze Age skeletons into state-of-the-art potions.[48]

The prescriptions of some physicians fell little short of cannibalism. The seventeenth-century German pharmacologist Johann Schroeder devised, as we have seen, a recipe for a cure-all that featured a fresh human cadaver as the prime ingredient.[49] This kind of medicinal cannibalism – or what was known as 'corpse medicine' – has in fact been used by ancient cultures of the Mesopotamians, Greeks, Chinese, Hebrews, Indians and Romans. Many ancient medical texts prescribed pollutant therapy (using human blood or body parts) to fight impurity or disease. In particular, the pulverized flesh and bones of Egyptian mummies were used by medieval Europeans as a cure for numerous ailments – poisoning, incontinence, migraines, abscesses, giddiness, paralysis, internal ulcers, concussions, contusions and even scorpion stings. Our word mummy, which conjures images of the bandaged and embalmed corpses of Egyptian pharaohs, originally referred not to the corpses themselves but to the medicines prepared from them. The strange belief that eating Egyptian mummies could cure ailments seems to have come about through the mistranslation of Arabic medical books. In Arabic the word bitumen was a general word for asphalt and other similar substances. Arab physicians spread bitumen on cuts, bruises and bone fractures, as well as using it internally to treat tuberculosis and ulcers. After years of practice, they discovered that the best results came from a Persian bitumen known as *mumiya*. Gerard of Cremona, who translated accounts of Egyptian embalming and their use of bitumen, may have inadvertently been the cause of this misunderstanding, since he wrongly assumed that *mumiya* – which was used in the embalming process – referred to the embalmed bodies themselves.

Mummy medicine became popular in the twelfth century as large numbers of Europeans, who fought in the Crusades in Palestine, witnessed firsthand how the Arabian medics applied *mumiya* to wounds, mistaking this tarry substance for ground-up bodies. If *mumiya* was also taken internally to cure tuberculosis, the Crusaders must have thought, then why not use it for other ailments? By the Middle Ages, people all over Europe commonly resorted to this form of cannibalism to cure their ills. There is no evidence that eating a mummy actually cured any one of these ailments, but it almost certainly tasted awful and induced vomiting – thereby possibly having, in some cases, a salutary effect.

Despite warnings about mummy medicine by the sixteenth-century French surgeon Ambroise Paré, who urged the banning of its internal use because it caused a 'paine of the heart or stomacke, vomiting and stinke of the mouth', the demand for ground-up mummies soon threatened to out-strip the supply.[50] Unscrupulous dealers, spotting an opportunity to make money, began mummifying dead criminals and selling them to unsuspecting European traders. Just as there was a trade in fake Egyptian antiquities, so too there emerged a market for fake mummy medicine. *The British Encyclopedia or Dictionary of Arts and Sciences,* published in 1809, claimed that apothecaries were being supplied with the flesh of executed criminals in place of ancient mummies, and that this flesh was spiced with cheap ingredients and baked in an oven 'till the juices are exhaled, and the embalming matter has penetrated so thoroughly that the flesh will keep, and bear transporting to Europe'.

If recent reports from India can be believed, people are still unwittingly consuming human body parts to cure themselves of various afflictions. In January 2006, Swami Ramdev, owner of the popular Divya Yog Pharmacy near the holy city of Haridwar, in northern India, was accused by the Indian politician Brinda Karat of using human and animal bones in his Ayurvedic medicine. Ramdev, who manufactures thousands of potions, denied the charge, accusing Karat of being an agent for multinational pharmaceutical companies. Karat backed her claims by having several of Ramdev's potions tested at government laboratories; the results appeared to confirm her accusations. However, samples sent to the Shriram Institute of Industrial Research, another government laboratory, proved the opposite. Finally, Tilak Raj Behad, India's Health Minister, informed the press that the reme-dies were purely herbal and contained nothing untoward. So the mystery lingers. However, sceptics became suspicious of the motive behind Karat's allegations when she produced ten ex-workers from the Divya Yog Mandir Trust who claimed that human skulls were powdered and mixed with Ayurvedic medicines. These ten workers had been sacked from Ramdev's company, alongside 103 others, when they campaigned for minimum wages and company insurance schemes. An agreement was reached, but the agitating workers lost their jobs and therefore may have had reason to wish ill upon the Divya Yog Pharmacy. What better way to exact revenge, Ramdev's supporters suspect, than to suggest that Ramdev was a purveyor of corpse medicine?

THROW MUMMY FROM THE TRAIN!

Mummies have also played a part in another misconception about human remains. In his book *Innocents Abroad,* published in 1869, Mark Twain entertained his readers with accounts of his experiences travelling in far-flung places. His Egyptian observations in particular caused fascinated comment in drawing rooms across Europe and America. Twain claimed to have ridden aboard an Egyptian train whose fuel was 'composed of mummies three thousand years old, purchased by the ton or by the graveyard for that purpose'. He even reported that the train drivers discovered that 'plebeian mummies didn't burn as well as a king'.

Twain was, not for the first time, pulling the legs of his readers. For the record, some Egyptians were known to burn mummy wrappings to heat their homes, but there is not a shred of evidence to suggest that mummies were ever used to fuel trains. If mummies had been used, the pollution from the bitumen used in the embalming process would have been extremely toxic and unpleasant for the train drivers. However, during the Siege of Paris by the Prussians in 1870, a macabre solution, not dissimilar to Twain's far-fetched claims, was proposed to the Scientific Committee for the Defence of Paris, which had been entertaining all manner of fanciful notions for withstanding the siege and defeating the Prussians. To solve their lighting problems (gas for street lamps was in short supply), a correspondent alleged to have discovered a method of obtaining light by distilling cadavers, which provided, he proudly declared, 'a very clear light, more powerful, softer and infinitely more economical than oil gas'.[51] The 'City of Light' would be illuminated thanks to hundreds of boiled corpses. There is no evidence that the bizarre proposal was ever put to the test, and Parisians remained in darkness during the four-month siege.

BODIES OF WORK

When mummies weren't being eaten or – in the apocryphal stories – used to power locomotives, they found quite another role: they ended up in artists' paintboxes. The pigment called 'Mummy Brown' was, as its name suggests, made from the ground-up remains of human cadavers – Egyptian mummies, to be precise. Sally Woodcock, senior lecturer in art history at the University of London, thinks that 'very many nineteenth-century painters might have used mummy as a pigment at one time or another', but it is, she claims, virtually impossible to identify its uses in specific paintings.[52] It is a deep brown that was sometimes mixed with other pigments and, more often than not, was used for painting shadows.

Artists were not necessarily aware of the origins of the useful brown pigment on their palette. Edward Burne-Jones, the British Pre-Raphaelite painter, was shocked to be told in 1881 by his friend Lawrence Alma-Tadema that Mummy Brown was actually ground-up mummies. According to his wife Georgiana, he immediately took his tube of Mummy Brown and 'insisted on giving it a decent burial there and then'. She described the interment: 'So a hole was bored into the grass at our feet, and we all watched it put safely in, and the spot was marked by one of the girls planting a daisy root above it.'[53] The obvious implication is that many of Burne-Jones's paintings produced before this respectful burial have traces of human remains.

Burne-Jones was not unique in his ignorance of the origin of his pigment, which is probably why Mummy Brown was so commonly used. Once its origins were exposed, its popularity among painters began to decrease. It is not known quite how ground-up mummies first metamorphosed into paint, but there is evidence that the substance was used as early as the twelfth century. The apothecaries who sold ground-up mummies as medicinal cures also sold paint pigments. Somehow – whether accidentally or deliberately – one of them discovered that mummy powder produced a distinctive colour. Apothecaries used different parts of the mummy: some preferred the fleshiest parts, while others ground up every bit (bones included) to produce a deeper pigment. One German source describes in detail how apothecaries would wash the mummy thoroughly before cutting it up and soaking the bits for days in water. Impurities were rinsed off and the remains ground in water. The filtering process took six to eight rinses in warm water until the residue was ready for drying and pulverizing.[54]

The Swiss artist Angelica Kauffman (1741–1807) is known to have used Mummy Brown in her paintings, since the English poet George Keates wrote a thirty-two page epistle praising her for allowing a mummy to live through her paintings. And an apothecary's sales ledger as late as 1902 records that the American artist James Jebusa Shannon, famous for his enchanting painting *Magnolia* (1899), now in the Metropolitan Museum of Art in New York, bought tubes of mummy paint. Visitors standing before *Magnolia*, the portrait of a beautiful young woman, may wish to spare a thought for the unsuspecting mummy who finds himself, as Keate wrote, 'Call'd from the Darkness of the Tomb' to create an artistic masterpiece.[55]

Many other artists made use of the dead body, often in much more alarming ways, in order to enhance their skills. The sixteenth-century Florentine painter known because of his reddish complexion as Il Rosso Fiorentino – the Red Florentine – used to dig up fresh corpses from their graves in order to study the effects of death and decomposition on human anatomy. (Rosso was a strange character: he also kept a baboon for a servant.) An even greater dedication to art, and an even more horrifying desecration of the human body, was practised by Jacopo da Pontormo, one of Rosso's contemporaries. Pontormo supposedly kept corpses floating in troughs of water in his house as he prepared a painting on the subject of Noah's Flood, making drawings of them as they bloated and blackened. Not surprisingly, the neighbours soon complained about the smell. Pontormo was a friend of Michelangelo, who was also a dedicated and accomplished anatomist. However, Michelangelo became so affected by the sight of dead bodies – which were supplied to him by a helpful hospital administrator in Florence – that he was sick to the stomach and unable to eat, and so he eventually abandoned the practice.

In more recent times, the controversial artist Anthony-Noel Kelly, a former butcher, has been caught using body parts in his art. An art lover visiting the London Contemporary Art Fair in 1997 was shocked to recognize in one of Kelly's sculptures the face of a recently departed friend, now cast in plaster, coated in silver, and showing part of his exposed brain. When the police discovered about thirty body parts on the premises of his studio in Clapham, South London, Kelly, a cousin of the Duke of Norfolk, admitted that they were indeed for use in his art. He moulded plaster casts from the remains – including one from the corpse of his grandmother – and gilded the plaster copies in gold and silver. It transpired that an employee of the Royal College of Surgeons was the source of his supplies. Kelly had sketched dismembered body parts on the premises of the Royal College of Surgeons but then paid a laboratory technician to smuggle out torsos, limbs and other body parts from which to make his plaster casts. In 1998, he was sentenced to nine months in prison, not for using the body parts in his art, but for stealing them. It was a difficult case to prosecute because under English law, no one can own a corpse. However, the judge ruled that the specimens were the property of the Royal College of Surgeons because 'skilled work' had been carried out on them by 'a previous generation of surgeons'. Kelly, the prosecution argued, intended permanently to deprive the 'owners' of their property.

Shortly after the high-profile Kelly case, another even more disturbing one hit the headlines. In 1999 it was discovered that 2,080 organs had been removed without parental consent from eight hundred deceased children at Alder Hey Hospital in Liverpool. Many parents had specifically asked that any organs removed for autopsy be returned for burial with the body. However, Professor Dick van Velzen, pathologist at Alder Hey Hospital between 1988 and 1995, used (or planned to use) them for research purposes, without getting the permission from either the coroner or the parents. Dr van Velsen's stockpile included 445 foetuses, 188 eyes and more than two dozen disembodied heads, many of them stored in dusty jars with inadequate levels of formalin. In 2001, van Velzen was convicted in Canada of improperly storing body parts after being sacked from W. K. Grace Hospital in Halifax, Nova Scotia, for similar practices. In the same year the General Medical Council in Britain suspended him after finding that he had 'systematically, illegally and unethically' stripped organs from the bodies of thousands of children at Alder Hey.

These two cases were responsible for a change to the law in Britain, with the introduction of The Human Tissue Act. This Act ensures that the coroner has the right to examine tissues and organs at an inquest, after which they must be returned to the next of kin. As the law now stands in Britain, a dead body is the property of the next of kin. After we die, that is, we belong to our spouses or children.

CHAPTER 5

Getting Stuffed

Embalmers, Plastinators and Headshrinkers

As the mummified head and swaddled skeleton of Jeremy Bentham show, 'ashes to ashes and dust to dust' does not necessarily apply to everyone. Embalming usually conjures up images of Ancient Egyptian mummies wrapped in reams of bandages; but the Egyptians were not the first (Australian aborigines and the Chinchorro Indians of Chile both preceded them) and certainly not the last to preserve corpses in this way. Embalming has been performed for a wide variety of reasons. Egyptians did it so that the soul wandering in the afterlife for three thousand years could return to a body that was intact and uncorrupted. For others, like the Chinchorro, it was done simply to delay saying good-bye to their loved ones. There are practical reasons too. As a corpse can decompose quickly, embalming allows it to be transported across long distances for burial. Embalming can also be carried out to aid the identification process of a corpse, or in the name of scientific research. Whatever the rationale, the methods and techniques are equally diverse – and sometimes truly bizarre.

THE MUMMY RETURNS

The thousands of Egyptian mummies that have been discovered intact over the last millennium are testament to the success of ancient embalming techniques. The Egyptians did not use, as later practitioners would, a system of arterial embalming. Instead, they used herbs, spices and salt to preserve their dead. First the viscera – the internal organs – were removed (through the anus) and treated with these preservatives. The brain was pulverized and scooped out through the nostrils with a metal hook. Methods of embalming varied from dynasty to dynasty, but Egyptian embalmers commonly packed the empty skull with linen strips impregnated with resin, while the removed organs were washed and mixed with herbs, spices and resins, after which they were either returned to the body or stored in jars. Cavities in the body were washed out with spiced palm wine, after which the corpse was left to dehydrate by immersion for anything from forty to seventy days in natron (sodium salt) collected from the dry lakes of the desert. This dehydration caused the finger and toenails to fall off, although they were promptly replaced to ensure the body was intact for its reunion with the soul. The cadaver was then cleansed, straightened, padded with stuffing and anointed with oils and gum resins designed to prevent insect attack. The abdominal incision was closed and the nostrils plugged with resin or wax. The mummy was then ready for wrapping. About twelve hundred yards of narrow bandages – the length of ten football pitches – were held together with gum or glue, and were used to wrap the body, thus protecting it from the environment and preventing swelling.

Medieval Europeans may have eaten Egyptian mummies as medicine, but they showed little desire – and had no aptitude – to embalm the corpses of their own dead. In England, for example, embalming was reserved in the main for the aristocracy and high-ranking ecclesiastics, possibly to keep their bodies intact for the Resurrection. However, techniques had much more to do with hermetically sealing coffins – using lead-lined coffins or wrapping the body in beeswax-coated shrouds – than with removing organs and using preservatives on the body itself.[56]

Sometimes this lack of expertise led to awkward moments at the funeral. In 1087, while sacking the town of Nantes in northern France, William the

Conqueror, victor at the Battle of Hastings in 1066, was mortally injured, not by the enemy, but by a fall from his horse. He was taken to Rouen, where he died on arrival. The king was hastily – and incompetently – embalmed so that his body could be shipped to Caen for burial in the Abbey of St Stephen. There, the Conqueror was lowered into his stone coffin with great difficulty due to his enormous size – and his bowels burst during the ceremony, giving off the most dreadful stench and putting the fear of God into everyone present.

Likewise, after Pope Alexander VI – the notorious Rodrigo Borgia, father of Lucrezia and Cesare – died in Rome in August 1503, his body was taken to the chapel of Santa Maria della Febbre, beside the basilica of St Peter's. There, due to the sweltering summer heat, his corpse rapidly began to putrefy, with the face turning black and the body steaming. Worst of all, the corpse swelled to such grotesque proportions that it had to be forcibly stuffed into the coffin by the horrified carpenters. So deformed was the pope's corpse that no one could believe he had died from natural causes; instead they thought he must have been poisoned by his son Cesare. In fact, malaria was probably the culprit.

It was the discovery of the circulation of blood by the Englishman William Harvey (1578–1657) that made arterial embalming viable. A Danish doctor named Fredrick Ruysch (1665–1717) was one of the first to experiment with the system of arterial embalming, which, in its essential form, is still in use today. Embalming in this period was developed in order to preserve the dead for anatomical dissection and study rather than for religious or other reasons. Ruysch was later to arrange his embalmed specimens in artistic poses, often with props, which a paying public queued to view. His exhibits were known as 'Ruysch's Repository of Curiosities' and carried titles such as 'Syphilitic skull of a prostitute kicked by the leg of a baby' or 'A drunken rat holding a small beer barrel'. Who could resist paying to cast an eye over such prodigies? Ruysch was not, however, good at keeping records, so it was Scottish anatomist, Dr William Hunter (1718–83), who was in fact credited with the discovery of arterial preservation.

Ruysch supposedly injected into the veins of his deceased subjects a concoction of chemical preservatives, including alcohol. Hunter took the procedure a step further by draining the blood and replacing it with mercury, essential oils, alcohol, cinnabar, camphor, saltpetre and pitch or rosin. Roasted gypsum was placed in the coffin beside the embalmed body in order to aid the preservation process. To draw attention to his new trade in 1775, Hunter embalmed the dead wife of his friend, a London dentist named Martin van Butchell. According to witness accounts, the technique was not entirely successful, since Mrs van Butchell was said to look dry and shrunken, not at all a pretty sight. Nonetheless, the unfortunate woman was then displayed in van Butchell's London home as a kind of advert for Hunter's business. This bold gambit was to attract enormous criticism because it allowed van Butchell to continue receiving an income from his wife for as long as she remained above ground. Van Butchell weathered the storm of disapproval and continued to display her until he remarried and his second wife, understandably fed up with stepping around her predecessor each day, shipped her off to a local museum. The first Mrs van Butchell finally ended up at the Museum of the Royal College of Surgeons in London, where she remained until 1941, when she was cremated by a German bomb.

STRIKING A POSE

Around the time that Dr Hunter was touting for business by displaying his dentist's wife as a sample of his merchandise, across the Channel a Frenchman was experimenting with a different technique of arterial embalming. Hidden away on the second floor of a nondescript building at the École Nationale Veterinaire d'Alfort, in a suburb of Paris, is the Musée Fragonard. The museum is filled – rather like a grotesque version of a Barnum & Bailey Circus – with row upon row of glass cases containing every animal and human deformity imaginable (and some, frankly, not): a two-headed calf, a wax cast of a man's head covered in pus-discharging abscesses, a chicken with four legs, and tragically deformed human foetuses. Drawing back the curtain that covers the entrance to the rear room – Fragonard's exhibits – one is confronted by a life-sized man, flayed of his skin, astride a galloping horse, also flayed. This tableau is entitled 'The Horseman of the Apocalypse'. To the right is 'Samson', another skinless cadaver, with a conspicuously large, blackened penis, who stands tall, waving a donkey's jaw in his hand.

This is the 'art' of Honoré Fragonard (1732–99), cousin of the more famous Rococo painter Jean-Honoré Fragonard and descendent of the famous family of Provençal perfumiers. Fragonard studied as a surgeon and, in 1765, took up the post of Principal and Professor of Anatomy at the first veterinary college in the world, situated in Lyons. It was here that, in order to promote science and education, he perfected his unusual embalming techniques. What made Fragonard different from other anatomists of the day was that he did not concern himself with making the skin look fresh and lifelike – a task which embalmers still find difficult today – but instead peeled it away to reveal the structures beneath.

Fragonard refined his technique into a fine art. After removing the skin, he fixed the corpse in the pose he required. The body would then be dissected, leaving the muscles carefully in situ. Often he would inject the nerves and vessels with coloured wax, and he developed the technique of adding aromatic spices to alcohol and injecting it into the arteries of his subjects in order to prevent putrefaction. To finish the process off, layers of varnish were applied as a seal. The result was a series of anatomical models whose veins and muscles could clearly be seen by eager medical students.

Sadly, Fragonard's career was less than glittering. Six years after taking up his post at the veterinary school he was fired by his superiors for his perceived eccentricities. His work apparently offended both his colleagues and the general public alike, and it was not therefore given the scientific merit it deserved. He was also seen to be unnecessarily macabre and theatrical, due to the way in which he exhibited some of his pieces. Fragonard's critics may have had a point. For example, his 'Horseman of the Apocalypse' once held reins of red ribbon, and he arranged another exhibit, three human foetuses, to look as if they were dancing a jig – a tableau that particularly offended the squeamish. After his dismissal, Fragonard disappeared from the public eye for several decades, though he was reputed to have created several further collections of 'curiosities' which he exhibited behind closed doors throughout France.

Fragonard's career briefly revived when, in 1795, he was employed as head of anatomical work at the École de Santé in Paris, where he promised to perfect his embalming techniques in the name of science. However, the eccentric Frenchman never really fulfilled these promises, dying four years later at the age of sixty-seven. Only twenty of his creations exist today, as most were destroyed during the French Revolution.[57]

Honoré Fragonard's modern-day successor – in terms of his scientific ideals, gruesome exhibits and dogged controversy – is the Austrian impresario of 'plastination', Gunther von Hagens. As visitors wander around von Hagens's BODY WORLDS exhibition they are confronted by a series of side-of-beef-complexioned figures in action poses, such as 'The Soccer Player', a naked, skinless athlete frozen in the moment of putting the ball into the back of the net, a flesh-and-bone montage worthy of Fragonard. Another, 'The Ponderer', sits in silent contemplation, his spine rising like a railway track to his brain, which has been exposed by a cleft in his skull. Through their rose-coloured muscles and cutaway organs, these and other well-preserved corpses reveal the wonders of the ways in which the human body moves, breathes, feels, ingests and defecates. It is, as one visitor commented, a 'silent pink factory', although one in which visitors, faced by the grinning, pop-eyed 'mannequins', may feel more than a little uncomfortable.[58]

Von Hagens developed his plastination process in 1977, with the aim of making human corpses so malleable that they could be bent into various poses to look as if they were running or jumping. Touring the world since 1995, the exhibition has been seen by millions of visitors. In addition, more than four hundred institutions worldwide use his method to preserve anatomical specimens for study and instruction. In 1983, he was even approached by the Catholic Church to plastinate the heelbone of Hildegard of Bingen, who died in 1179 – an assignment that then led him to offer to plastinate Pope John Paul II. The Church authorities demurred after apparently showing some initial interest in the plan.

Von Hagens, who was born Gunther Liebchen, has been able to halt decomposition by adding reactive plastics – silicone rubber, epoxy resin or polyester resin – to the body, using a vacuum technique that extracts moisture. He is no stranger to controversy, as the Roman Catholic Church now – ironically – condemns his preparation and exhibition of corpses as a 'serious violation of the dignity of the dead and their reduction to the status of objects'.[59] Another row has erupted over the origins of his corpses. Von Hagens was accused by the German magazine *Der Spiegel* of buying and then plastinating the cadavers of executed Russian and Chinese prisoners – a charge he categorically denied, claiming that all the bodies had either been bequeathed by relatives or were unclaimed corpses provided by the local authorities in China and Russia. Indeed, in 2005, von Hagens took an injunction out through the German courts against *Der Spiegel*, which is now banned from repeating such accusations. On his official website, von Hagens boasts of having a donor roster of 6,593 individuals, including 140 Americans. Of these volunteers, 350 are already deceased and therefore ready for plastination. Such large numbers of donors do seem to suggest there would be no need to receive illegal bodies. Indeed, anyone interested in becoming part of one of his future exhibitions can download the donor consent form from his website. By completing and signing the form, donors agree to being shipped off to one of von Hagens's embalming facilities within twenty-four hours of their death. Additionally, von Hagens holds a meeting every two years for potential donors at the Heidelberg Institute for Plastination – recruitment drives, of a sort, to enlighten and encourage prospective plastination subjects.

STEP RIGHT UP

The ancient Egyptians developed embalming techniques for religious reasons, while Europeans, such as Fragonard, did so for anatomical research. However, as Dr Hunter's exhibition of Mrs van Butchell shows, embalming is sometimes done for less lofty reasons: in other words, to make a quick buck. There is, in fact, a long and somewhat disreputable history of embalming human specimens for public display, often in carnival sideshows.

People of non-European origin were often displayed in Europe and America, from Christopher Columbus's Arawak Indians to the 'Hottentot Venus' – a Khosi woman from South Africa named Saarjite Baartman who was exhibited to paying crowds in London early in the nineteenth century.

The proprietors of these 'exhibits' often continued to display their subjects even after they died, aided by the efforts of the embalmer, the ghoulish prurience of the paying public, and an alarming lack of any moral sensitivity. One of the more famous cases is that of Julia Pastrana, a young Mexican woman who was forced on a worldwide tour, billed as the 'Bearded and Hairy Lady' and the 'World's Ugliest Woman'. When Julia died in Moscow in 1860, aged twenty-six, the man who discovered her, an impresario named Theodore Lent, employed a Russian professor to embalm her. Thereafter she continued her world tour inside a glass cabinet, remaining on display in Norway until as late as the 1970s.

A similar fate has befallen a number of Native Americans, though in their cases the original motive was not money so much as revenge. Victims included Ma-ca-tai-me-she-kia-kiak, known to white American settlers as Blackhawk. A Sauk warrior born in 1767 in what is now Illinois, Blackhawk led a series of uprisings against settlers and the US Government until his defeat at the Battle of Bad Axe in 1832. When he died six years later, his grave was desecrated and his body stolen. The remains were eventually recovered, only to be sent to Burlington, Iowa, where they were put on display in the local museum. When the museum burned in 1855, the body was destroyed. A much more fitting tribute to Blackhawk has since been created, an heroic statue that stands on a bluff across the river from the town of Oregon, Illinois.

The Native American 'Captain Jack', whose Modoc name was Kintpuash, was hanged in California in 1873 for the murder of General Edward Canby. Due to white expansion in the region, the Modoc tribe of northern California was resettled in 1864 on the Klamath reservation, on the California-Oregon boundary. The Modocs were to share this reserve with the Klamath tribe, the land's original owners, and Pit River Indians. After many conflicts with the Klamath tribe, Captain Jack left the reservation in the early 1870s with a small band of followers, hoping to return to their original hunting grounds. General Canby, a Civil War veteran, was despatched to negotiate Captain Jack's return to the reservation, but he was killed on arrival, shot twice in the head. Captain Jack, captured soon afterwards with three of his warriors, was hanged and then buried at Fort Klamath. One day after his burial, he was exhumed by graverobbers, embalmed, and for the next few years he travelled around various American cities as a carnival exhibit. His head was eventually sent to the Army Medical Museum in Washington DC.

The story of one of the stranger examples of exhibiting embalmed bodies for profit began unfolding on 7 December 1976, during the filming of an episode of ABC's *The Six Million Dollar Man* at the Nu-Pike Amusement Park in Long Beach, California. The director of the episode asked one of the crew to move a mannequin – a long-time resident of the fun house – that was dressed as a cowboy and dangled from a rope. As the crew member pulled on the dummy, its arm came off in his hand. To the horror of everyone on the set, the mannequin proved to be no ordinary attraction, for the detached arm was human. So, it quickly became apparent, was the rest of the body. This life-like dummy was in fact the embalmed body of one Elmer McCurdy.

Embalmed cowboys are not necessarily what one expects to find when visiting an amusement park, so how did Mr McCurdy end up in Long Beach? Working with clues such as a 1924 penny and a ticket from the Museum of Crime in Los Angeles – both of which were found, oddly, in Elmer's mouth – forensic investigators were able to piece together his life story. Born in 1880, McCurdy became an outlaw after robbing a train near Okesa, Oklahoma, in 1911. Sadly for McCurdy, there was only $46 in the train's safe, but this modest sum did not deter a posse of men from chasing the bandit and killing him in a Wild West-style shoot-out. His body was taken to the funeral parlour in Pawhusha, Oklahoma, and when no one came to claim it, the undertaker, shrewdly sensing a business opportunity, embalmed McCurdy, charging punters a nickel each to see 'The Bandit Who Wouldn't Give Up'. After five years of earning his keep as a curiosity, McCurdy was claimed by two tricksters who informed the enterprising undertaker that they were relatives wanting to give poor Elmer a decent burial. No such luck: McCurdy then embarked, like Captain Jack, on a career as a sideshow exhibit in a travelling carnival. He was eventually retired, some years later, to the Nu-Pike Amusement Park, where his true origins were evidently long forgotten.

When his identity was confirmed, Elmer McCurdy was finally returned to Oklahoma in April 1977. More than six decades after his violent death, and after years of posthumous peregrinations, he was given a worthy send-off, being taken to his final resting place, the Summit View Cemetery, in a horse-drawn, glass-sided hearse that had been arranged by the Oklahoma State Historical Society.

THE INCREDIBLE SHRINKING MEN

Ruysch, Fragonard and von Hagens all claimed that they were first and foremost scientists, using embalming as a means to promote scientific knowledge. It was only as an afterthought, apparently, that they went on to exhibit their creations for public viewing. However, when does exhibiting embalmed bodies in demeaning ways cross the line from science and art and merely become disrespectful to the dead? The curators of New York's National Museum of the American Indian were faced with this ethical question when, in the early 1980s, it was decided to remove one of their most popular exhibits for being ghoulish as well as morally dubious.

No one has ever solved the mystery of why the 'Little Men', two shrunken bodies, one thirty-one inches high, the other a truly miniature twenty-six inches, were embalmed in this way. These Liliputian corpses are now in deep storage until a decision is made as to where to repatriate them. The smaller man has Afro hair and was bought for the museum in 1920 from Juan Krateil, a Polish mining engineer based in Latin America. However, an Ecuadorian named Gustave Struve claimed the body had been stolen from him a few years earlier. After much deliberation, the museum paid Struve $500, which he quickly accepted and then offered the other specimen. This second body, sporting white hair and a beard, was thought to be of Spanish origin.

The Jivaro Indians of Ecuador, with their skilful preservation techniques, whereby they shrank the disembodied heads of their enemies and wore them around their necks as trophies, were initially thought responsible for the 'Little Men'. But members of the tribe were incredulous when asked if it was customary for them to shrink whole bodies.[60] The shrinking of the two bodies therefore seems to have had less to do with tribal ritual and more to do with financial gain. Only two examples of Struve's handiwork have ever come to light, but the mind boggles as to the number of corpses he must have practised on to reach such a high level of expertise.

Struve's method of embalming, the motives behind it, and the source of the bodies have never been revealed. It is thought, however, that he copied the techniques of the Jivaro. Unlike Struve, the Jivaro had specific reasons for shrinking heads: they hoped to boost their own personal power. The head – known as the *tsantsa* – was believed to hold magical powers: possessing the head of an enemy benefited both the warrior and his ancestors, preventing the spirit or soul of the slain foe continuing into the afterlife and harming both the living and the dead.

The process of preparing a shrunken head, which took about a week, was undertaken with a care and precision worthy of Fragonard or von Hagens. Firstly, the skin and hair were carefully peeled away from the skull, which was thrown into the river for the anaconda to feed on. The eyelids were sewn shut with natural fibre and the mouth skewered with pegs that were eventually replaced by strings of chonta seeds. The head was then simmered in a sacred pot for about an hour and a half; care had to be taken to avoid over-cooking in case the hair fell out. Once cooked, the head had reduced to a third of its size, with a blackish rubbery appearance. The skin was then ready to be turned inside-out like a rubber glove and the leftover insides scraped out, after which it was flipped back into its original shape. The slit in the rear of the head was sewn back together, leaving a small gap for hot stones to be slipped inside to sear the interior and shrink the head further. Rotating the head constantly ensured the stones did not scorch the skin during further shrinkage. Hot sand was then forced through the nose and ears to fill the gaps left by the stones. Finally, stones were applied to the outside of the face to seal and shape the features, while a heated machete was pressed against the lips to dry them out.

The shrunken heads of several Amazonian tribesmen called the Shuar are still on display at Oxford University's Pitt Rivers Museum. Like the 'Little Men' in the National Museum of the American Indian, they are one of the most popular exhibits in a museum that houses the remains of some two thousand humans, most collected in the nineteenth century by General Augustus Pitt-Rivers. The Pitt Rivers's curator, Dr Laura Peers, has been struggling with the same ethical questions as the curators in New York, and in 2007 she admitted that she felt 'uncomfortable' about the presence of her turnstile-spinning exhibit and speculated about the need to canvas the people of Ecuador for their opinion and perhaps send the heads back whence they came.[61] A replacement part was then offered to the Pitt Rivers to make good its loss. Inspired by Dr Peers's repatriation plans, an American-born Oxford artist named Ted Dewan decided to fill the empty space in the Victorian display cabinet by donating his own head for shrinking. Even though Mr Dewan offered to leave enough funding to cover the costs of shrinkage ('using traditional methods'), storage and maintenance, the Pitt Rivers declined his offer.[62]

The shrunken heads in the Pitt Rivers are part of a display called 'Treatment of Dead Enemies'. Desecration of an enemy's head was not limited to the Jivaro or the Shuar, though often the treatment involved considerably less artistry and craftsmanship. The city of Pistoia, in Italy, claims to be the home of football. Today A.C. Pistoiese play their football in bright orange uniforms in the twelve thousand-seat Stadio Comunale in Pistoia. But five hundred years earlier their ancestors played a much more violent version of the game. In the early 1500s, a violent feud between two leading families, the Cancellieri and the Panciatichi, led to much butchery, bloodshed and the mutual burning down of houses. After one particularly grisly encounter, the Cancellieri exposed the disembodied heads of twelve of their rivals on lances, after which they kicked them about the streets in a game of *calcio*.[63] No doubt the Cancellieri clan, like the Ecuadorian Indians, or like the vengeful settlers who put Blackhawk and Captain Jack on display, felt greatly empowered by humiliating their enemy in such a way.

A MOST LASTING LOVE

Embalming can also be done for kinder and more compassionate reasons. The ancient civilization of Chinchorro Indians, from the northern coast of Chile, who flourished 5000–500 BCE, embalmed their nearest and dearest for reasons that had nothing to do with money or vengeance: they simply could not bear to be parted from them – especially from their children. Examination of Chinchorro mummy remains shows that this little-known race spent much time and skill embalming their loved ones, turning them, in effect, into poignant scarecrows.

The first Chinchorro mummies were accidentally discovered in 1917 by German archaeologist, Max Uhle, but it was not until the 1980s, when ninety-six more were unearthed, that a clearer picture of their lives could be made. New technology shows that these surviving mummies are, in fact, the oldest in the world. Dissection by paleopathologists – a discipline that combines archaeology, pathology and physical anthropology – also showed that many of the children had died of bacterial, viral or parasitic infections, and it is believed that grief was the driving force behind their artful technique of mummification.

The process used by the Chinchorro was very different from the ancient Egyptians or the Jivaro Indians. It began with the Chinchorro embalmer removing the skin from the body in a single piece and setting it carefully aside; the flesh was then removed, reducing the corpse to bones. The remaining skeleton was reinforced with sticks and tied back together, the empty spaces being filled with reeds and a clay-like paste that was moulded to the body in order to produce a lifelike human appearance. The skin that had been set aside was then fitted back onto the body, after which a wig was added and a coat of blue-black paint applied to the entire figure. Finally, the deceased was fitted into a red body suit and given a face mask. These mummies were not buried, rather they were placed on top of sand dunes where the families would come and tend them. If they became damaged, they were lovingly repaired.

The Chinchorro preservation ritual continued for over three thousand years, eventually evolving to include all members of the family. At some point, the mummies became go-betweens for communication with the spirit world, and families would routinely sit with the mummies and ask for wise counsel.

The reverence for mummies – a kind of ancestor worship – did not die out with the Chinchorro. The Incas, whose civilization covered vast areas of Latin America, took this practice a step further, believing that if they treated their mummies with respect and tended to their physical needs (such as leaving out cocoa leaves for them to chew on and beer to drink, and even lifting their garments so they could 'relieve' themselves), they would in return be offered advice and bountiful harvests. Each new Inca king built his own palace, leaving his predecessor's palace to house the former king's mummy, complete with a staff of servants to tend to it.

Mummy worship was eventually wiped out by the Spanish, but remnants of that special relationship with the dead flourishes today in many parts of South and Latin America, for example in Mexico, during the Day of the Dead celebrations, when families wait joyfully in cemeteries for their ancestors to visit with them during the first two days in November. The first of November celebrates deceased infants and children – the *angelitos*, or 'little angels' – while the following day is set aside to honour the dead adults. Entire families congregate at funeral plots, construct altars, and lay out flowers, food and other offerings for the departed. Few modern cultures celebrate death and the family so openly and wholeheartedly. But when the Nobel Prize-winning writer Octavio Paz wrote that the typical Mexican had no fear of death, but rather 'chases after it, mocks it, courts it, hugs it, sleeps with it; it is his favourite plaything and his most lasting love', he could have been writing about the Chinchorro tenderly ministering to their rows of mummies on the windswept coast of Chile.

A COMMUNIST PLOT

Embalming may have been available to everyone in the Chinchorro tribe, but in some cultures it was reserved only for royalty, the aristocracy or political icons. The Scythians, for example, who lived in southern Russia between 8000 and 4000 BCE, were famous for mummifying their kings. After death, the king's viscera were removed and replaced with a mixture of chopped cypress, frankincense, parsley-seed and aniseed. The cavity was sewn up and the body encased in wax, to be paraded around the villages over which he had ruled. Taking a job as the king's servant was not perhaps a wise career move, especially if the king was elderly, since immediately after his death the servant would be strangled, embalmed and then interred with his erstwhile employer. On the first anniversary of the king's death, fifty more of his servants would be killed and mummified, along with fifty horses. Each mummified servant was staked through the spinal cord so he could sit perched on his horse, heroically protecting his dead king forever.

Mummifying royalty or other political figures can be a way of enabling citizens – or forcing them, as in the case of the Scythians – to pay their respects. A similar case is that of Vladimir Ilyich Lenin (1870–1924). Though Lenin's expressed wish was be buried quietly next to his mother in St Petersburg, his successor, Josef Stalin, was quick to spot the propaganda value of putting his dead predecessor's body on permanent display. Lenin was initially embalmed by Dr Alesksei Ivanovich to delay putrefaction only until his funeral, six days later. However, watching the proletariat's adulation of Lenin as they trooped past his body, heads bowed, Stalin realized that preserving the corpse of his late comrade was a way of keeping the revolution on track. The Russian leader's embalmed corpse would, he hoped, replace the Christian saints that many Russians still secretly worshipped. Stalin therefore asked Ivanovich to extend Lenin's shelf-life for another forty days so he could remain on display. In the meantime, a crack medical team was put together to develop new embalming techniques. Doctors V.P. Vorobev and R.I. Zborsky took a great risk in volunteering for the project, since failure meant certain death. They practised their art on unclaimed bodies until they came up with a chemical solution composed of formalin, glycerine, alcohol and various secret ingredients that were to make them world leaders in embalming techniques.

The very same techniques were used to embalm numerous other Communist leaders, such as Georgi Dimitrov of Bulgaria in 1949; Marshal Horloogiyn Choybalsan of Mongolia in 1952; Klement Gottwald of Czechoslovakia in 1953; Ho Chi Minh of Vietnam in 1969; Mao Zedong of China in 1976; Agostinho Neto of Angola in 1979; and Kim Il-Song of North Korea in 1994. No Communist despot, it seemed, missed getting the Vorobev-Zborsky treatment and having his pickled corpse displayed for the edification of posterity. Even Stalin, the man who first saw the political potential of embalming, was to get the treatment two hours after passing away in 1953. For eight years he lay in state next to Lenin until he fell out of favour and – as a consequence of de-Stalinization – was removed by Nikolai Krushchev, who regarded his predecessor's violent legacy as too negative a reminder of the more unsavoury side of Communism. Stalin was finally discreetly buried under the Kremlin wall.

Lenin was not so lucky. Over ninety years after his death, Lenin's mummified body – looking as if he has just dropped off to sleep – can still be viewed in a mausoleum in Moscow's Red Square. Overseen by the Scientific Research Institute for Biological Structures in Moscow, he receives a dapper new suit every year and enjoys a trip to the beauty parlour for an embalming fluid treatment before returning to the display cabinet where all and sundry can gaze at him. However, all may not be what it seems, for rumours are rife that fungus is growing on Lenin's neck and the skin around the ears is mysteriously turning blue. Alas, there is no money for the expensive chemicals that would be needed for repair.

Lenin's mummification has produced many sceptics. Gail Johnson, a funeral director and embalming historian, thinks the body is actually made of wax.[64] John Chew, former director of the Institute for Funeral Service Education at Boca Raton's Lynn University in Utah, and Desmond Henley, OBE, a London embalmer, are both likewise doubtful whether Lenin was indeed embalmed.[65] They argue that in 1924 the Russians would not have possessed the skills to preserve a corpse for so long a period, especially following an autopsy. Indeed, it has been suggested that the corpse is merely an effigy made – rather like the Chinchorro mummies – from the skeletal remains. The public only sees the face and hands under low lights and through thick viewing glass, so it is impossible to tell if it's the 'real' Lenin or simply a waxwork imposter. As the Russians refuse to allow international experts to examine the body and to give details of their formulae, it is one secret that Lenin will take to his grave – if, that is, he ever gets there.

DON'T CRY FOR ME

As the example of Stalin shows us, political vicissitudes mean that a corpse, no matter how well embalmed, has no guarantee of immortality. Perhaps the most tragic of political icons to be embalmed, and then to fall from political favour, was Eva Perón, wife of the Argentine president Juan Perón. Known affectionately as Evita, she was the darling of Argentina before dying in July 1952 of stomach cancer at the age of thirty-three. Her husband, devastated by her death, spent over $100,000 having her embalmed. Dr Pedro Ara, cultural attaché to the Spanish embassy at the time, and also, fortuitously, a professor of anatomy, a pathologist and professional embalmer, was commissioned to do the job. He was later accused of having been present at her deathbed in order to ensure that doctors avoided prescribing her drugs that might counteract the effect of embalming chemicals – though this was never proved. The task of embalming Evita took him a year to complete, as he injected and re-injected her body with various chemicals, submerged her in baths of acetate and potassium nitrate, and coated her face with layers of transparent plastic. When Dr Ara had finished, the beautiful Evita had rarely looked as stunning in life.

Perón planned to build Evita a mausoleum in which, like Lenin, she could be permanently on display; however, before it was completed, he and his government were overthrown, a circumstance forcing him to flee Argentina, leaving Evita behind. The new government, unsympathetic to the Evita cult, determined that she should be removed from the political arena so as not to become a rallying-point for defeated Perónistas. Intriguingly, Evita's family, exiled in Venezuela, declined to take her, while the Catholic Church refused to allow her to be cremated and the Argentine Navy ruled out burying her on a remote island where its headquarters were based. To his credit, the new president, General Pedro Eugenio Aramburu, showed little enthusiasm for dumping her in the ocean from an aeroplane, as had been suggested by some bright spark. Secret burial was attempted but then abandoned as the Perónistas always found the proposed sites and left flowers and candles as marks of respect. For a time her corpse was concealed in the apartment of an Argentine army major, then in a wooden crate labelled 'radio equipment' in the attic of Military Intelligence headquarters. In 1957 she was secretly sent, via the Argentine embassy in Bonn, to a cemetery in Milan, Italy. There, finally, she was interred under the alias Maria Maggi de Magitius.

Evita did not rest in peace for long, however. In 1970 Juan Perón, having settled in Madrid with his third wife, was asked to return to govern Argentina, which was in its usual state of political chaos. He agreed only on condition that Evita's body would be returned to him. Evita was duly despatched to Madrid; soon after, in 1972, Perón departed for Argentina, albeit without his dead wife. Before he could organize her homecoming, he died unexpectedly, on 1 July 1974. Evita was eventually flown back to Buenos Aires a few months later. After reposing on public display for two years and experiencing yet another military coup, she was finally laid to rest in her family's vault in the Recoleta cemetery in Buenos Aires.

Like Lenin, Evita's mummified body was surrounded by professional suspicions, since rumours flourished that she, too, was a wax effigy. Although not commenting on these stories, her two sisters, Blanca and Erminda Duarte, wrote years later that when they saw Evita's body in Spain she had hammer blows to the temple and forehead, a gash on the cheek and arm, a sunken nose, a near-severed neck, fractured kneecaps, an amputated finger, tar on her feet, deep slashes on her chest, and hair like wet wool. When she went on display in Buenos Aires, there was no evidence of any such injuries. Either the embalmer had done a near-miraculous job, or a body-double made of wax was substituted.

DR LIVINGSTONE, I PRESUME?

Eva Perón's transatlantic travels were made possible by jet engines and embalming techniques so sophisticated that her husband's successors believed her corpse to be a clever replica. But those who died in foreign lands in previous eras faced trickier tasks for their homecomings, and ingenious methods had to be devised. After his death in Babylon in 323 BCE, Alexander the Great was shipped back to Alexandria submerged in a clay pot of honey. Horatio Nelson, killed at the Battle of Trafalgar in 1805 on his ship *The Victory*, was preserved in brandy for his journey back to England. Legend goes that Nelson was preserved in naval rum and not brandy, and that the barrel was half empty when it reached England, the alcohol having been illicitly siphoned off and drunk through straws by his men. This is where the saying 'tapping the Admiral' – meaning illicit drinking – comes from.

The Crusaders devised a particularly clever plan for preserving a body. They were known to disembowel and cut up their dead before casting them into cauldrons of boiling water to steam off the flesh. In this state, the remaining bones were easily transportable for the long journey back to their homeland – usually wrapped in a bundle and tied to their faithful horse – for a Christian burial. This practice continued until Pope Boniface VIII's edict of 1299 condemned the practice, rendering it illegal.[66]

When Dr David Livingstone, the famous British explorer, died in a remote village in Zambia in 1873 while searching unsuccessfully for the source of the Nile, few thought it possible to transport his body over a thousand miles across central Africa to a homeward-bound ship that would return him to England for burial. However, two of his most loyal African companions, Susi and Chuma, were adamant that their employer should be returned to his homeland, and so they worked out a way of preserving him for the long and dangerous journey. With the permission of Chief Chitambo, in whose village Livingstone had died, they built a special wooden platform for the procedure. First Livingstone's body was eviscerated, and his heart and other organs were buried under a mulva tree in the village. His body was then packed with salt, while his face was bathed in brandy and exposed to the sun. Each day he was turned a fraction – rather like a bottle of expensive wine in a cellar – so that each part was equally dried. On the fifteenth day, his body was wrapped in calico, encased in a bark cylinder, and stitched into sailcloth. Finally, to complete the process, the sailcloth was tarred to make it waterproof, then lashed to a carrying pole in such a way that it looked like a bundle of goods, thus avoiding native superstitions about dead bodies passing through villages.

After losing ten of their party to disease, violence and various other hardships, Susi and Chuma reached Bagamoyo, in Tanzania, nine months later, in February 1874. Chuma sailed to Zanzibar to inform the British authorities of Livingstone's whereabouts; they in turn sent a ship to pick him up and take him home, still swaddled in sailcloth. He arrived in Southampton on 15 April 1874, a shrunken, desiccated little bundle that was not quite so readily identifiable, one presumes, as the good doctor had been when tracked down by Henry Morton Stanley sixteen months earlier. Three days later, he was laid to rest in Westminster Abbey. As a mark of respect for such a great man, a national day of mourning was declared.

HOMEWARD BOUND

Returning a body to its homeland for burial was a strong factor in the popularization of embalming in the United States. Dr Thomas Holmes (1817–1900) was a medical practitioner who, while working as a coroner in

New York in the 1850s, spent years experimenting with chemicals to produce an effective embalming solution.

Dr Holmes really found his calling during the American Civil War. Soon after it commenced, President Lincoln's security guard, Colonel Elmer E. Ellsworth, was killed while snatching a Confederate flag from the roof of a hotel in Alexandria, Virginia. Ellsworth was highly regarded in Washington, so it was agreed that his body should be sent back to the White House for a lavish funeral. Holmes offered to embalm the body for free, and so successful did he prove that by the end of the war, in 1865, he had embalmed over four thousand bodies, including those of eight generals. He charged $7 for enlisted men and $13 for an officer. It was partly due to this sudden popularity of embalming that the tradition of wearing dog-tags was adopted by many Northern soldiers in order to make identification easier if the worst were to occur on the field of valour. However, embalming was a Northern practice only, since the Confederate surgeons had neither the chemicals nor the technical know-how.

Dr Holmes was influenced by the *History of Embalming*, a text published in 1838 by an apothecary named Jean Gannal (1792–1882). Gannal worked in the medical department of the French Army during Napoleon's campaigns of 1808–12 and at the Battle of Waterloo. He proved himself a clever chemist, who, after starting up several factories producing dyes, waxes and glues made from animal gelatine, drifted into the science of embalming to maintain the freshness of his animal specimens. In 1837, Gannal patented an embalming solution – quite different from William Hunter's – that consisted of equal parts of acetate of alumina at 50°F (10°C) and chloride of alumina at 68°F (20°C), which were injected into the carotid artery without the blood having been removed. Although Gannal won the Monthyon Science award for this work – a monetary prize donated by the French lawyer Baron de Monthyon – his patent was challenged in 1844 by other embalmers who claimed they had been using a similar preservation technique for years. The patent was removed when their charge was proved correct. The Frenchman was also later to admit to adding small amounts of arsenic to his solution – which proved to be lethal for anyone dissecting an embalmed cadaver. When this secret ingredient came to light, the use of arsenic in embalming solutions was quickly banned in France, although it remained in use in the United States until 1910.

The discovery of the chemical formaldehyde in 1859 by Alexander Butlerov (1828–66) and August Wilhelm von Hofmann (1818–92) would eventually prove decisive for modern embalmists. The benefits of formaldehyde include the ability to destroy the enzymes responsible for decomposition and the micro-organisms that spread disease. These disinfectant properties were not actually discovered until 1888; in the beginning it was expensive to produce so was not commonly used – for example, during the time of Dr Holmes – in embalming fluids. However, by 1900 production costs were reduced, coinciding with growing realization that arsenic and mercury, previously used in embalming solutions, were highly dangerous. Formaldehyde was universally adopted by 1906.

Formaldehyde, still used in embalming today, proved to be both more economical and more effective than previous solutions. Formaldehyde is a simple chemical made of hydrogen, oxygen and carbon, and is produced naturally in the body. Today formaldehyde has an enormous number of uses, including the manufacture of furniture, insulation, vaccines, photographic film, shampoos, toothpaste, cosmetics and deodorant, to name but a few. Indeed, the production of formaldehyde and formaldehyde-containing goods accounts for about $500 billion of the annual US gross national product – of which embalming fluid amounts to only a small percentage.[67] Not bad for a product that is naturally emitted when Brussels sprouts and cabbage are boiled.

Whether formaldehyde will still be used in Europe in any of its guises after 2010 is in doubt. Stravros Dimas, the European Union environment commissioner, wants it evaluated under the EU directive on biocidal products (adopted in 1998) to ascertain its effects on the environment. The Irish MEP Brian Crowley has challenged this directive, claiming that such a ban would kill off the Irish wake, a custom where corpses are kept in an open coffin for days on end while relatives celebrate the deceased's life. Irish funeral directors have been told by the EU that, whatever the outcome, they can ask the authorities to apply for an exemption for embalming substances. The EU is not, it insists, threatening the traditional Irish funeral. American retailers who use formaldehyde products may not be so lucky.

According to Karen Caney, the National General Secretary of the British Institute of Embalmers, there are no annual statistics available on the number of embalmings carried out in the UK, but she claims to have seen an increase since qualifying twenty-five years ago.[68] However, in North America, where statistics are kept, roughly sixty-eight per cent of the population is embalmed at death.[69] This means that over half of all Americans are chemically preserved before interment or cremation. The American tradition of an open-coffin funeral and an open-house to view the body – traditions that have almost disappeared in Britain – probably accounts for this prevalence.

An embalmer's place of work today might be mistaken for an operating theatre. The walls are scrubbed clean, with shining stainless steel and rubber tubing everywhere; steel surgical instruments adorn work benches, and jars of pink chemicals are lined up on shelves. In the middle of the room stands the embalming table. And, in a way, an embalmer's workroom is indeed an operating theatre.

Although it might be possible (as the example of Lenin demonstrates) to keep a body preserved indefinitely, modern embalmers aim to stave off putrefaction for weeks rather than years; in other words, just until the funeral and mourning periods have taken place. The first step, once the body has been placed on the embalming table, is to wash it thoroughly with disinfectant. A dead body is not dangerous to handlers unless its late owner had an infectious disease, but protective clothing and gloves are worn as a precaution throughout the procedure. The eyes of the deceased are closed by putting a small curved plastic disc – an eye cap – under the eyelids. Sometimes a gel is added to secure the closure. To avoid a ghoulish appearance, the mouth is also closed, usually by placing a tack in the upper and lower jaw. Each tack has a fine wire attached, and if the two wires are twisted together the jaw can be closed, rather like a medieval drawbridge. Severed limbs can be sewn back on, while cuts and gashes can be smoothed over with cosmetic wax.

Before embalming fluid can be injected, either through the carotid artery (where the neck meets the shoulder) or the femoral artery (in the leg at the groin), the embalmer must assess the state of the body. What was the mode of death and the weight and general condition of the remains? Did the deceased suffer from any diseases? Such factors will determine the type and strength of embalming fluid to be used. As unadulterated embalming fluid can make a body look grey and listless, dyes are now added to give it a more realistic glow.

The embalming machine has a two to three gallon reservoir and an electric pump. Dr Holmes used an injection pump that resembled a large hypodermic syringe attached to a cannual. Filling the syringe with bodily fluids and emptying it into a large bucket was a slow process. Today, a tube is attached to the embalming solution (made up of eight ounces of the embalming fluid to one gallon of water) and then inserted into the artery, while another larger tube, leading to the sewer system, is placed into an accompanying vein. The embalming solution is then pumped into the artery, forcing the blood out through the second tube. It takes about three gallons of fluid to complete the job, which continues until the liquid coming out of the tube runs clear. The process takes about an hour. The tubes are then removed and the incisions sutured shut.

The next step is to embalm the internal organs. First, a small incision is made above the navel, and a long needle called a trocar is inserted into the abdominal and thoracic cavities. The blood and other fluids are evacuated via suction, after which embalming fluid is injected via the trocar into the organs before these incisions are also closed. The body is cleansed again, the hair is washed, the nails are trimmed, and the nose and ear hairs are removed. The body is now ready for the final treatment: a complete beauty and wardrobe makeover.

After Lenin died, Alexander Pasternak, brother of Boris Pasternak, author of *Dr Zhivago*, was asked to paint a watercolour of Lenin's face. Today Alexander Pasternak's picture is still supposedly used as a reference point for the beauticians touching up Lenin's skin colour, but it would be highly unusual in modern times for embalmers to use a painting of the deceased in order to achieve the exact skin tone. Instead, they are more likely to rely on trial and error, using mortuary cosmetics and clever lighting in the slumber (or viewing) room.

Although most body preservation nowadays lasts merely until the funeral has taken place, there is nevertheless one company in the United States that claims it can stave off putrefaction forever. Summun was set up in 1987 by Summun Borum Amen Ra (né Claude Nouvell), a fitness guru and wine merchant, and Ron Temu (né Ron Zeffener). The company is headquartered, appropriately enough, in a three-storey pyramid in Salt Lake City, Utah. The firm uses a process that includes the removal of the internal organs but the retention of the brain, which is injected with a hardening chemical preservative. The body and internal organs are soaked in vats of a solution of salt, oils and chemicals, including formaldehyde, fluoride and alcohol. The organs, coated with polyurethane and wrapped in linen, are then returned to the body before it is slathered in glycerine, wines, oils and more polyurethane. Two hundred feet of linen, seasoned with herbs and spices, swaddle the body itself, which is finally covered with fibreglass and sometimes, if requested, with gold leaf.

Eternity does not come cheaply and, according to their website, prices for this mummification start at $67,000. Costs can quickly escalate. The mummy is interred in a sarcophagus which is sculpted in clay, then cast in bronze or stainless steel to resemble – if desired – an Egyptian mummiform. This is then welded shut and the air sucked out, to be replaced by an inert gas. Some sarcophagi can cost up to $500,000 depending on how elaborate they are. The founders of Summun plan to build a huge mausoleum in Utah's Manti-Lasalle mountains to house their mummified clients. Customers will be able to purchase a private granite sepulchre with viewing glass for families and friends to pay homage.

All very well, but one only has to take a short walk amongst dilapidated, overgrown headstones visible in some cemeteries to realize how few years it takes the dearly departed to be forgotten by their nearest and dearest. If that isn't warning enough, look no further than the ancient Egyptian mummies themselves. Not long after they were preserved – supposedly for the required three thousand years – many have been eaten as medicine, used as paint, dissected for entertainment, placed in Victorian drawing rooms, or thrown on bonfires for urban clearance. (During the raising of the Egyptian Aswan Dam in 1907, thousands of mummies were uncovered and disposed of in this way.) They, too, fell short in their quest for immortality.

CHAPTER 6

The Ultimate Makeover

Incorruptibles and Self-embalmers

As we have seen, there are many ways to preserve a body: injecting it with formaldehyde, scooping out innards and sprinkling them with spices, encasing it with von Hagens's plastination, or giving it the mysterious Vorobev-Zborsky treatment. But some bodies are preserved naturally, by accident, without the helping hand of the embalmer – or, in some cases, with what has been interpreted as divine protection. These well-preserved corpses include everyone from the most revered Catholic saints to obscure hunter-gatherers who had the misfortune to topple into peat bogs after too many glasses of prehistoric wine.

CALL ME INCORRUPTIBLE

The rue du Bac, a narrow street on Paris's Left Bank, boasts two major tourist attractions. One is Le Bon Marché, the world's first department store, which occupies an elegant building designed by Gustave Eiffel. Directly across the street – and at least as popular with the tourists flocking along the rue du Bac – is the Chapelle Notre-Dame de la Médaille Miraculeuse, the chapel of 'Our Lady of the Miraculous Medal'. The devotees who arrive at the small church wait their turn to kneel and pay their respects to a female figure who lies in an ornate glass box, her head and feet propped on pillows, her hands clasped in prayer and clutching a rosary. This star attraction – what might be mistaken at first for a waxwork effigy from Madame Tussaud's – is a nineteenth-century nun, St Catherine Labouré. Lenin and many of his fellow Communist leaders from around the world required the offices of skilled embalmers and morticians before going on display in their particular glass boxes. But St Catherine's well-preserved features are the result, apparently, of more natural – or perhaps even supernatural – conditions.

Christian teaching frequently emphasizes the perishability of the physical body: 'Dust you are, and unto dust shall you return,' Genesis 3:19 states portentously. Yet the Fathers of the Church, such as Tertullian, made much of the fact that the word cadaver comes from the Latin *cadere*, meaning to fall – and what falls, they argued, could also rise. Accordingly, Christian doctrine holds that at the Resurrection the bodies of the dead will be 'raised incorruptible' (1 Corinthians 15:52). Long ago, however, it was discovered that some bodies showed signs of incorruptibility long after death – but long before the trumpet blast of the Resurrection.

St Catherine of Labouré is only one of the more recent examples. Born in 1806, Catherine is revered for having received an apparition of the Blessed Virgin Mary, who instructed her to make and distribute medals bearing her – that is, the Virgin's – image. All who wore the medals, the Virgin told her, would receive great grace. Catherine duly created and distributed the medals before dying of natural causes in 1876. When she was exhumed over fifty years later, in 1933, her body was found to be in a state of perfect preservation. Catherine was an 'incorruptible': someone whose body was not subject to the normal ravages of decomposition and disintegration. As such, she joins an illustrious list of saints whose bodies have retained their freshness long after death, from St Francis Xavier to St Bernadette of Lourdes, the latter of whom died in 1879. Exhumed in 1909 by a commission investigating her claims to sainthood, Bernadette's body was found by those present – including a bishop and two physicians – to be in a near-perfect state of preservation. A third exhumation, in 1923, was followed by an autopsy that pronounced her liver supple and virtually normal in its consistency. Since 1925 St Bernadette has been on display in a crystal coffin in the Church of St Gildard in Nevers, France.

Incorruptibles date from the earliest decades of Christianity. Mysteriously, irrespective of the manner of burial, temperature and moisture, rough handling, proximity to other decaying corpses, or even the application of corrosive quicklime, their bodies have remained free of decay. The oldest incorruptible is St Cecilia, who was martyred in 117 CE. She was married off to the nobleman Valerianus of Trastevere, a Roman pagan who, far from being a model husband, frequently beat her. Some might argue that his patience had been pushed to the limits: on their wedding night Cecilia informed him that he must not touch her body, as she was betrothed to an angel who jealously guarded it. Desperate to meet his love-rival, Valerianus was told by Cecilia that this would only be possible if he was baptized as a Christian. Happy to make a virtue of necessity, he went off to meet Bishop Urbanus, who baptized him. On his return to Rome as a Christian, Valerianus and Cecilia were duly showered by the angel with roses and lilies, after which, presumably, the young husband enjoyed his conjugal rights. Valerianus was so impressed – or, perhaps, relieved to have outsmarted his rival – that he asked the angel if his brother could also be baptized. Christians, however, did not fare well in Rome in the early decades after Christ's crucifixion, and Valerianus and his brother were eventually martyred for the crime of having buried other Christian martyrs. The same sad fate awaited Cecilia when she was seen burying Valerianus and her brother-in-law. An attempt to suffocate Cecilia in her bath was unsuccessful, so her executioner tried instead to decapitate her. This, too, was unsuccessful and she lived for three days with horrendous injuries. When she did finally expire, Pope Urbanus buried her in the Catacomb of Callistus, among eminent bishops and confessors. When her tomb was opened in 1599, almost a millennium and a half after her martyrdom, her body was found to be in superb condition.

Looking slightly worse for wear in his glass box in the Basilica of Bom Jésus in Goa, India, is St Francis Xavier. After he died in India in 1552, he was placed in a wooden coffin and given two coats of quicklime to accelerate the decomposition of his flesh so that his bones could be returned to Spain. The casket was buried and then, two months later, exhumed in preparation for the transport of the remains. However, neither the quick-lime nor the passage of two months had made the slightest mark on St Francis – indeed, a sweet smell issued from the coffin (the last thing one would expect in the hot Indian climate).

Considering his age, St Francis Xavier has actually weathered the centuries remarkably well. Not only is he not in a hermetically sealed glass box (he is still prey to the fierce Indian heat and humidity), but he has suffered from the ravages of the faithful. In 1554 his little toe was bitten off by a devout Portuguese woman who wanted a relic of the great man; soon afterwards three more of his toes were amputated for use as relics. Then in 1614 he lost his right arm below the elbow when the Jesuits had it removed and shipped to their church in Rome, and several years later what remained of the arm, including the shoulderblade, was cut off and sent to Japan. Various fingernails, toenails and bits of bone have been harvested from these amputations and dispersed to churches around the world. In 1952, on the 400th anniversary of his death, he survived the gruelling ritual of being kissed by 817,000 pilgrims.

There have been some one hundred incorruptibles. The appearance of so many well-preserved corpses meant that by the Middle Ages most candidates for sainthood were exhumed for the inspection of their remains, with bodily preservation becoming, along with at least two miracles, a necessary prerequisite for canonization. Typically, the incorruptibles have a lifelike appearance and, like St Francis Xavier, a sweet smell. Sometimes they perspire, shed tears or drip blood; and all of them – this is what they truly share in common – happen to have been devout Christians: they prayed incessantly, they helped others, they were self-sacrificing, they believed devoutly, and many (such as Bernadette of Lourdes and Catherine Labouré) had visitations from 'special' people such as the Virgin Mary.

Caring for others was also an important attribute of incorruptibles, as revealed by the example of Margaret of Castello, who spent much of her adult life taking care of the sick and attending to prisoners. She had been born into a wealthy family in 1287, at the Castle of Metola, near Florence in Italy. Sadly, she was an unprepossessing physical specimen: a blind, hunch-backed dwarf with one leg shorter than the other. These daunting handicaps did not seem to bother Margaret, but her parents were so dreadfully embarrassed by her appearance that they locked her away in a room in the castle, where she spent her days praying. Eventually, her parents abandoned her, at the age of twenty, at the tomb of a holy man, Father Giacomo, who was known for his miracles. Margaret was taken in by nuns and during her remaining years was reputed to have the power of curing people with her prayers. The miracles did not cease when she died in 1320, aged only thirty-three, since hundreds of miracles were later attributed to her intercession. Two hundred years later, in 1558, when Margaret was exhumed so her remains could be moved from the rotting coffin, her body was found to be perfectly preserved. Today it can be seen on display – the little body still sadly deformed if perfectly preserved, right down to the eyelashes and fingernails – under the high altar of the Church of St Domenico in Città di Castello in Umbria.

Incorruptibility may not have helped St Margaret's hump or mismatched legs, but divine intervention sometimes makes incorruptibles look better dead than alive. This is exactly what happened to St Theresa Margaret, who died of a strangulated hernia at the age of twenty-two in 1770 at the Carmelite monastery in Florence where she lived with other nuns. Immediately after death, her face became bloated and discoloured, while her extremities turned black. She looked so frightful that the nuns feared her body would decay – rather like Pope Alexander VI's some 270 years earlier – before funeral rites were performed. As the funeral was planned for the following day, she was hastily removed to the funeral vault. It was not long, though, before the nuns noticed a dramatic change had taken place: the horrible disfigurations of death disappeared as Theresa Margaret began to regain her natural colour. As Theresa Margaret's body gradually turned soft and flexible, making it look as though she was asleep rather than dead, the nuns requested that the funeral be delayed for fifty-two hours. To capture this miraculous event, Anna Piattoli, a Florentine portrait painter, was called to paint a picture of the deceased nun. When the work was completed, a beautiful fragrance was said to have wafted through the crypt. Theresa Margaret was finally buried eighteen days later, looking beautiful, lifelike and serene. Thirty-five years on, she was still found to be incorrupt. She may now be seen in a glass case at the Monastery of St Theresa in Florence.

But are incorruptibles the products of divine intervention or the result of more earthly powers? Peter Mitchell, from Peter Mitchell Associates, in Maidstone, Kent, is responsible for exhuming bodies from churchyards and other burial sites and relocating them. Mitchell explains that occasionally he exhumes a body that is perfectly intact, despite the headstone proclaiming it to be over two hundred years old.[70] He thinks, however, that the preservation has more to do with perfect environmental conditions than with the hand of God. If a casket is made from the right wood, lined with lead and then buried in a heavy clay soil, a vacuum is sometimes produced, sealing off the body from water, insects and bacteria. Many of the incorruptibles were interred in burial vaults under church floors prior to their exhumations. Churches tend to keep a steady temperature throughout the seasons, creating conditions conducive to preserving the body. It is now known that interred bodies decay at a rate that depends on, among other things, the acidity and moisture in the soil. Soft tissues can be preserved for some time in a moist, airless location with an acid soil. Indeed, the dank climate of England has proved a surprisingly congenial home for incorruptibles, such as Cuthbert, Guthlac and Queen Etheldreda – the latter's disembodied hand, still intact despite the centuries, may be seen in the church of St Etheldreda, in Ely, Cambridgeshire. Yet none of this quite explains how St Francis Xavier could have survived the layering of quicklime, or how some of the other saints remained intact for many centuries, while nearby corpses rotted away.

There was a thrilling display of posthumous preservation early in 2001 when the remains of Pope John XXIII, who died in 1963, were moved to a more conspicuous location inside the basilica of St Peter's in Rome. The process required his exhumation, and those present for the opening of the coffin, including the Vatican's secretary of state, reported that the pontiff looked as if he had died only a day or two earlier. Vatican officials downplayed talk of a miracle, however, and the preservation of 'the people's pope' was probably the result of the circumstances of his interment: embalmed with a formaldehyde-based fluid, he was placed inside three caskets – made of oak, lead and cypress – which were in turn placed inside a marble casing. 'The body of the Holy Father was well protected,' Vincenzo Pascali, from the University of Rome, was quoted as saying. After exhumation, the body was squirted with an antibacterial agent and rein-terred in a hermetically sealed lead casket – thus probably safeguarding the pope's appearance for another thirty-eight years.

The Vatican is highly sensitive to the issues raised by the incorruptibles. Ezio Fulchereri, a pathologist from the University of Genoa and an expert on incorruptibles, has – with the Vatican's blessing – examined many of these apparently miraculously preserved bodies of saints. He claims that quite a number have actually been artificially embalmed. On further inves-tigation he also discovered that the Church was not necessarily trying to cover up these embalmings, but that records had simply been lost or over-looked. For example, when examining the body of St Margaret of Cortona he found obvious embalming incision scars. In 1297, when St Margaret died, the people of Cortona asked the Church to embalm her since she was so beloved, and the officials complied, duly recording the fact. When examining St Clare, the founder of the convent of the Poor Clares in the thirteenth century, Fulchereri found the saint was not quite everything she seemed. All that was actually left of her was her bones, which were carefully held together with silver wire. Her 'body' had been padded with cloth and pasted with pitch, while her 'face' was a porcelain mask. She was, in other words, a mummy not dissimilar to those fashioned by the Chinchorro. Once again, the Catholic Church did not deliberately set out to deceive people: St Clare's body had at some point simply decayed and, as she was so beloved, it was decided to make a *corpus sanctus* (a holy body) out of the bones rather than put them in an urn.

In the 1980s, researchers at the University of Padua suggested that there are seventy saints in the same state, as a result of which the Roman Catholic Church has officially dropped posthumous preservation as one of the cri-teria required for beatification. However, there are some saints, experts claim, who show no signs of external interference. They include St Ubaldus of Gubbio, Italy, who died in 1168; the Blessed Margaret of Savoy, famous for founding a monastery for nuns, who died in 1464; and, more recently, Blessed Savina Petrilli, founder of the Sisters of the Poor, who died in 1923.

When another incorruptible, St Zita, was examined by the pathologist Gino Fornaciari, no incision marks – the telltale signs of interference – were found. St Zita had gone to work as a domestic servant for a wealthy family in Lucca. After a life of devotion and hard work mopping floors, serving meals and polishing furniture, she died in 1278. Her casket was opened in 1446, 1581 and 1652, and on each occasion her body was discovered incorrupt. Fornaciari was able to confirm that all her internal organs were still in situ. She is now the patron saint of butlers, housemaids, servants, waiters and waitresses. Today she reposes in a crystal coffin in the basilica of San Frediano in Lucca, wearing a lace shawl and a blue satin dress, looking like she's taking a well-deserved rest.

ALL DRESSED UP AND NOWHERE TO GO

For several hundred years the possibility of becoming an incorruptible, and of staving off the encroachments of death, was offered to the citizens of Palermo, Sicily. The results of this practice are now on show for tourists with €1.50 in their pockets and a taste for the gruesome. The scene they encounter is not unlike the one that must have greeted Bronze Age visitors to the coast of Chile. Bodies are arranged in orderly rows that line the damp, whitewashed corridors. Many are dressed in their Sunday best – bonnets, shawls, long dresses – while others are more cheaply attired in what look like burlap potato sacks. Some repose on shelves; others stand upright, their hands folded over their groins like nervous footballers before a penalty kick. One or two look like they've just nodded off to sleep; most of the others give a less peaceful account of themselves: missing jaws, empty eyesockets, painful grimaces, ghoulish leers, contorted limbs, silent screams. These are the residents of the Catacombe dei Cappuccini, or the Catacombs of the Capuchins.

The Capuchin monks arrived in Palermo in the middle of the sixteenth century and buried their dead in a grotto behind the church of Santa Maria della Pace. When the grotto became full, a new, larger cemetery was required, and so the bodies of the dead were exhumed with the intention of relocating them. To the monks' surprise, they found some forty-five of the bodies were in near-perfect condition despite having been dead for a decade or more. The mummification seems to have been the result of natural conditions, such as the limestone in the grottoes.

Learning of these 'miraculous' preservations, the residents of Palermo soon wanted their own place in the cemetery. By the 1630s a number of nobles were given the privilege, and inhumation in the catacombs became the ultimate status symbol. The limestone may have helped preserve the original Capuchin monks, but embalming techniques were developed to aid the natural conditions. The most usual method was to place the dead in underground cells called 'strainers', where their bodies were naturally dehydrated for some eight months before being washed in vinegar or dipped in arsenic – that old friend of the embalmer – and then dressed for display, usually in their finest frocks. Money, as well as arsenic and limestone, was required to preserve the body, with devout relatives obliged to pay handsomely for the privilege of keeping their loved ones in this museum of the dead. If the cash dried up, the body would be downgraded, that is, moved to a shelf in a less conspicuous position in more undesirable surroundings.

In the space of almost three hundred years, some eight thousand bodies have been placed in the catacombs, which meant a new arrival, on average, every two weeks. The only foreigner who managed to bag a spot was Giovanni Paterniti, the American Consul in Sicily, who died in 1911, and who reposes in an open coffin. Fortunately, he has yet to experience the decay of some of his fellow inmates, since his face remains distinguished and lifelike. He sports a moustache that must have been the height of fashion in Palermo in 1911. The last to be interred was Rosalia Lombardo, an extremely lifelike two-year-old who died in 1920. Her placid and well-preserved features make her look like she has fallen into a light sleep, something that has earned her the poignant nickname of 'Sleeping Beauty'.

THE ICEMEN COMETH

The hand of God may be one way of 'naturally' preserving bodies; another, as the Capuchin monks discovered, is a combination of environment and the elements. Ice, deserts and bogs can also halt the decomposition process and preserve a body for hundreds if not thousands of years.

In 1991, two mountain walkers in the Otzal Alps on the Italian-Austrian border, stumbled across Ötzi the Iceman – probably the most famous of the ice-preserved mummies. Radiocarbon dating of the remains estimated Ötzi to be between 5,000 and 5,350 years old, his body having been frozen at glacial temperatures of -20°C (-4°F), 10,400 feet above sea level. He was found with skin and hair attached to his body and most of his clothes still intact; various weapons and tools lay at his side. Scientists were able to discover the state of his health and what he had eaten immediately before his death. It seems Ötzi had been in a fight, as an arrowhead was embedded in his shoulder. Experts now believe he fled up the mountain but collapsed and died from blood loss, hunger and cold. Today he can be seen at the South Tyrol Museum of Archaeology in Bolzano, Italy. However, modern science appears to be failing where the glacier succeeded, since Dr Eduard Egarther Vigil, Ötzi's official caretaker at the museum, says there are signs of bacteria eating away at the iceman's knee. The necessary precautions have been taken, but it is very difficult permanently to stem the decomposition process once the body has had contact with the air.

Ice is such a good agent of preservation that it has also entombed the Pazyryk ice mummies – two females and one male – found by Servey Rudenko in the Altai Mountains of Siberia in 1947–8. They, like Ötzi, were dated between the fifth and third centuries BCE. A further fully clothed male mummy, also found in ice in Khahasia in 1969, was stored with others in the State Hermitage Museum in St Petersburg until 2003, when a remarkable discovery was made: after his clothing was removed, evidence of a faint tattoo appeared on the ice mummy's shoulder. Using infrared rays, scientists could clearly see drawn on his body a pattern of commas, rosettes, monsters, and bows and arrows. After re-examination, the other three Pazyryk mummies were likewise found to have tattoos, in their cases ones depicting tigers, leopards, horses, wild mountain sheep and deer, winged monsters and scenes of mauling: the prehistoric equivalents, presumably, of the death's heads daggers and roses offered by more modern tattoo artists.

Sand is another effective medium for preserving the body. Indeed, the early Egyptians – royal, common, rich, poor – originally buried their dead in shallow pit-graves on the edges of deserts. The heat of the sun and the dry sand created the right conditions for mummifying the bodies. It was only later that Egyptians invented their artificial mummification techniques for use on the middle and upper classes.

One of the most remarkable collections of sand-mummified bodies is the Tarim mummies of Xinjiang province in China. Several well-preserved bodies were found in 1985 in the Takla Makan desert and dated to around 2000 BCE. The most startling thing about these mummies, apart from their great antiquity, is that some had red hair and all were clothed – like members of Scotland's 'Barmy Army' – in what look like Celtic tartans. DNA testing confirmed that they were of European ancestry, but no one knows why or how they died so far from home. The Chinese government was unwilling to investigate further for two reasons. First of all, the Uyghurs, a Muslim minority who live in the region, have claimed the mummies as their own. The Uyghurs number only seven million but are eager for political independence from Beijing. Although the Uyghurs migrated from Mongolia less than two thousand years ago, experts argue that in all probability it was the Uyghurs who slaughtered the descendents of the red-haired mummies, assimilating the rest of the travellers into their tribe. However, the Chinese authorities fear that if a partial DNA link connects the mummies to the Uyghurs it will strengthen their claim for a separate state. The Chinese are by no means inclined to grant independence, not least because geologists have estimated that eighteen billion tons of crude oil lie under the Tarim Basin. A few ginger-haired mummies, murdered far away from home, could make an independent Uyghur nation extremely wealthy.

Another natural preservative is a bog. A bog is a living carpet of sphagnum moss that consists of two layers: on top, the acrotelm, through which water can move freely; and, underneath, the amorphous layer of peat known as the catotelm. There are two different types of bog: the 'raised bog', which consists of about two per cent peat and ninety-eight per cent water, and the 'blanket bog', which is only eighty-five per cent water. Either one can prove a deadly morass for the unwary, as Jack Stapleton discovers to his cost in Arthur Conan Doyle's *The Hound of the Baskervilles*.

Whatever the bog type, the lower catatelm layer is protected from any environmental changes above it, thus becoming a great natural preserver of anything that should topple into it. Moreover, peat and sphagnum moss are believed to release a chemical preservative called sphagnol. Some scientists argue that the acid in bog water, combined with the anaerobic conditions, delays the action of putrefactive bacteria. Interestingly, dried moss, known to have antibacterial properties, was used in the First World War to bandage wounds; sailors also took bog water on sea journeys as it stayed algae-free longer than well or spring water. [71]

One of the oldest bog bodies is that of the Tollund Man, discovered in a Danish bog in 1950. He was thought to have died in 200 BCE, at about the age of thirty, and to have been strangled with a leather belt. It appeared that he had been ritually executed before being thrown into his peaty grave. On display in the Sileborg Museum in Denmark, Tolland Man has amazingly human features, from his wrinkled brow and closed eyelids to the stubble on his chin. He was so well preserved that scientists were able to identify from his stomach contents that his last meal (the final dinner of a condemned man, apparently) was a rather meagre helping of barley and other seeds.

Perhaps the most controversial of the bog bodies were those known, appropriately enough, as the van der Peats. Discovered in the Bourtangemoor peat bogs of the Netherlands in 1904 by a peat cutter named Hilbrand Gringhuis, Mr and Mrs van der Peat, as they were affectionately dubbed, were believed to be over two thousand years old. The two bodies had been arranged with the right arm of the larger encircling that of the smaller body, enabling them to hold hands. The poor state of the bodies made it difficult to confirm the sex of the smaller of the pair, though a penis was visible on the larger body. The larger body had also been disembowelled, with the entrails showing on top of his abdomen. In 1990, however, a re-examination found that the smaller of the two bodies was sporting stubble – a decidedly unfeminine five o'clock shadow – on what was left of his chin. Much to the delight of the Dutch gay press, Joan van der Peat seems actually to have been John. No one knows if they were indeed a homosexual couple, but one possible explanation for their pose is that the larger of the two was disembowelled in battle and then buried with his servant and/or sexual partner. In any case, their touching embrace has lasted for two millennia.

THE RAINBOW BODY

In 1975 an earthquake struck the remote Spiti district of Himachal Pradesh, a desolate, mountainous area of Tibet close to India's border with China. Two Indian soldiers were sent to repair a damaged road, which lay a dizzying twelve thousand feet above sea-level. In the process the soldiers came across the mummified body of a man crouched in a meditative pose with a strap placed around his neck and knees. Beside him lay a scroll, which disintegrated when touched. Locals rescued the body and built a small spirit house to shelter him. His name turned out to be Sangha Tenzin, and he was – as scientists eventually discovered – over five hundred years old.

Because of the restrictions imposed on entering the area, the outside world only learned of Tenzin's existence in 2004, when an Indian journalist managed to visit the shrine and take photographs. When Victor Mair, an anthropologist from the University of Pennsylvania, got wind of the monk's existence, he organized a team of scientists and set off to take a look. Mair suspected something quite incredible: that this monk had actually embalmed himself. X-rays and hair samples were soon to prove Mair's alarming hypothesis to be correct. But why – and perhaps more to the point – how would someone go about embalming himself?

To find the answer, Mair took a trip to Japan, where there are twenty known self-mummified priests, sacred to followers of the Shingon Buddhist sect. The priests of the Shingon sect were so devout it was thought by their followers that they could control droughts, plagues, earthquakes and typhoons. Yet life was not easy for Shingon priests: they were known to find crevices in the mountains and meditate alone for days on end, or to bathe for hours in freezing waterfalls. Kuukai, the first Japanese priest to undergo self-embalming, lived over a thousand years ago at a temple in Mount Kooya, Wakayama. Kuukai believed that enlightenment came only through physical punishment, which taught a practitioner to detach himself from his bodily form. The Shingon Buddhist sect was established around this somewhat macabre belief. Those able to master their bodies in this way were acclaimed as Buddhas with protective powers. They were – and still are – worshipped and idolized by their followers.

The process of self-embalming, outlawed in Japan since the nineteenth century, is a typically arduous one, taking a total of ten years to achieve. For the first thousand days the monk eats only nuts and seeds from the surrounding forest, while at the same time undergoing hard physical labour and following a strict ascetic practice, the aim being to reduce body fat – the fleshy bits that are first to decompose after death. For the second thousand days, he is allowed to eat only the bark and roots of a local pine tree. Soon he begins to resemble a skeleton as the moisture in his body reduces. Near the end of this second period, the monk drinks only a special tea made from the sap of the Urushi tree. This very poisonous sap is more ordinarily used to make lacquer for bowls and furniture. The tea causes vomiting, sweating and excessive urination, further reducing the water content of the monk's body. The poison also kills off maggots and bugs when the decomposition process begins. During the final thousand days, the monk is entombed, barely alive, in a stone room just big enough for him to sit in the Lotus position. He has a bell which he rings every day; his failure to sound the clappers indicates to the outside world that the tomb can finally be sealed, thereby cutting off the air supply.

In 1877 the last known monk successfully completed the process; today he can be seen at the Nangakuji temple in Tsuruoka, Japan. There are eighteen mummies in total on show in other temples; all have been dressed in religious robes and are lovingly cared for. With their flowing robes, pious poses and grinning skulls, these Buddhist mummies would not look out of place in the Catacombs of the Capuchins, or in a crystal box in a Catholic shrine.

The Tibetan monks, Mair was to discover, followed a process similar to the Japanese priests. However, they did not eat pine bark to aid the process of self-embalming, though they did fast and meditate intensely. A devout Tibetan Buddhist sect practised a form of Tantric meditation that was so powerful it was only transmitted verbally to a few special monks. They believed that this form of meditation, if performed at the precise moment of death, created a 'rainbow body' of pure light that could channel the spirit to Nirvana. If a monk were to achieve this divine state, it was maintained, his 'pure' body would naturally be preserved as a relic.

For the average person today, unable to eat only one peanut from the jar or resist the dessert trolley, it might seem an impossible task to self-preserve oneself with the aid of meditation or a special diet of pine bark and Urushi tea; but Dr Herbert Benson, from Harvard University's Medical School in Boston, believes it possible. He conducted a host of tests on Tibetan Buddhist monks to assess the effects of meditation on metabolism. The monks practised Tumo (yoga of inner heat), which enabled them to raise their body temperatures to phenomenal levels when meditating. In temperatures of 40°F (4°C), the monks wrapped in ice-cold wet sheets were able to increase their body temperature so much the sheets would steam and dry out. If such feats are possible, Benson concluded, there is no reason why an adept could not reduce his body fluids and self-embalm himself.[72]

More research from Mair and his team discovered that a particular region of Tibet had suffered from famine caused by several years of crop failure. An unassuming monk, Sangha Tenzin, determined to sacrifice himself by meditation in the Tantric way in order to achieve the rainbow body, with the added bonus of protecting the valley of his people. His death, he believed, would bring blessings to this infertile land. To ensure success, he fasted beforehand, then attached a special meditation strap to his neck and knees in such a way that if he lost meditative concentration for one second he would fatally throttle himself. It is not known if Tenzin was successful in making the land fertile, but he would have certainly captured the hearts of the locals for his bold attempt.

Interestingly, the likes of Tenzin were not an uncommon sight in Tibet. After the Chinese annexed Tibet in 1951, hundreds of mummified monks were gathered up and publicly burned in an attempt to wean the devout away from Buddhism. Several centuries earlier, on a different continent, another occupying force was to do the same: hundreds of Inca mummies were rounded up by the Spanish and publicly burnt. The intention, too, was to wean the natives away from mummy worship. Whether Lenin, Evita, St Francis Xavier or obscure Tibetan monks, some bodies, it seems, can be as evocative and inspirational in death as they are in life.

CHAPTER 7

Stone Angels to Space Rockets

Commemorating the Dead

Not so long ago, a funeral in many British or American homes used to be a simple and unvarying affair: a black hearse, a wooden coffin, a few traditional hymns, a graveside ceremony, all capped off by a headstone or a statue of an angel. But it needn't end so solemnly and discreetly. Today people are looking for ever more creative and personal ways to say farewell to loved ones. These include blasting human remains into space, submerging them in artificial coral reefs, or burying them in personalized coffins in the colours of the deceased's favourite football team. Even the hymn is no longer traditional as old favourites such as 'Abide with Me' and 'Amazing Grace' give way to top 40 hits. According to the Bereavement Register, a group that works to remove the names of the deceased from direct mailing databases in Britain, Canada and France, fifty-one per cent of the five thousand people polled have considered having a specific song – not a hymn – played at their funeral. 'Goodbye my Lover' by James Blunt and 'Angels' by Robbie Williams have been among the most popular.

One of the more innovative ways of conducting a funeral comes from China. In August 2006, five people from Jiangsu province were arrested for running striptease send-offs at funerals: the guests were being treated, it seems, to the sort of erotic performances that, in the UK at least, are more commonly associated with boozy stag (bachelor) parties. This type of farewell had become so frequent that local officials in Jiangsu ordered that funeral plans must be submitted in advance to the authorities to put a halt to such 'obscene performances'. The locals were not happy. The more people who attend a funeral, the more the deceased is honoured, and what better way to swell the congregation than by offering a pneumatic young woman in a G-string?

BACK IN BLACK

Funerals and mournings, at least in Britain and America, used to be considerably more sober affairs. In 1827, when the Duke of York died, the Earl Marshal, the Twelfth Duke of Norfolk, issued an order that it 'is expected that all persons do put themselves into deep mourning'. Mourning was taken extremely seriously in nineteenth-century Britain, whether for the second in line to the throne, such as the Duke of York, or a close relation like a husband or father. Fashion magazines of the day, such as the *Ladies Monthly,* produced illustrations of suitable mourning attire. But it was the Victorians, a few years later, who truly turned mourning into a fine art. Taking their lead from Queen Victoria, who herself spent forty years mourning her husband, Prince Albert, a whole etiquette of funerary protocol emerged, with middle and upper class women bearing the brunt of this formality.

Victorian mourning customs seem to have had all the strictness for the women of Afghanistan under the Taliban. By the late 1860s, for example, widows were effectively excluded from society. For the first year they were not permitted to accept any invitations or to be seen in a public place. For a year and a day, they were expected to be in deep mourning and to wear nothing but black crape, known for its lack of light-reflecting sheen. In *The Gentlewoman's Book of Dress,* published in 1890, Mrs Fanny Douglas described, with deadly seriousness, the life of a mourning widow who finally ventured out in public: 'If she lifts her skirts from the mud, she must show by her frilled black silk petticoat and plain black stockings her grief has penetrated to her innermost sanctuaries. If she put up her parasol, it is at once evident that she would deem it wrong even to shelter from the sun beneath anything less emotional than black chiffon arranged in puffs.' A widow was evidently expected to grieve right down to her underpants. Men, on the other hand, simply wore plain black suits and black armbands and, unlike widows, could marry as soon as they wished after the death of their wife, thus continuing life much as before.

After a year of deep mourning, the widow entered the half-mourning stage, where she could exchange her black crape dress for a silk one. As time went by – a further twelve months – the black could be replaced by a purple or mauve dress, or, after aniline dyes were invented in the 1850s, violet, pansy, lilac, scabious and heliotrope ones. Mourning timescales depended on the degree of closeness to the deceased. Parents who lost children, and vice-versa, wore full mourning for nine months and half-mourning for three. The death of a sibling required three months of deep mourning and three of half-mourning, while the deaths of in-laws, aunts, uncles and cousins demanded a mere matter of weeks. These rules were helpfully outlined in Cassell's *Household Guide,* published in 1874.

Once a woman entered the half-mourning stage, she could wear certain types of jewellery. Pearls and amethysts were allowed, but the most popular was made from jet, a type of hard coal formed from a prehistoric monkey-puzzle tree. Jet was washed up on the North Yorkshire shores around Whitby, and it was also mined at Bilsdale, in Yorkshire's Cleveland Hills, until the early 1890s, when over-mining made it scarce and expensive. In Ireland, mourners tended to wear carved Bog Oak jewellery made from Irish peat, while others favoured tortoiseshell mourning jewellery known as piqué and introduced originally by French Huguenots in the seventeenth century. In 1887, the year of Victoria's Silver Jubilee, the Queen finally agreed to relax mourning etiquette by putting off her widow's weeds and wearing silver on state occasions. This was the beginning of the end of excessive mourning, at which point silver – the new black – started to flood the market.

Several fortunes were made from this Victorian cult of mourning. Courtaulds of Braintree, in Essex, enjoyed a monopoly on the fast-growing crape industry. George Courtauld, a descendant of Huguenot silk-weavers, had founded the firm in 1809, and by the end of the nineteenth century Courtauld was a household name throughout Britain, Europe and the

Empire. Indeed, during the Franco-Prussian War in 1870, demand for crape was so high that the company was hard put to keep up with orders. Crape was expensive, but Courtauld was clever enough to develop a cheaper version called the 'Albert crape', enabling the working classes to follow the fashion. This version was a mixture of cotton and silk, and it was even more coarse and uncomfortable to wear than the original.

After a Victorian funeral, a memorial card would be sent out to inform people of the death. Originally sent as reminders to pray for a departing soul, the Victorians adopted the custom as part of their funerary etiquette. About 80 by 120mm (3⅛ by 4¾ inches) in dimension, these cards, made by specialist firms, could be quite ornate, with doleful-looking women sitting under weeping willows a common theme. Space was left for local printers to fill in personal details. By the beginning of the twentieth century these were replaced by the folding cards that we are more familiar with today.

The First World War finally brought to an end the lavish and prolonged mourning customs in Britain. With an unprecedented 745,000 British men killed in the war, the government encouraged the use of black armbands to replace formal Victorian funerary wear, in the hope that morale would not dip nor women disappear into the cloisters of mourning. Nearly a hundred years later, in twenty-first century Britain and America, the grief may be just as strong but mourning customs have dwindled to almost nothing. Employers are not legally required to give people time off even to attend funerals (although most in fact do), and workers are generally expected to return to their jobs on the following day. There is no differentiation in mourning the loss of a spouse or other family member or friend, and mourning attire no longer need be black, merely a dark colour. The regimented ritual of celebrating a death has long disappeared, only to be replaced by more novel and personalized ways of commemorating a life.

Other cultures, however, are more intransigent about mourning rituals. In the Greek Orthodox Church, widows are instructed to wear black for two years. The colour of mourning clothes for Hindus is white, and a widow was once expected to remain in mourning for the rest of her life. She must shave her head once a month, and she is forbidden to wear jewels or to attend festivities such as marriage feasts. If she is a member of the Saiva sect, her forehead is smeared with ashes.[73] In China, the children of the deceased wear black, but the grandchildren wear blue and the more distant relatives dress in white. The children, furthermore, don't cut their hair for forty-nine days after the death of their parent.

One of the more notorious mourning customs was the Hindu practice of sati, in which a widow, as proof of her love and loyalty, would be burned to death (voluntarily or otherwise) on her husband's funeral pyre. Prevalent among the noble classes in India, it originated over seven hundred years ago in order, supposedly, for the wives of men captured in battle to avoid being taken as captives, but also, no doubt, as a way for a male-dominated society to dispose of unwanted women who would pose a financial liability. A religious dimension was soon added, with victims being venerated as goddesses and given places in heaven from which they could redeem their less fortunate forebears. Even though Protestant missionaries to India vigorously opposed the custom, by the first decades of the nineteenth century more than five hundred women a year were immolating themselves. The custom was finally outlawed by the Governor-General, Lord William Bentinck, in 1829. However, some forty cases have been reported since India gained independence in 1947, including, most famously, that of a pretty, well-educated eighteen-year-old named Roop Kanwar in September 1987. After her husband died of a burst appendix eight months into their marriage, Mrs Kanwar donned her wedding sari, climbed onto her husband's pyre, cradled his head in her lap, and urged her brother-in-law to light the fire. He apparently obliged, and she was engulfed in flames.

In recent years there have been two cases of sati in the central state of Madhya Pradesh. In the summer of 2002 a sixty-five-year-old woman named Kuttu Bai threw herself on the burning pyre of her dead husband. She was watched by an appreciative crowd of four thousand that included her two sons, who made no effort to restrain her. Policemen who attempted to stop the widow's self-immolation were pelted with stones and prevented from rescuing her. Four years later, in August 2006, the charred remains of a woman in her forties, identified only as Janakrani, were found on the funeral pyre of her dead husband. The authorities have suggested that Janakrani's death was a simple act of suicide, not sati, but the claim did nothing to dissuade tourists from flocking to her home village to witness the scorched pyre or another widow, a twenty-seven-year-old named

Mithlesh Prasad, from attempting to follow suit. Mrs Prasad, fortunately, was restrained by her relatives.

A HIGH PRICE TOUPÉE

The rigid rules and crape costumes may have disappeared, but not all Victorian mourning rituals have been jettisoned in twenty-first-century Britain and America. Preserving and venerating a keepsake of the beloved, such as a lock of hair, enables people to feel close to the recently departed. Wearing the tonsorial remains of a loved one became common practice amongst the wealthier classes in Britain in the eighteenth and nineteenth century. Brooches, lockets, bracelets, ribbons and even watch chains incorporating the hair – lovingly scissored from the head of the deceased – were worn by the middle classes in Victorian Britain. The trend soon spread across Europe and to America. Plaiting and the preparation of hair for jewellery spawned an industry of hair artists whose skills were highly sought after. Those who couldn't afford their exorbitant fees tried to go it alone using Alexanna Speight's manual, *Lock of Hair* (1891), with varying degrees of success. Like death masks, hair jewellery only lost its appeal when photography became available to the masses at the end of the 1880s, at which point brooches containing strands of hair were replaced by miniature photographs – an altogether cheaper option.

It is still possible today to have strands of hair of departed loved ones safely enclosed in a brooch, bracelet or necklace. Cremation Keepsakes, in Parker, Colorado, proposes to do this, offering a wide choice of jewellery that includes the popular hearts and crosses, to the more unusual: golf clubs, cowboy hats and even boots (the latter of which puts an altogether new meaning on the derogatory phrase 'my mother-in-law is an old boot'). The company has also incorporated a modern equivalent of this Victorian tradition by offering to incorporate a thimbleful of cremains (human ashes) instead of human hair into the jewellery.

A century or two after its vogue, the custom of clipping a lock of hair from the deceased has fuelled a strange trade not unlike the one for medieval relics. Historical luminaries whose hair was snipped for keepsakes on their deathbeds, or whose barbers surreptitiously kept their trimmings, are today making appearances at auctions and in valuable collections of curiosities. There are now several hundred hair collectors in the United States alone. Snippets from the heads of John F. Kennedy and Princess Diana have even been offered on eBay. Among the most prolific and successful of these collectors is John Reznikoff of Westport, Connecticut, whose collection features more than a hundred different locks of hair: Charlotte Brontë, Napoleon, the Duke of Wellington, Abraham Lincoln (a snip at $750,000), Henry Ford, Albert Einstein, Marilyn Monroe and Elvis Presley (from when he received his GI haircut). Reznikoff recently ran into trouble, though, when he bought hair from a living rather than a dead subject: for $3,000 clippings from the head of Neil Armstrong entered his collection. Armstrong's barber, Max Sizemore, had secretly been sweeping up the astronaut's hair after each of his visits to the barber's chair. Armstrong threatened to sue Sizemore, who, unable to get the hair back from Reznikoff, donated the money to charity.

So if the medieval trade in relics, with its fingernails and vials of blood, seems distastefully gruesome, it's worth considering how today it continues in only a slightly different form – albeit with celebrities and politicians rather than venerated saints being shorn of their bodily possessions and sold to the highest bidder.

DIAMOND GEEZERS

Hair in a locket or brooch is one thing, but the more extravagant can have their loved ones made into a diamond to be worn as jewellery. Two companies, one American and one Swiss, have discovered a way to turn human ashes into diamonds, producing hundreds of 'diamond geezers' a year, at a cost that can run as high as £14,000. Humans are carbon-based, so when their ashes are heated to 3,000°C they turn into graphite, which can then be compressed into a diamond. The average person yields enough carbon to make fifty to a hundred diamonds, so it would be possible to wear a dead spouse around the neck.

LifeGem Memorials, based in Chicago but with a UK office in Brighton, takes sixteen weeks to turn cremains into patented diamonds, which they have certified by the European Gemological Laboratory. LifeGem's diamond cutters are able to facet the stone in any way desired, or to laser etch it with distinctive markings. They can also mix the diamonds with other minerals so the client can choose if they want their loved one to become a blue, red or yellow-toned stone. The Swiss company, Algordanza, claims, on the other hand, that their diamonds are completely natural and additive-free. They maintain that the diamond will change colour naturally depending on the diet of the deceased: a vegetarian, for example, will produce a blue tinge.

LifeGem state that in 2005 they helped over a thousand families give their deceased relatives a sparkle. The company announced that it intended to auction three diamonds made from Ludwig van Beethoven's hair, the proceeds to go to charity. LifeGem teamed up with John Reznikoff, who gave LifeGem eight strands of the maestro's hair. Reznikoff's vast collection raises the possibility that dead presidents and movie stars will in future be given this bio-bling treatment. This was probably not quite what Marilyn Monroe had in mind when she sang 'Diamonds are a Girl's Best Friend'. On 18 September 2007 the company put the first one up for sale on eBay, hoping to make over $1,000,000 (£500,000). The diamond was sold, but the price achieved and the name of the lucky buyer are both unknown.

OBJETS D'ART

As the LifeGem diamonds show, cremation has led to an entire industry devoted to disposing of or commemorating a loved one. No longer need the loved one repose underground after making his or her quietus. Besides wearing the dearly departed around the neck or on the finger, it is now also possible to turn them into, for example, a beautiful ornament. One company in California, Crystal Eternity, mixes human ashes with molten glass to make these glass mementoes. Each piece is unique and guarantees admiration long after the deceased passed away. Alternatively, it's also possible to become a post-mortem painting. Such was the destiny of Marvel Comics editor Mark Gruenwald, known for the comics *Captain America* and *Quasar,* who died in 1996. Carrying out his request, his wife mixed his ashes with ink for a limited poster run of the comic *Squadron Supreme:* a few strokes of the brush later and Gruenwald became part of the comic trade that he so adored. Strange as that sounds, others are following suit. Artist Bettye Brokl, from Mississippi, came up with the idea for Eternally Yours Memorial Art after sprinkling her mother's ashes in a series of abstract paintings which she subsequently gave to her family as mementoes. Unlike the Egyptian mummies who got turned into 'Mummy Brown', the cremains were not mixed with paint but rather scattered over the finished product and sealed for posterity with a clear film. Brokl's work has become so popular that she now hires other artists to meet the demand. Tailormade paintings cost between $350 and $900.

More robust mementoes are also available. Ed Headrick, who patented the Frisbee in 1967, was himself made into Frisbees for his friends and relatives to throw around in the park. Four years after his death in 2002, a few of these 'Steady Ed's Memorial Discs' were still being offered for sale, at $210 a pair, on the website of Disc Golf Association (a Frisbee game invented by Headrick). All proceeds were earmarked for the building of a Frisbee museum California.

For the sporty or outdoorsy type, Canuck's Sportsman Memorials, in Des Moines, Iowa, might be the ticket. They will encase cremains in duck decoys and shotgun shells as well as, for dedicated anglers, in fishing bait and tackle boxes. Jay Knudson started up this company specializing in personalized commemorations in 1991. One of his first commissions was to insert the ashes of seventeen-year-old car crash victim Erik Brown into the lining of a basketball. As Erik had been a keen basketball player, his brother thought this a fitting tribute, and the mounted ball sits pride of place on Erik's family's mantlepiece.

Green options are likewise available. Carleton Glen Palmer, who died in 1998, wanted his cremains used to save the environment. Palmer's son-in-law Don Brawley, a keen environmentalist, ran the Reef Barrier Development Group, which sank environmentally friendly concrete balls in the ocean to replace deteriorating reefs. Before his death, Palmer requested that his cremains be mixed into one of these balls and placed in the ocean to form part of a reef – and in this way Eternal Reefs was born. The process can cost between two and five thousand dollars, depending on the choice of reef. Relatives are encouraged to help mix the cremains with the concrete; they can also place a handprint in the damp concrete during casting and take a rubbing of the bronze plaque fixed to each ball. When the ball has been shaped and cured, relatives can be taken out in a boat to witness the sinking of the memorial ball: a new twist on the idea of burial at sea. The more intrepid can dive near it whenever they wish in order to see their loved one sleeping with the fishes.

Yet cremation is not necessarily the most environmentally friendly way to dispose of a body. True, the process avoids the toxic embalming fluids that can potentially contaminate the soil and groundwater, and the scattering of remains over water or in the wilderness does away with the need for the herbicides and petrol-powered mowers that keep cemeteries neatly trimmed and looking smart. But nearly all crematoria use gas, a finite resource that pollutes the environment, and the burning of chipboard coffins likewise causes harmful emissions. The coffins themselves raise sustainability issues given that as many as fifty million board feet of timber are committed to coffins each year in the United States.[74] Most serious of all, fillings in the teeth of cremated dental patients emit mercury into the atmosphere, poisoning the soil, waterways and wildlife. With three grams of mercury in the teeth of the average person in Britain, crematoria are poised to become the country's biggest mercury polluters. In 2007 the British government therefore stipulated that by 2012 all of them must be fitted with special filters.

It is with such problems in mind that an enterprising Swedish woman has invented a different kind of technology for disposing of our loved ones. In 2005 media reports stated that Susanne Wiigh-Masak, an environmental biologist in the Swedish town of Jönköping, was developing a method called 'promession'. Touted as a green alternative to cremation, it involves the deceased being dipped in liquid nitrogen after death. The brittle body is then vibrated in a machine until, like a Ming vase in an earthquake, it shatters into a million pieces. A metal separator then carefully picks through the powder, looking for artificial hips, metal plates, or dreaded dental fillings. The powdered remains are placed in a box made of corn or potato starch and interred in a shallow grave, where in a matter of a few months they become so much compost.[75]

GOING OUT WITH A BANG

Not everyone wants such a discreet and efficient finale as the one proposed by Susanne Wiigh-Masak, and a market has grown for more ostentatious send-offs. From the depths of the ocean to the infinity of outer space, anything is now possible where the distribution of human remains is concerned. Billionaires spend as much as $25 million to become space tourists, but for a mere $995 a person can have his cremains blasted into space. Celestis Inc., of Houston, Texas, offers memorial space flights where either one or seven grams of cremated remains are put into individual capsules about the size of a lipstick container and placed in a memorial spacecraft attached to a satellite. These capsules stay in orbit for anything from two to two hundred years depending on the final altitude of the primary satellite – at which point it re-enters the earth's orbit and explodes with a satisfying bang. Hardly the greenest way of disposing of a body, but full marks for special visual effects.

The company launched its inaugural flight in April 1997 with twenty-four 'passengers', including Gene Roddenberry, creator of the popular TV series *Star Trek,* who boldly went where no man's cremains had gone before. Also on board was the LSD guru Timothy Leary, who took, as the *Washington Post* reported, 'one final, far-out trip'.[76] The capsule orbited the earth for five years before the passengers were cremated for a second time as they re-entered the atmosphere. Punters can choose from several options, starting with the basic Flight Capsule Service, which includes one gram of cremains being placed in a capsule, to the $12,500 Lunar or Voyager Services, in which cremains are launched into either the lunar orbit or deep space. Included in all the packages is the opportunity for friends and family to attend the launch, receive a memorial DVD, and have a biography of the deceased permanently displayed on the company's official website. In 2007, Roddenberry was followed into space by one of his actors, James Doohan, better known as 'Scotty', chief engineer on the *Enterprise.* Scotty was 'beamed up' for one last time on board the twenty-foot-long SpaceLoft XL rocket developed by UP Aerospace, Inc.

For those not tempted by the extraterrestrial option, fireworks are another choice. In 2005, thirty-four fireworks carried the ashes of the 'Gonzo' journalist Hunter S. Thompson into the sky with a fantastic display of colours. The actor Johnny Depp, who played Thompson in the

1998 film version of his life, *Fear and Loathing in Las Vegas,* paid a reputed $2.5 million for the fireworks, which were blasted from a 153-foot-long gun built around an industrial crane.

Spending a couple of million dollars on a loved one's final send-off might seem a little excessive, but there are less expensive options. For between £900 and £1,800 the Heavens Above Fireworks company based in Essex will modify fireworks to include cremains. Their service provides a display of personalized fireworks synchronized to your favourite music. The writer Philip Pullman, author of the bestselling *Dark Materials* trilogy, decided to commemorate his step-father in this way. He commissioned Scottish Fireworks and Displays, a company based in Edinburgh, to work out how many rockets were needed. The rockets filled with his step-father's cremains – forty in all – were then ignited on a small headland called Starley Point, on the north side of the Firth of Forth. 'Having seen how that worked,' Pullman has declared, 'I'm inclined to echo the words of my niece, "That's the way I want to go!"' [77]

Cremains can also be scattered from an aeroplane over the ocean or a favourite patch of the countryside. In Britain there are no laws preventing the scattering of ashes, but in the United States it varies state by state. A word of warning, though. In May 2002, panic spread as a container spilling grey dust was seen being cast from a small Cessna airplane over Seattle's SAFECO baseball stadium, where the Seattle Mariners are based. The hazardous materials team from the Seattle Fire Department rushed to the scene as officials from the Federal Aviation Administration (FAA) – understandably jumpy in the months after 9/11 – urgently set about contacting the pilot. The bemused pilot told the authorities he worked for a company hired to disperse cremains. Dave Miller, of the FAA, was anything but sentimental: 'Their choice of locations would appear to be extremely imprudent.' [78] Imprudent, perhaps – but highly appropriate: the cremains were those of a devoted Seattle Mariners fan.

PERSONAL SPACE

Inner space as well as outer space is also an alternative. Electing for burial rather than cremation no longer means a plain and discreet six-sided pine box and tooth-shaped granite headstone. It is now possible to personalize gravestones and coffins in virtually any style imaginable. Lesley McGuiness, from Newcastle, erected a tombstone for her husband, who died from cancer in his thirties, that was in the shape and colour of his favourite football team's shirt. Made from granite by Simon Richard, who works in his family firm of masons, Joseph Richmond and Son, it was in the black and white colours of Newcastle United. This 'Magpie' tombstone was unique enough to win the gravestone industry's award for Most Original memorial of the year in 2006. As it was carved partly in China, it cost only £2,000 as opposed to the more than £5,000 price tag it would have carried had it been made from scratch in England.

Requests for these sorts of unique headstones are becoming more and more common: only one-fifth of those produced by Joseph Richmond and Son are plain memorials with only the name of the departed carved on them. Likewise, coffins and urns now carry a more personal stamp. J.C. Atkinson, an independent maker of coffins based in Tyne and Wear, will decorate a coffin or urn with personal images that range from the religious or the picturesque to sporting or floral designs. The most popular are countryside scenes or football club colours. The most unusual, according to Julian Atkinson, the director of the company, featured an engraving of a brandy glass, cigar and baked beans – the favourite indulgences of the deceased. Another was from a farmer who requested an image of a flock of sheep on his coffin 'so he could fall asleep while counting them'. Charges vary depending whether the coffin is lined and furnished, but the average price is around £600. And all the coffins are created using ecologically friendly paints and wood that comes from a sustainable source.[79]

However, it is the Ghanaians from the Ga community of Accra who are truly the leaders in the field of novelty coffins. Traditionally, chiefs were transported around their villages in elaborate chairs. One such Ga chief, early in the twentieth century, requested that his chair be made in the shape of a cocoa pod, cocoa being a major crop in Ghana. Sadly, he died before he could be borne aloft around the village, but the giant cocoa pod then did duty as his coffin. Then, in 1951, one of the apprentices of Ata Owoo, who made such chairs for chiefs, asked his boss if he would make a coffin in the shape of an aeroplane for his grandmother who had recently died. Owoo obliged, and the trend for personalized coffins soon caught on. Today there are workshops all over Teshi, a suburb of Accra, making coffins in the shape of cars, boats, birds, fish and anything that might have a special meaning to the deceased. There have even been coffins shaped like mobile phones and Coca-Cola bottles. It's not uncommon for Ghanaians to commission a design before they die so they can admire their final resting vessel before it is too late. And why not? After all, they'll be spending eternity inside, so it might not be a bad idea to inspect the craftsmanship and admire the design.

Most people today tend to make do with a small gravestone if buried or, if cremated, a sundial or garden seat. However, the wealthiest and most powerful members of a society have, since time immemorial, been burying their dead in fantastic tombs and mausoleums, constructing ever bigger and more impressive monuments to commemorate their nearest and dearest. The Taj Mahal in Agra, India's most beautiful and bewitching mausoleum, was completed in 1654 to house the body of Mumatz Mahal, favourite wife of the Mughal Emperor Shah Jahan. It took twenty-two thousand workers and seventeen years to build. But perhaps one of the most spectacular mausoleums of all times is that of the First Emperor of China, Qin Shi Huangdi (King Zheng). In 1974 a group of peasants digging for a well at the foot of Mount Li in Shaanxi province unearthed some pottery. Archaeologists confirmed that it was from the Qin Dynasty (221–206 BCE), and began digging in earnest. What they discovered was over seven thousand life-size terracotta soldiers, horses, chariots and even weapons, all guarding the burial chamber of King Zheng.

The major states in China had battled continuously from 453 BCE until the state of Qin, proving far superior in tactics and organization to any others, successfully conquered its neighbours in 227 BCE. For the first time, one dynasty united all the Chinese states. Records found in the tomb of a high-ranking official who died in 217 BCE showed that the Emperor had divided his newly acquired domain into thirty-six provinces. One of his greatest achievements was the standardization of the language and currency, a legacy which continues to this day. From his capital at Xi'an the Emperor ordered a brand new palace to be built, together with the strengthening of the Great Wall. Chinese emperors, like Egyptian pharaohs, traditionally began building their tombs as soon as they took the throne to ensure they would be in a good location for the afterlife. The construction of this emperor's mausoleum commenced in 246 BCE – forty years before he died – taking eleven years and 700,000 conscripts to complete.

The tomb itself has not been opened, but it is surrounded by pits containing the Terracotta Army. Pit number one contains the infantry soldiers, each with individual features and characteristics; the second pit houses the cavalry, with over one hundred horses and chariots; while a third houses the army headquarters staff. From written records, the historian Sima Qian suggests that the tomb itself is encased in bronze with exquisite furniture and fittings ready for the emperor's future needs. Treasures of an unknown quantity would have been buried within its walls. Whether they remain no one is sure, as historic accounts show that General Xiang Yu and his army plundered it only a few years after the emperor's death. It is likely that riches, if still there, were not the only valuables entombed with him, for it was decreed that all the emperor's wives who had not borne him sons should be buried with him, alive. The construction team fared no better: all workers involved in the building or interior design of the tomb were executed, and the pits of these unfortunates have been found nearby.

LOOK ON MY WORKS, YE MIGHTY

For lesser mortals, building a mausoleum protected by a seven thousand-strong terracotta army is hardly an option, but among those with money there has recently been a revival in ostentatious burial chambers. In 2004 the Forest Lawn Cemetery in Buffalo, New York, advertised 'a once-in-a-lifetime opportunity to join your legacy with that of America's greatest architect' – that is, by purchasing a crypt in Frank Lloyd Wright's Blue-Sky Mausoleum. Those enamoured of Wright's work – the great American architect designed over three hundred buildings, many with sharp, elongated façades – can take the opportunity to have their remains interred in one of the twenty-four granite sarcophagi in the mausoleum. Depending on the location of the sarcophagus within the building, the privilege will come with a price-tag between $300,000 and $1.5 million. A guarantee comes with each sale: the tomb will be maintained 'forever', since Wright's mausoleum has been deemed a national monument, which brings with it the appropriate funds for maintenance.

The Blue-Sky Mausoleum was completed in 2004. The industrialist Darwin D. Martin commissioned the project in 1925 but pulled out after losing all his money in the stock market crash of 1929. Wright had enjoyed a lifelong friendship with Martin, designing his residential complex in Buffalo, New York, his summer house on the edge of Lake Erie and the Larkin Soap headquarters in Buffalo, where Martin worked as an executive. The plans for the Blue-Sky Mausoleum were kept secret until an architect trained by Wright was commissioned to erect the monument exactly as it was originally envisaged.

Interment no longer necessarily means a six-foot-deep plot in a church-yard, topped by a humble gravestone and exposed to wind, rain and cold. Burial preferences have recently been shifting towards above-ground interment. Wright's Blue-Sky Mausoleum is only one of any number of architecturally stunning mausoleums in which crypt or niche space may be purchased. These modern mausoleums have all the beauty and splendour of medieval churches, with domes, skylights, stained glass, polished mar-ble, and sometimes even gardens and waterfalls. They include space for hundreds of coffins in niches and crypts, and the purchaser has the option of having his or her name inscribed in the allotted space in a variety of fonts. Some mausoleums even provide air filtration and circulation systems for the crypts themselves, to ensure that the deceased reposes in a healthy atmosphere. The industry leader is Carrier Mausoleums Construction of Ville St Laurent, Quebec. One of their most impressive offerings is St Anthony's Mausoleum, located at the Queen of Heaven Cemetery in Vaughan, Ontario, a short distance north of Toronto. Featuring more than four thousand crypts, it is a vast and elegant building with Doric columns of Italian marble, patterned carpets and chandeliers – all of the elegance one normally associates with the lobbies of five-star hotels. It also includes a columbarium room where glass- and marble-fronted niches cater to the growing demand for cremation options.

For those with deeper pockets and grander visions of their last resting places, private mausoleums can be purchased. In 2005 the Cold Spring Granite Company sold two thousand of these personal monuments, compared with an average of only sixty-five per year in the 1980s. The reason for this increase no doubt has much to do with baby boomers coming towards the end of their lives. Many have achieved extravagant material success and live in huge mansions that showcase their wealth and power. Many of them, like Chinese emperors or Egyptian pharaohs of the past, now want this grandeur to continue after their death.

A company called Matthews, purveyors of 'memorial products' in Pittsburgh, Pennsylvania, offers any number of designs for those plumping for statement-making above-ground entombment. Purchasers can choose from four distinct styles, including the 'Colonnade', which features fluted granite columns, and the 'Pagoda', which comes with a cast bronze roof and bronze foo lions standing guard. The granite may be selected from a variety of colours – everything from 'Sunset Rose' to 'Galaxy Black' – and purchasers have the choice of more than nine thousand emblems to reflect their religious beliefs or personal interests. They can even have their portraits carved and placed on display.

One of the more impressive of the private mausoleums is that constructed to house the mortal remains of Florida millionaire L. Gale Lemerand. A noted philanthropist, Lemerand sold his residential insulation company in 1995 for an estimated $150 million. Since then he has built a huge mausoleum for himself and his family at Daytona Memorial Park. Costing a total of $650,000, the tomb is made of red granite, stands on the edge of a lake, and features a pair of Medjool date palms that set him back almost $10,000. Mr Lemerand's mausoleum is all the more impressive considering that in 2007 the average price of a four-bedroom house in Daytona Beach was only $414,809.[80]

Even more ambitious is the plan of the controversial British businessman Nicholas van Hoogstraten. He has spent some twenty years and perhaps as much as £40 million constructing an enormous mansion – reportedly the largest and most expensive private home built in England for more than a century – near Uckfield in East Sussex. Known as Hamilton Palace, it boasts a copper dome, a hundred acres of parkland, and a six hundred-foot-long art gallery. Its *pièce de résistance*, though, is a gigantic and impregnable mausoleum in the east wing where Mr van Hoogstraten plans to repose, along with his artwork, for five thousand years, like a pharaoh entombed among his treasures. 'It's the nearest I can get to taking all my wealth with me,' he says, 'and ensuring that nobody else benefits from it.'[81]

Wealthy men such as Lemerand and van Hoogstraten may wish to pause for thought, however, before signing cheques for their granite and palm tree slices of immortality. In his poem 'Ozymandias', Percy Bysshe Shelley describes an arrogant monument to the ancient ruler Ozymandias, 'king of kings', which has fallen into ruin in the middle of trackless desert wastes. This 'colossal wreck' may foreshadow the fate of tombs of even the wealthiest baby boomers. No longer do people spend their Sundays visiting cemeteries to pay their respects as was done in the nineteenth century. Many grandiose tombs from the nineteenth century, in cemeteries such as Père-Lachaise and Highgate, have now fallen on Ozymandias-like hard times. Mr van Hoogstraten's house and mausoleum have even begun falling apart during his own lifetime. In 2006 a newspaper reported how a building inspection by the local council discovered vegetation growing on the uncompleted roof and problems with damp that made the house's walls look like a 'contour map'.[82] With Hamilton Palace decaying so soon, can Mr van Hoogstraten truly hope for five thousand years of grandiose and undisturbed repose?

It is partly because people are so quickly forgotten that every April the Natural Death Centre (NDC) in the United Kingdom organizes a National Day of the Dead. The National Day of the Dead enables people to pay their respects to the dead and share memories with family and friends. Those who can't make any of the organized events of the day are encouraged to light a candle at a mealtime to share memories of the deceased. Launched in 1991, the NDC, a charitable project, aims to improve the quality of dying and helps people arrange inexpensive, environmentally friendly funerals. For some, this celebration might provoke a few uncomfortable feelings; for the Wari tribe of Brazil, it would have caused severe anxiety as they didn't want to relive memories of loved ones and therefore commemorated their dead in a very different way.

THE LAST SUPPER: ENDOCANNIBALISM

Before 1956, the Wari lived an isolated existence. They hunted, they gathered, and they ate their in-laws after they died – a practice known to anthropologists as 'endocannibalism'. The Wari weren't the only South American tribe to undertake endocannibalism, but what makes them unique is the openness and pride with which they talked about it. From a Western perspective, the very thought of eating another human, let alone an in-law, is somewhat unappealing; by contrast, the idea of being buried and left to rot in the cold, wet ground was just as abhorrent to the Wari. A deep compassion for both the deceased and the bereaved underpinned their actions. A corpse left intact was a painful reminder of the deceased, prolonging the grieving. Eating the deceased, on the other hand, made the painful memories disappear more quickly, as did the burning of the deceased's house and belongings. According to the anthropologist James W. Dow, endocannibalism symbolized a 'reverence for the dead, an incorporation of the spirit of the dead into living descendants, or a means of insuring the separation of the soul from the body'. He cites the case of a man from another Amazonian tribe of endocannibals, the Mayoruna, who expressed a wish to remain in his village and be eaten by his children rather than be consumed by worms in the white man's cemetery.[83]

The Wari never ate their own blood relatives. This task was left to the in-laws, and it was regarded as a social obligation: to refuse to eat a relation was an unpardonable insult. Eating Wari flesh was often an extremely disagreeable experience as the body would begin decomposing while the mourning rituals were performed. Mercifully for the hapless relative discharging his familial obligations, not all of the decomposing flesh – which was at least roasted – needed to be consumed, since part was cremated. As with other South American tribes, the Wari were also known to eat their enemies. However, the emotions attached to this type of cannibalism (known to anthropologists as 'exocannibalism') were rather different. The Wari believed that to eat a fellow Wari was an honour and a mark of respect to the deceased; to dine on an enemy, on the other hand, was the ultimate insult to the deceased.

The Wari no longer eat their friends or, for that matter, their enemies. By 1962 all of the Brazilian Wari tribes had been contacted by the outside world searching for rubber and medicinal plants. The outsiders brought with them infectious diseases such as influenza, whooping cough, mumps, measles and malaria, thus decimating the tribes by sixty per cent. Today only about two thousand remain. The missionaries and government officials persuaded the Wari with medicines and material bribes to abandon their traditions and instead to bury their dead; some elderly Wari, who remember the good old days, still find this practice sits uncomfortably with them. One of them, Jimon Maram, explained to the anthropologist Beth A. Conklin what he felt about burying one of his children: 'We keep remembering our child, lying there, cold. We remember, and we are sad. It was better in the old days, when the others ate the body. Then we did not think about our child's body much. We did not remember our child as much, and we were not so sad.'[84]

There are certain hazards to endocannibalism. The 1976 Nobel Prize winner for physiology or medicine, Daniel Carleton Gajdusek, discovered that the Fore people of Papua New Guinea, who practised endocannibalism for nutritional as well as symbolic reasons, were prone to a disease they called Kuru, the Fore word for trembling. It was particularly common in women and children, and one of the symptoms was a tendency to laugh uncontrollably in between bouts of aggression. After years of research, Gajdusek found Kuru to be related to Creutzfeldt-Jacob Disease and other similar diseases, such as Bovine Spongiform Encephalopathy, or BSE, popularly known as 'Mad Cow Disease'. So why did the Fore succumb to Kuru while other human flesh-eating tribes did not? Partly it was due to bad luck or, as the Flanders and Swan song, 'Eating People is Wrong', says: 'Must have been someone he ate.' Some unsuspecting unfortunate in the tribe picked up an agent such as scrapie, which could have been contracted by butchered meat. Once in the body it manifested itself as CJD. One unlucky person, infected by chance, died as a result and then was eaten by other tribesmen, who subsequently developed the disease.

But perhaps the Wari and the Fore were ahead of their time. In 2006 a forty-four-year-old German computer technician named Armin Meiwes was jailed for life for eating Bernd Jürgen Brandes. This was no ordinary case of cannibalism, however, since Brandes had freely consented to be eaten: the two men had met in 2001 after Brandes replied to Meiwes's internet advertisement for a victim to be 'slaughtered and then consumed'. A video of the proceedings showed Brandes urging Meiwes to slice off his penis so the pair could fry and eat it. Meiwes obliged, sautéeing the severed organ in garlic. 'If I'm still alive in the morning,' Brandes wisecracked, 'we can eat my balls for breakfast.'[85] Evidence suggests that Brandes was not alive in the morning, since he expired from blood loss in the bath while Meiwes lounged nearby reading a *Star Trek* novel. In December 2002 police investigators found part of Brandes's butchered body stored in Meiwes's freezer, hidden under pizza boxes and sealed in packets inscribed with best before dates. He also took a photograph of his victim's amputated foot on a dinner plate, impaled by a fork and covered with sauce. Meiwes managed to eat an estimated twenty kilograms of his victim in the twenty-one months before he was caught. One delicacy he was denied, found in the bottom of his freezer, was labelled 'Fillet of Neck'.

The quest for ever more original and outlandish feats to perform with cremains has witnessed a number of claims that might find Amazonian tribal elders nodding approvingly. Larry Hagman, the American actor famous for his TV roles in *I Dream of Genie* and *Dallas*, has quite specific ideas regarding how he would like to be commemorated. Hagman claims he wants to be minced in a wood chipper and have his remains planted over an acre of land mixed with wheat and marijuana seeds. When the crops are ready for harvesting, he requests that a huge cake is made and on his birthday his friends and relatives can dance and be merry for three days dining on his remains.[86]

It is uncertain whether his closest friends would be agreeable to this 'last supper'. It is equally questionable whether Bert Richards – despite his son claiming otherwise – would have been entirely happy about how his life was celebrated. In 2007 the Rolling Stones guitarist Keith Richards admitted to a modern, rock 'n' roll version of endocannibalism. Richards's father Bert was cremated after he died at the age of eighty-four. But Mr Richards's cremains were not destined, like those of so many other deceased parents, to sit unobtrusively and half-forgotten on the mantlepiece, in a tasteful urn. It was possibly an unwise decision of the funeral director to hand over the powdery, whitish substance to as dedicated and prolific a drug-user as 'Keef'. What followed was, perhaps, inevitable. Richards confessed to a journalist for the British music magazine, *NME*, that he had been unable to resist mixing his father's ashes with a bit of 'blow' and then snorting him. 'It went down pretty well,' he boasted, 'and I'm still alive.' The indestructible old rocker is no doubt right that the concoction (or the human as opposed to the cocoa-leaf element, at least) did him little harm. The cremains would have been sterilized by the intense heat in the crematorium, and the carbon driven off as carbon dioxide. The cremains would therefore have been composed largely of minerals such as potassium, sodium, iron and calcium – and so snorting the ashes would have been rather like popping a multivitamin. As for Bert Richards, health experts speculate that his remains would have been enveloped in his son's mucus and expelled with a cough or a sneeze.

CHAPTER 8

Ghost Festivals and Purifying Fire

Safeguarding the Soul

These days, anything can be sold on eBay. Or so, at least, believed a young Chinese man from Jiaxing, a city near Shanghai. According to Reuters, in 2006 this opportunist offered a unique item on Taobao, eBay's Chinese equivalent: his soul. Taobao, or rather its parent company, Yahoo-backed Alibab.com, decided to pull the posting – which attracted fifty-eight bidders – as they didn't have a specific policy on selling souls. Taobao called an emergency meeting, eventually decreeing that members would be allowed to sell their souls, but only if they obtained written permission from a 'higher authority'. The young man in question is still waiting for confirmation from such an authority but anticipates closing the deal once the necessary paperwork is completed.[87]

As Taobao discovered, determining the relationship of the soul to the material world is not always easy. According to the *Oxford English Dictionary*, the soul (also sometimes referred to as the spirit) is the 'spiritual or immaterial part of man, held to survive death'. Depending on one's belief system, surviving death can entail a great many things, as the spirits of the dead can undergo many and various posthumous adventures. The soul can end up being reborn into another body, languishing in a fiery hell, or receiving its rewards in heaven. It can receive begging letters from the living and, once a year, feast on cakes and other treats; some cultures, we shall see, even provide the souls of the departed with supplies of Viagra. Souls find their way through the material world with the help of incense and paper lanterns or else get frightened away by sprigs of herbs, tolling bells and noisy salutes from cannons; and they make their way to the underworld by learning to scrutinize handbooks and perform magic spells. In some cultures, their hearts are eaten by vengeful gods; in another, a Lord of Death drinks their blood and licks their brains. And every summer, apparently, they make their passage in large numbers to communicate with mediums who have set up shop at a small town in upstate New York.

SPIRITS IN A MATERIAL WORLD

Not all cultures welcome contact from the dead. Indeed, the possibility of the dead returning was often so frightening to medieval Europeans that all manner of precautions – or superstitions – were invented to prevent such an eventuality. As soon as a person died, the fear of a ghostly return prompted relatives to open doors and windows so the spirit could depart from the house. The deceased was even carried feet first through the door to prevent his spirit from looking back and beckoning another family member to follow him into the realms of the dead. To further discourage a return, thresholds were scrubbed, floors were sprinkled with dill and fennel, frankincense and myrrh were burned in the fireplace and garlic was hung over doorways.

   In Britain, the custom of wearing black and donning a veil after a death stemmed from the desire to conceal the identities of the mourners from any malevolent spirits lurking about the churchyard. Curtains were drawn, mirrors covered and clocks stopped until the funeral had passed, all to ensure that the house of the deceased would be unfamiliar to a lingering spirit, forcing it leave. In Holland it was once the custom to install false doors in farmhouses to confuse spirits who tried to return. Coffins were often provided with coins and other trinkets in order to appease the spirit of the dead and dissuade it from returning to haunt the living, while in ancient China it was believed that, by inserting into tombs figurines of fierce guardians known as Qitou, the spirit was trapped inside and other spirits were prevented from entering. The Saxons even amputated the feet of their dead to prevent them from going walkabout at night. And in some ancient tombs, such as that of the Etruscan general Lars Porsena, mazes were built at their entrances to keep the deceased from finding his way back to the world to haunt the living.

Some dates in the calendar were regarded more likely to produce returning spirits. The ancient Celts (circa 600 BCE) thought there was a specific time when the shadowy boundary separating the living from the dead became blurred. The first of November, known as Samhain (pronounced sow-in), began the Celtic year at a time when the harvest had been collected and people battened down for a harsh winter. The eve of Samhain, 31 October, was a day that did not exist, a time when the material world collided with the world of the dead and the spirits returned to walk amongst the living. The Celts, unlike many other cultures, welcomed their ghostly guests. Food and entertainment was laid out in their honour, while celebrants dressed in animal heads and skins danced around a huge bonfire. Samhain was also a time when priests could obtain the help of spirits for their predictions. Hallowe'en, introduced into England by the Scots in Victorian times, is thought to have its roots in Samhain. Emigrants took Hallowe'en with them to the United States, where it is now a hugely popular annual event.

Some cultures have such a good relationship with the dead that once a year they actually invite them to come back and party. Each October in Mexico and other Latin American countries, street stalls begin selling papier-mâché skulls and skeletons, sugared skulls, and *pan de muerto* – a rich coffee cake decorated with meringues that look like bones. These treats are for the *Día de Muertos,* Day of the Dead, one of the biggest festivals in their calendar. On 1 and 2 November, the Mexicans believe, the souls of the dead return to eat, drink and be merry with their relatives. Traditions vary throughout Mexico, but often shells are placed on clothing, candles are lit, and incense is burnt to guide the dead to their families. Sometimes bells are rung to summon the departed spirits. The festivities are an excuse for ancestral graves to be cleaned and then covered with orange marigolds, brand new toys for dead children, and, for the adults, special food and alcohol such as tequila, mescal, pulque and atole. These *ofrendas* are eventually eaten by the living, but the food lacks nutritional value as the dead are deemed to have eaten its 'spiritual' essence (a handy prospect to contemplate, presumably, for anyone counting their calories). Even pillows and blankets are provided in case the dead get tired with all this frivolity and require a rest. In the homes, altars and shrines are built to continue the celebration.

Of course the majority of people do not actually see the dead on the *Día de Muertos*, but they are celebrating an ancient Mesoamerican tradition that believes bodily death is not the end. Before the Spanish conquerors brought Catholicism to Latin America, the indigenous population viewed death as a continuation of life. Life was a dream, and only in death did they awaken. The sugared skulls are eaten because skulls symbolize not only death but also rebirth. The celebration originally took place over the months of July and August until the Spanish priests moved it to coincide with the Christian holiday of All Hallows Eve in November. It is now celebrated on the first two days in November, having evolved into a fusion of Mesoamerican and European traditions.

The ancient Celts and modern-day Mexicans are not the only people to celebrate death with an annual festival. Ancestor worship plays an important part in Chinese culture, where traditionally families gather once a year on Tomb Sweeping Day, two weeks after the vernal equinox, to clean the graves of their ancestors. Whatever an ancestor might need in the afterlife – money and other items, such as limousines, mistresses and Viagra – are made of paper and symbolically burnt as their families picnic by the grave and fly kites shaped like frogs and dragonflies. Food offered to the dead includes 'grave cakes', which are made from a red-dyed rice dough that is imprinted with the image of a tortoise and stuffed with peanut powder or a paste made from red beans. The food is deliberately bland to minimize the chance of attracting hordes of free-loading ghosts.

The Ghost Festival is another holiday, celebrated by Buddhists, Taoists and believers in Chinese folk religions. In Japan it is known as O-bon or Bon. On the fourteenth night of the seventh lunar month in the Chinese calendar – which in Japan falls in July – the gates of hell are opened, permitting all ghosts to receive food and drink from their relatives. The origins of this festival derive from the story of Mahamaudgalyayana, a disciple of the Buddha. One day while deep in meditation he saw a vision of his mother trapped in the Realm of Hungry Ghosts, where she had ended up as a consequence of her selfish actions. When the disciple asked the Buddha how he might release his mother from this realm, he was told to provide a feast for the past seven generations of dead on 15 July. That day would also become a day of prayer for the dead souls and the provision of food for hungry ghosts. Mahamaudgalyayana's mother was released from her hell to be reborn as a dog in a kind household. Although the festival varies regionally, paper lanterns are floated to guide the spirits to their families, graves are cleaned, refreshments laid out, and in Japan a special dance is performed in which groups of people in special costumes dance in unison around a Yagura – a high wooden building constructed for the festival.

SPOOKSVILLE

The Mexicans and Chinese are not the only ones to court the favours of the dead. Today many people still think it possible to make contact with the souls of the dead. The American hamlet of Lily Dale, known to sceptics as 'Silly Dale' or 'Spooksville', is a place where the barriers between this world and the spirit world are believed to be particularly thin. This small collection of clapboard houses and picturesque, tree-lined streets, founded in 1879, is situated sixty miles south of Buffalo, New York. It provides a home for thirty-six resident mediums or spiritualists who regularly talk to spirits of the deceased. Each summer Lily Dale opens its doors to twenty thousand visitors, all seeking advice from the next world. Mae West was a frequent visitor, though she might have come for more earthly reasons as it was rumoured that she was having an affair with one of the resident mediums, the Revd Jack Kelly. In any case, the actress was a great believer in the spirit world. In a 1976 interview she claimed that the Revd Kelly returned from the afterlife to visit her, as did one of her deceased pets, a monkey that reappeared to her on the cornice of her bedroom wall.[88]

Visits from dead monkeys are presumably quite rare, but virtually all cultures have in some way attempted to communicate with the dead. Unusual as Lily Dale seems, attempting to make contact with the dead is an ancient and widespread practice. The ancient Egyptians used to write letters to recently deceased relatives in the hope that they would help solve their earthly problems. When the dead person received such a letter, written on linen or papyrus, he or she was expected to intervene from the afterlife, even attending the court of the underworld if necessary. The Greeks consulted oracles for a similar purpose, the Assyrians and Romans practised divination, while the Inca emperors rarely made a major decision without first consulting the preserved bodies of their ancestors. Even in the Old and New Testaments references are made to physical mediumship, healing and talking in tongues. However, at the Council of Nicea in 325 CE, the Catholic Church decreed that only priests were worthy of contact from the 'other side' and that this communication should only come through the Holy Spirit. All other contact was deemed unholy, and anyone suspected of psychic dabbling was accused of being a witch and put to death.

This ruling was not openly challenged until the eighteenth century, when the Swedish scientist and astronomer Emmanuel Swedenborg (1688–1772) wrote extensively about how he could commune with deceased spirits when in a trance. These spirits, according to Swedenborg, mediated between God and humans. In Swedenborg's world, a single Heaven and Hell did not exist; instead, he envisaged a series of spheres that a spirit passed through as it progressed, drawing nearer and nearer to God. Each sphere was dependent on how the person lived his life on earth. For example, a murderer might find himself in a sphere with fellow murderers, in fear for his own safety. Not long after Swedenborg's ideas began circulating, another radical thinker, an Austrian physician named Franz Mesmer (1734–1815), invented the technique of hypnotism by means of which he claimed to be able to contact the spirits of the deceased by means of trances.

It was, however, two little girls from rural New York who were ultimately responsible for the birth and subsequent popularity of what has been termed spiritualism. In 1848, nine-year-old Catherine Fox, known as

Kate, and her sister Margaret told their mother they could hear tapping coming from the cellar of their farm in rural Hydesville. The girls devised a system of communicating with the noise: two taps meant yes, and one, no. Eventually, after extensive questioning, the girls and their mother apparently learned that the mystery rapper was a pedlar who had been murdered and buried in the cellar.

The girls' older sister Leah was quick to spot the financial potential of Kate and Margaret's talents, promptly turning them into a stage act. News quickly spread of the Fox sisters' ability to communicate audibly with a spirit, and they were invited to give public demonstrations. The showman P.T. Barnum jumped on the bandwagon, taking them to New York, where their fame spread rapidly. Critics tested the girls by tying them up, raising them off the floor and even strip-searching them, but no devices were ever found. The more famous they became, the more famous were the spirits with whom they talked: Benjamin Franklin regularly conversed with them. And yet their lives were not particularly happy ones. Both women became alcoholics; Kate was to die of the disease in 1892, followed by her sister, ill, disillusioned and destitute, a year later.

Few could have predicted the effect the Fox sisters and their rapping pedlar would have on the public's imagination. In a short space of time, mediums claiming similar talents began materializing all over the place and, of course, charging handsomely for their services. Spiritualism attracted radical thinkers in the nineteenth century who were eager to reject the established churches, which, in their view, did nothing to fight slavery or advance women's rights. Women in particular were attracted to spiritualism because it provided them with a role as mediums and allowed them to address mixed public gatherings. It came as a blow to the spiritualist movement when Margaret converted to Catholicism and in 1888 confessed that it had all been a hoax. The clicking noises, she explained, were surreptitiously made by their knee and toe joints: their communication with the world of the dead was in actuality a mere matter of cartilage and bone. It seems that the Fox girls were bored one day and innocently decided to frighten their mother. Events got out of hand so quickly that they became too scared to admit it was all a prank. Many people, however, still refused to believe the toe-joint explanation, and Margaret did not help matters by recanting her confession shortly before she died in 1893. When human bones were excavated from the cellar of the Fox's farm in 1904, believers seemed confirmed in their conviction that the pedlar had indeed existed. He was even named as Charles B. Rosma, but further investigations have not so far traced any such person who matched that name.

The public may have been so receptive to the Fox girls' hoax in part because of the time and location of their performance. Long before Lily Dale, New York State was a place where spiritual happenings were not uncommon. In 1823, Joseph Smith announced that he had received a set of golden plates from an angel named Moroni, which he had found buried in a hill near Palmya, in rural New York. Smith translated these plates, first by using some supernatural spectacles given to him by Moroni and then by placing a seer stone in his hat and burying his head in it. The result was the *Book of Mormon* and the creation of the Church of Latter-Day Saints, which today has over twelve million followers. Several years before the Fox girls first made contact with the dead, a New York farm worker and Baptist preacher, William Miller, announced that the world was going to end on 22 October 1844. The result was that thousands of people sold their belongings in anticipation of the Judgement Day. Later, the Shakers, also believers in spirits, set up their Holy Sanctuary of the New World in New York.

In 1852, the new trend of communicating with the dead was brought over to Britain and championed by the Boston medium, Mrs Hayden. She was ridiculed in the press and criticized heavily by the Church of England, but a year later the first Spiritualist Church was established in Keighley, Yorkshire, by David Richmond. Demonstrations of mediumship in the form of séances and automatic writing became popular in living rooms all over the English-speaking world, proving to be a profitable business attracting many charlatans and fraudsters. When Queen Victoria contacted the medium Robert James Lee to speak with the recently departed Prince Albert, spiritualism was given further endorsement. By 1900, however, the public on both sides of the Atlantic began to lose interest, in particular after a series of investigations into fraudulent claims by mediums became public. However, recent statistics show that in the late 1990s there were over six hundred spiritualist congregations in the United States with more than 210,000 members.

One of the most famous believers of recent years was Princess Diana who, before her death in 1997, regularly consulted the medium Simone Simmons. And now, appropriately enough, Diana allegedly communicates regularly with mediums all over the world. Indeed, in March 2003, an American TV company charged viewers $14.95 (£9.50) to watch a live broadcast of British mediums, Craig and Jane Hamilton-Parker, as they contacted the late Princess of Wales via a séance. Princess Diana, we are led to believe, was able to tell them that she was very happy in the afterlife and that she now spends her time with Mother Theresa. She also imparted to the Hamilton-Parkers the information that she had intended to marry Dodi al-Fayed.

Perhaps there is a reason why the dead are always with us. Dr Michael Jackson, in his doctoral thesis 'A Study of the Relationship between Psychotic and Spiritual Experience' (Oxford University, 1991), claims that spiritual experiences are a central component in a normally adaptive process of problem-solving common to the general population. This might explain why, as long as we have anxieties about the future and uncertainties about our place in the world, we will continue to believe that the dead can intervene and influence our lives – and that they should therefore be treated with respect, and maybe even offered the odd piece of cake.

PURGING THE SOUL

The nearest equivalent to a death festival in the Christian calendar is All Souls' Day, celebrated on 2 November, the day after All Saints Day. All Souls' Day emerged in France in the eleventh century, established by St Odilo, the fifth abbot of Cluny. According to legend, a pilgrim returning from the Holy Land was cast ashore on a small island. The hermit who lived there informed him that beyond the rocks could be heard the groans and cries of tortured souls in Purgatory; the devils, meanwhile, could be heard lamenting that the prayers of the faithful allowed their victims to escape from their clutches. Unlike cultures holding that spirits may return to haunt the living, Christianity maintains that souls can be consigned to Purgatory, the realm where they spend time – indeed, thousands of years – before entering Heaven or Hell. Purgatory (whose name comes from the

Latin *purgare*, 'to make clean or purify') awaits those who have not fully atoned for their sins, but prayers from the living can help them pay for these transgressions and thereby reduce their time.

Arriving back in France, the pilgrim informed the abbot, who set aside 2 November as a day of intercession to pray for the souls doing time in Purgatory. This practice quickly spread throughout the Western Church. After the Reformation, All Souls' Day was abolished by the Church of England but revived by the High Anglicans late in the nineteenth century. In 1980 its observance was encouraged in the alternative Church of England Service Book.

Purgatory did not always exist in Christian doctrine. Early Christians regarded death as a release from the trials and tribulations of a sinful world; it was a joyous event representing a return to God. Indeed, the anniversary of a death, in the early centuries after Christ, was far more important than a birthday. Death was viewed as the surrender of the self to destiny, with friends and relatives, including children, gathering around the deathbed to hear the dying ask forgiveness for all his or her bad deeds. However, things were soon to change. The concept of Purgatory was introduced in the early fifth century by St Augustine of Hippo, receiving papal ratification from Pope Gregory I (590–604). It was no longer enough to make your peace only with friends and family before safely entering the gates of heaven; the faithful now had to pass through the purifying fire – the *ignis purgatories*. Henceforth in the Christian world, death became a gloomy affair. By the eleventh century, medieval man began to love his life and his possessions, and he feared death would take away these pleasures.

By the end of the twelfth century the idea of being judged by God at the end of one's life – and of ending up in Heaven, Hell or Purgatory – was firmly established in Christian doctrine. Dying was transformed from a happy and inevitable event to something to be feared. Elaborate ceremonies and prayers were devised to help the soul pass through Purgatory and find its way to Heaven. People could lessen their time in the purifying fires by performing prayers and making sacrifices – attending mass, embarking on pilgrimages, or purchasing letters of indulgence – as ways of cancelling out their sins on earth. Even after they died they were still able to see to it that time was trimmed from their sentence. For a fee, priests chanted prayers for the deceased in order to speed the soul's passage through Purgatory. Many people left money in their wills so that a mass for the dead would be chanted at their funeral and then sung on the third, seventh and thirtieth days following the burial, with a final mass on the first anniversary. For the truly devout – and for those with deep pockets – it wasn't unheard of for masses to be sung for up to ten years following a death.

In the Middle Ages, only the rich could afford such spiritual support, since mourning cloaks were required, new candles had to be purchased for each sitting, and the poor were invited to the service, expecting in return to be fed. The priest also had to be paid and a donation made towards church funds. Some people willed their houses and land to the Church to cover these costs, while the wealthier members of society founded chantries, private chapels in which priests performed masses and said prayers for their souls. In order to establish such a chapel, a person or organization had to gain permission from the King of England guaranteeing that the priest to the chantry would not interfere with the duties of the local priest. An endowment was then paid for its erection and upkeep. A typical example was the building in 1437 of an almshouse for thirteen poor men at the manor of Ewelme in Oxfordshire by the Duke and Duchess of Suffolk. A royal licence was issued and, in return for food and accommodation, the thirteen lucky men spent their time with the chantry priest, praying for the souls of the chantry founders, their friends, the King and the faithful.

It didn't seem fair that the rich could reduce time in Purgatory while the poor were consigned to a long wait, so many people joined religious guilds, paying a fee for a chantry priest to say masses for their souls and thereby cut down their years in Purgatory. Some guilds were quite large, especially in the towns and cities, and they could therefore afford to retain their own chantry priest, as well as altars or chapels within a church. Larger guilds also took responsibility for charitable services, such as running schools, hospitals and almshouses; grammar schools were initially founded by chantries.

When Henry VIII was excommunicated by the Roman Catholic Church in 1533 for divorcing his wife and marrying Anne Boleyn, the Reformation in England began in earnest. Declared Supreme Head of the new Church of England, Henry dissolved the monasteries with their close links to Rome, claiming their treasures and possessions as his own. Chantries, with their Catholic obsession with Purgatory, were also targeted. The King urged Parliament to pass the first Chantry Act of 1545, decreeing that all chantries and their properties belonged to him. Few chantries were actually closed in this period, but after Henry died in 1547, his successor, Edward VI, reinstated the Act and successfully suppressed 2,374 chantries and guild chapels. The monies appropriated were supposed to go to charitable causes but never got much further than the pockets and purses of Edward's advisors. With the suppression of the chantries, many of the periphery facilities such as grammar schools disappeared, representing a great loss to the community.

Strangely, nearly three hundred years later, in 1837, the chantry system was introduced into the Anglican Church. Three laymen, Joseph and Walter Plimpton along with Edward Frederick Croom, from the parish of St James, Hatcham, in London, formed the Guild of All Souls. It still exists today, employing a chantry priest who is based at Little Walsingham, Norfolk, and masses are held in twenty-one dioceses.[89] The Guild is somewhat cagey regarding what good these prayers do for the dead. According to their information leaflet, supporters of the Guild 'do not know, and we do not need to know, the precise conditions of the after-life'. Followers 'believe only that the departed are in the hand of God, as they have been in their earthly life . . . that God will supply whatever they may need and that they may grow in grace as they respond to his will for them'.[90] There are chapters in the United States and Australia that are similarly maintained by donations and bequests.

MAKING A MEAL OF IT

It must have been reassuring to know that someone was prepared, even if it was for a fee, to pray for one's soul to be released from Purgatory. But what if your sins could be wiped clean before you even reached Purgatory? One way of getting on this direct route to Heaven was to lead a pious life, devoting oneself to good works. There was, however, another option. What if you could find someone to absorb your sins – to take them upon himself – before you got to Purgatory?

According to John Aubrey, writing in 1686, such a creature actually existed: 'In the County of Hereford was an old Custome at Funeralls', he wrote, 'to hire poor people, who were to take upon them all the sinnes of the party deceased.'[91] How precisely were these sins transferred? In 1852, a Mr Moggridge of Swansea provided testimony how this practice was carried out in Llanderbie, Wales, as late as the 1820s: the 'sin-eater', Mr Moggridge said, 'would be given bread and salt which had been laid on the corpse's chest, plus half a crown, after which he quickly left, for he was regarded as a mere pariah, as one irremediably lost'.[92] The act of physically consuming food that had been in contact with the dead was sufficient, it seems, to effect a transfer of sin from one person to another. Sin-eaters, it was said, were feared and ostracized from any social interaction. They lived isolated lives on the outskirts of villages and were contacted only when a death occurred. Any utensils used in feeding the sin-eater were burnt or disposed of after the event.

Finding other examples of sin-eating proves difficult. Nor is the origin of this custom clear, but it may be based on the scapegoat of the ancient Hebrews, whereby a sacrificial goat was burnt after taking on the sins of the Jews. Sin-buying was not widespread amongst Jews, although the Jews of Brody in Poland, now in the Ukraine, were known to follow the custom.[93] An undesirable could, for a fee, take upon himself the sins of another – something bound to make him even more of an outcast.

Sin-eaters may never have existed in large numbers in the British Isles, but the custom of consuming cakes, wine, bread or ale around the coffin was common in the eighteenth and nineteenth centuries in the Midlands and in the northern counties of England. The custom derives from medieval times, when alms and food were given to the poor in return for their prayers. A farmer's daughter from Derbyshire explained to Sydney Oldall Addy, the famous English folklorist, in 1895: 'When you drink wine at a funeral, every drop that you drink is a sin which the deceased has committed; you thereby take away the dead man's sins and bear them yourself.'[94] This was evidently partaken by all of the mourners, not simply by a scapegoated sin-eater. Notorious old reprobates presumably called for quite a number of bottles.

THE ART OF DYING WELL

Most cultures have fixed ideas about where the soul ends up, whether it is in Purgatory, Heaven, Hell, or even rebirth into human, animal, mineral or supernatural form. And many cultures have also produced guidebooks for the post-mortem condition, treatises that not only explain death to the living but, even more, provide the dead with a handbook of instruction. One of the oldest texts for the newly deceased, *The Book of the Dead*, was produced by the ancient Egyptians around 2600 BCE. However, this title is a misnomer invented by the German Egyptologist Karl Richard Lepsius in 1842, since the original text does not resemble a modern book bound with cover and spine. Originally inscribed on the exterior of tombs and later written on papyrus scrolls, the texts were buried with the deceased in the sarcophagus. Initially they were named the *Pyramid Texts* as they were produced only for the King and his family in Egypt's Age of the Pyramids. Eventually, they were replaced by the *Coffin Texts*, and anyone who could afford a sarcophagus was able to commission one for insertion in his tomb. In its final incarnation, the *Book of the Dead* incorporated writings from the previous texts and added even more insights to the life beyond.

Unlike the Bible or Koran, which reveal to humanity knowledge from a supreme, single deity, the *Book of the Dead* deals exclusively with guiding the deceased into the afterlife. It consists of magic formulas and spells that can be used to reach the underworld. Hieroglyphics and pictorial images illustrate the trials that await the deceased, the most important of which is the weighing of the heart against Ma'at (Truth), which Anubis, the god of embalming and guide and friend of the dead, carries out. The heart is weighed on scales against a feather: if it is lighter than the feather, the deceased is permitted to continue with his journey; if the heart, weighed down with sin, is heavier than the feather, the hideous hybrid monster Ammit emerges from the shadows to eat it.

No two copies of the book were exactly the same as they all were personalized. Indeed, the *Book of the Dead* for the Scribe Ani was originally seventy-eight feet (twenty-eight metres) long. People of lesser importance had to make do with much shorter versions, keeping fingers crossed that vital magic spells were not omitted from their version, thus hindering their safe passage to the underworld.

From the sixth to the first century BCE in southern Europe, followers of the cult of Orpheus were also buried with instructions for the afterlife. According to Greek legend, Orpheus, by singing and playing the lyre exquisitely, could charm wild beasts, arrest rivers in their courses, and move rocks and trees. Perhaps the most famous legend surrounding Orpheus, however, is when his wife Eurydice was bitten by a serpent and died while fleeing from Aristaeus. Orpheus was so sad that he entered the underworld and played his music to Hades and Persephone. Touched by his melancholy, they allowed him to return to earth with his wife on condition he walk in front of her without looking back. He foolishly disobeyed them, and Eurydice disappeared for ever.

The cult of Orpheus was concerned with the emancipation of the soul from physical matter. Each soul, it was believed, was immortal and of celestial origin, but was doomed to the laws of reincarnation. Due to original sin, which, according to Orpheus, began when Zeus copulated with his mother Rhea-Demeter, a soul could be reborn into human, animal or even vegetable matter. Orphics believed the whole human race had been polluted and, in order to help the deceased to return to its celestial origin and escape the 'sorrowful, weary wheel' of never-ending reincarnation, gold plates or laminae-inscribed instructions on how to escape reincarnation and attain a blissful afterlife were buried with them. 'I come from among the pure, O pure queen of the netherworld', said one lamina written in the fourth century BCE. 'In fact, I too declare myself to belong to your blessed lineage . . . I flew out of the woeful cycle, heavy with care, and ascended to the coveted crown with swift feet. O happy and truly blessed, you shall be a spirit and not a mortal.'[95]

Followers of Orphism were few in number, living mainly in southern Italy and Crete. Not much is known about this sect as initiation involved purification rights and the imparting of secret knowledge by word of mouth. Members lived in their own communities and became strict vegetarians so as to avoid inadvertently eating a reincarnated soul – not dissimilar from the beliefs of Buddhists that were emerging in the mid-fifth century BCE in India.

Another great user's guide to the post-mortem state is the *Tibetan Book of the Dead*. Written in the eighth century for a Tibetan king by the Indian

Yogi Padmasambhava, it describes the journey of consciousness through the three stages (called bardos) of dying: the moment of death; the intermediate state between death and rebirth; and the process of rebirth. The original text was written in a cryptic language and hidden in a mountain in Tibet. Five hundred years later, fifteen-year-old Karma Lingpa, who was engaged in esoteric practices, found the text and was able to crack the code and later pass on the teaching orally to his son. It was many years before the information was written down and became a central teaching in the Tibetan Buddhist canon. Not until 1927 was a tiny portion of the work, 'The Great Liberation by Hearing', translated into English by an American Theosophist, Walter Evans-Wentz. This particular teaching was designed either to be committed to memory by the dying person or to be read to them after death as they went through distressing states in the afterlife. However, despite the vivid and sometimes terrifying encounters, there is, at each stage, a chance for the deceased to gain liberation, if the soul can recognize that what it is experiencing is not real.

The first stage of death, according to the *Tibetan Book of the Dead*, is when the inner mind is engulfed with a radiant white light. If this light is recognized as the true nature of the mind, the deceased is immediately liberated and rebirth becomes unnecessary. If unsuccessful, the deceased enters the next stage, in which terrifying images flood the mind. Recognizing these images as aspects of the mind ensures liberation, but if the mind is weighed down with confusion and negative thoughts attached to lifetime memories, the deceased plummets down further. The book teaches that at some stage the deceased will experience a 'life review' where all his good and bad deeds will be broached, and he will tremble with fear, awe and terror. His actions will be reflected vividly and precisely and, most alarmingly, the Lord of Death, Yama, will cut off the deceased's head, remove his heart, pull out his entrails, lick his brains, drink his blood and eat his flesh. And yet he will not die as he is hurtled towards rebirth as a god, a demi-god, a human, an animal, an anguished spirit, or a hell-being, until finally he emerges through rebirth.

The *Tibetan Book of the Dead* has gained popularity over the years with New Age seekers and converts to Buddhism. It has recently been translated and, in 2005, published in its entirety by Tibetan monks and edited by

Graham Coleman, president of the Orient Foundation and himself a prac-
tising Buddhist. At a lecture at the Oxford Literary Festival in March 2006,
Coleman explained how the Dalai Lama once said that, if someone is taking a holiday, it is typical for him to prepare beforehand by researching the
area and buying a map and a guidebook. 'People happily do that for a holiday,' says Coleman, 'but they don't want to do it when they know they're
going to die. The *Tibetan Book of the Dead* is that guidebook.'[96]

Medieval Europeans once also used the equivalent of a guidebook to prepare them for death. *Ars Moriendi,* or the 'Art of Dying', were Latin texts
originally composed in 1415 by an unknown Dominican friar. Before the
Black Death decimated the population of much of Europe in the mid-
fourteenth century, the priest delivered prayers and rituals at a deathbed.
However, the Black Death was undiscriminating, hitting the ranks of the
clergy as badly as other sections of society and leaving a shortage of priests to
console the dying. *Ars Moriendi* emerged, in effect, as a 'virtual priest',
enabling a ravaged society the opportunity to follow the correct death rituals with or without a clergy present. Offering advice on how to die well, they
depicted images of the struggle between vices and virtues in a dying man's
mind, showing how good and evil were contesting his soul. It was translated
into most European languages and was particularly popular in England,
with copies appearing in various guises until the seventeenth century.

There was originally a long version of the text called *Tractatus artis bene
moriendi,* or 'Treatise on the Art of a Good Death', which consisted of six
chapters that, among other things, consoled the dying man that death was
nothing to fear and provided his relatives with the appropriate prayers to
help him get through the gates of Heaven. Once block-books became available around 1450 – that is, books printed from carved blocks of wood with
both text and images – a shorter version of the *Tractatus,* known simply as
Ars Moriendi, came on the market. This concentrated on the second chapter of the *Tractatus,* which dealt with temptation, and consisted of eleven
woodcut pictures. The first ten woodcuts were divided into five pairs; on
the one hand the devil presented temptations to the dying man, and on the
other, a picture showed the proper remedy for that particular temptation.
The final block illustrated the dying man being accepted into Heaven, with
the vanquished devils returning whence they came.

Whatever the belief of the afterlife, the fact remains that we are no nearer in gaining tangible, scientific evidence of post-mortem existence than James Boswell over 250 years ago: 'Five thousand years have now elapsed since the creation of the world, and still it is undecided whether or not there has ever been an instance of the spirit of any person appearing after death. All argument', he concludes succinctly, 'is against it; but all belief is for it.' From ancient Egypt to Lily Dale, the power of this belief endures.

CHAPTER 9

Bodies of Evidence

Murder Most Foul

Today, the causes and effects of death are studied, quantified and documented as never before. Dead bodies, especially those that have met with foul play, are now subjected to the most rigorous scientific investigation. Highly trained experts seek clues to the identity and origins of human remains by scrutinizing everything from their fingerprints and dental records to the isotopes of oxygen in their teeth, the polonium in their bones and the pollen in their nasal passages. The public fascination with this kind of post-mortem investigation is reflected by the success of the novels of Patricia Cornwell (a one-time technical writer and computer analyst for the Chief Medical Examiner of Virginia) and CBS's Emmy Award-winning *CSI: Crime Scene Investigation*, the fifth series of which, in 2004–5, averaged more than twenty-six million viewers per episode in the United States. In 2007 the Museum of Science and Industry in Chicago even opened an exhibit called 'CSI: The Experience', in which visitors enter various 'crime scenes' and collect the scientific evidence to crack murder cases. The Museum even runs Saturday courses in which, for a mere $12, participants can study techniques of fingerprint analysis, toxicology and forensic microscopy – all vital tools of the trade, as we shall see, for the forensic scientist.

The more dedicated may wish to attend a five-day 'Workshop in Forensic Archaeology and Anthropology' at Cranfield University's campus in Shrivenham,Oxfordshire. According to its literature, the university aims to 'introduce participants to the subject of forensic archaeology'. For a cost of £650, participants are offered 'interactive' sessions dealing with forensic skeletal analysis, gunshot and blast wounds, and the processes of decomposition. Also among the attractions is a demonstration by a 'cadaver' dog – an animal (not unlike an airport sniffer dog) that has been trained to sniff out dead bodies. All of this may seem ghoulish to the squeamish or uninitiated, but the dead body has been the focus of such high-tech scientific investigation that some people receive more care and attention after their death than they ever did in their lifetime.

BEFORE THE FORUM

The three-acre site, with its dozens of rotting corpses, looks like a Civil War battlefield or possibly the favoured dumping ground of a prolific serial killer. Found on the outskirts of Knoxville, Tennessee – not far, in fact, from where 813 Confederate soldiers died at the Battle of Fort Sanders in 1863 – it is situated near the banks of the Tennessee River, surrounded by razor wire, in woodlands where the nearby University of Tennessee Medical Center used to incinerate its waste. A few of the corpses are buried in shallow graves, as if by a killer in haste, while others are entombed, submerged in water, wrapped in body bags, left in the open for exposure to the elements, or stuffed in the boots of abandoned vehicles. Here they remain, in temperatures that in July average 30.5°C (86.9°F), as the rodents, bugs and elements do their worst.

As readers of Patricia Cornwell's 1994 bestseller *The Body Farm* will know, this ghoulish landscape is the University of Tennessee Forensic Anthropology Facility, more popularly known as the Body Farm. The facility was founded in 1981 by the distinguished forensic anthropologist Dr Bill Bass, who convinced the university to set aside a parcel of land in order for him to study the rate and nature of a corpse's decomposition. Since the first subject arrived (a half-pickled seventy-three-year-old alcoholic with emphysema and heart disease, who was donated by his daughter and promptly christened 1–81), hundreds of other bodies have been distributed across this open-air laboratory in the name of medical science. Thirty to fifty bodies are donated each year, though in 2005 more than a hundred people put their signatures on the university's Body Donation Document.[97]

Dr Bass was originally motivated by the most basic questions about a decaying body: 'At what point does the arm fall off? What causes that greasy black stain under decomposed bodies, and when? When do the teeth fall out of the skull?'[98] Dr Bass and his colleagues have since discovered all that and much more – for example, how dead bodies emit gases and acids (some four hundred volatile compounds have been identified) and how a corpse participates in such things as the life-cycle of the fly and the growth of the fungus *malassezia*. The FBI now holds training courses for its agents at the facility, and forensic experts from around the world regularly visit. In 2006 a second facility opened in Cullowhee, North Carolina, as part of the Western Carolina Human Identification Laboratory. Plans are afoot for others in Texas and Iowa, though in 2007 the proposed farm in Texas was hampered by a typically Wild West problem: vultures circling the site in hopes of a meal were considered a danger to passing aircraft.

Cutting edge the Body Farm may well be, but forensic science is actually nothing new. The word forensics originated over two thousand years ago, following one of the most famous murders in history. On 15 March 44 BCE, Julius Caesar was summoned to the Forum to accept a petition requesting him to hand powers back to the Roman Senate. As the fifty-six-year-old Emperor began reading the petition (unbeknownst to him, a clever fake by a band of conspirators) he was struck a glancing sword-blow in the neck by a man named Casca. As he appealed for help, the other conspirators unsheathed their weapons and Caesar was (as Plutarch reports) 'hackled and mangled among them, as a wild beast taken of hunters. For it was agreed among them that every man should give him a wound, because all their parts should be in this murder'. Caesar received twenty-three stab wounds in all, with Brutus, according to Plutarch, wounding his leader 'about his privities'.[99]

Several hours later, after Caesar's body had lain for three hours in a pool of blood, 'all bemangled with gashes of swords', the physician Antistius was summoned and given the task of discovering which of the twenty-three wounds was fatal. Examining the dead Emperor's body, he soon discovered that the fatal blow came from an upward thrust, under the left shoulder blade, which had pierced Caesar's heart. He announced his findings before the Forum, an area in Rome set aside for political and social activity, and where speeches and announcements were made. The word forensics, from *forensis*, 'before the forum', derives from Antistius's announcement.

Antistius did not even perform the world's first forensic investigation. Forensic assessments have been found in China, written on bamboo slips dating as far back as 221 BCE. It was not until 1248, however, that advice on examining dead bodies was made available, at least in China, to those in authority investigating a murder. *Hsi Duan Chi Yu* ('The Washing Away of Wrongs'), a Chinese treatise written by Sung Tz'u, describes, amongst other things, how to distinguish drowning from strangulation, and how to ascertain the time of death by assessing a body's decomposition, taking into account the season and its effects on the corpse. It was written during the Sung Dynasty (960–1279) by the man who served as the Judicial Intendant in Hsin-feng region. Sung Tz'u wrote the treatise because those holding inquests were administrators, not doctors, and consequently they were often woefully ignorant of medical matters.

Sung Tz'u gives useful advice on deciding if a death occurred due to such things as 'sexual excess', which can be determined, his treatise points out, if the man's erection has not subsided. It also covers determining death by tiger bites, prodding, lightning strikes and trampling by a horse. In the latter case, the corpse 'will be slightly yellow in colour, the hands open, and the hair in disorder'. On the other hand, a person crushed to death by a cart's wheels will have open mouth and eyes but 'the hair will be in order'.[100] Strange as these conclusions appear, Sung Tz'u does show an impressive knowledge of forensic entomology, giving as an example the case of the body of a man found in a ditch, slashed and bloodied. The villagers feared bandits were responsible, and so the Provisional Death Investigator was sent for. As the victim had not been robbed, however, the Investigator concluded bandits were not involved. He ordered everyone to bring their farm sickles for examination; it would be tantamount to guilt if anyone refused, and so over seventy blades arrived for inspection. It was a hot day, and the flies gathered on one sickle in particular – the sickle, the

Investigator correctly surmised, of the murderer, since he understood that the flies were attracted to the odour of blood left behind on the weapon. On further investigation, it was discovered that the murderer had lent the dead man money and, when it was not returned, murdered him with his sickle.

As the Provisional Death Investigator and Sung Tz'u both understood, a dead body always leaves its mark behind. Wrongs can be washed away with the help of forensics. The tell-tale signs of the dead body, fortunately for forensic analysis, linger in dozens of ways.

I HEARD A FLY BUZZ

As the Provisional Death Investigator understood, insects play an important role in the death cycle. 'I heard a fly buzz when I died', wrote the American poet Emily Dickinson – and no wonder. Certain flies can smell a body, within minutes of its death, from up to a mile away. Through their body hairs, blowflies and flesh flies can smell acetic, butyric, valeric acids, indole, acetone, phenol and methyl disulphide, all of which are emitted by cadavers as they begin the process of decomposition. The chemical receptors on these hairs guide flies to the source, with (in Dickinson's words) 'blue, uncertain, stumbling buzz'. Their sole ambition is to deposit their eggs on tender flesh that will feed their young.

Forensic entomologists, the bug experts who study these insects and arthropods, are called upon for their invaluable insights. By eating dead bodies, arthropods contribute to recycling organic matter back into the ecosystem, and understanding the speed at which larvae or maggots develop helps pathologists to determine the time of death, which is particularly helpful in cases of murder. Laboratory studies as well as those at places like the Body Farm have given an insight into the life-cycle of flies and maggots. Depending on the species of fly, hatching can take between fifteen and twenty-six hours if the temperature is, say, a steady 72°F (22°C). Once hatched, the maggots move into the body to feed. Maggots are eating machines: they have evolved with nostrils beside the anus, a novel design that allows them to respire even as they feed with their heads burrowed deeply in rotting flesh.

The first and second instar, or life stages of a maggot, last between eleven and forty-eight hours, and the third instar, the final stage, between thirty-six and sixty hours. A mature third-instar maggot at the end of its feeding cycle might crawl off the body to find a dark hideaway in order to develop into a pupa. It then evolves into a mature fly and the cycle begins all over again. By studying the development stage of maggots and flies on or near a dead body, forensic teams can estimate the time of death, especially if the decomposing process is well under way. When taking samples of maggots at crime scenes, the entomologists must therefore remember to spade soil up to three feet away or, if the body is indoors, inspect a nearby carpet or sofa to see if mature maggots have fled to pupate.

Until the seventeenth century, science still followed Aristotle's belief in 'spontaneous generation'. After observing cold meat producing maggots, flour producing mealy bugs and weevils appearing from nuts, Aristotle concluded that flies and fleas did not come into the world via parents but rather from decaying earth and excrement, from which they materialized fully formed. It was not until 1894 that Jean-Paul Mégnin, a veterinarian and researcher into parasites at the Museum of Natural History in Paris, published *The Wildlife of Cadavers: The Application of Entomology to Forensic Medicine*, that forensic entomology was put on a solid footing. To Mégnin's horror, his carefully researched 214 pages became the reference book for European homicide cases, even though Mégnin argued strenuously that his observations might not hold outside Paris because, as he realized, the soil and weather conditions responsible for attracting insects could differ substantially. It was, however, a start.

The study of insects took off a little earlier in the United States than in Europe, not for solving homicide cases, but to stem insect-related crop damage. By 1862 agricultural colleges had begun springing up all over the country. In 1874 and 1876 terrible plagues of locusts hit the Great Plains of Nebraska, Colorado, Iowa, the Dakotas and Minnesota, destroying large areas of crop land. Laura Ingalls Wilder, author of *The Little House on the Prairie* series of memoirs, wrote of the swarms that engulfed her family's homestead. The Rocky Mountain locusts ate everything in their path, from barley and buckwheat to spruce and tobacco; they even ate the blankets put over crops to protect them. The Entomological Commission resulted from this calamity, having been established to develop effective pesticides. These particular locusts eventually left on their own accord – no one really knows why – and they are now extinct. Soon afterwards, in 1881, the Systematic Entomology Laboratory at the National Museum in Washington DC was founded to identify and study insects, in particular flesh-eating flies that were causing havoc with livestock. Much knowledge about the development of insects and bugs was being developed, but it was not yet systematized as a helpful tool for the police in solving murder cases.

Jerry Payne, a graduate student at Clemson University in South Carolina, was the person to bring the study of forensic entomology some scientific credibility. In 1962, he was funded by his university to undertake pioneering research into insects on dead pigs. Payne deliberately selected pigs for his observations since their skin and hair is similar to that of humans. Placing some dead piglets in insect-proof cages and others in open cages, he patiently watched and recorded their different stages of decomposition. He collected 301 different species of insects and eighty-one invertebrates from the dead pigs. Discovering that the invisible gases of decay attract different insects at different times, Payne described the now famous six stages of decomposition – fresh, bloated, active decay, advanced decay, dry decay and remains – that are still used today. Although Payne was offered positions in forensic entomology after he graduated, he opted to work for the United States Department of Agriculture, researching pest control on crops.

Forensic entomologists must take into account – as Jean-Paul Mégnin pointed out – the microclimate of the place in which a body was found. Furthermore, when arriving at an estimate of the time of death, they must factor in access points for the insects. Flies are particularly versatile, often squeezing through the tiniest of cracks in closed doors and windows. The presence of greenbottle (*Phacencia sericata*), for example, suggests that the body originated in an urban, sunlit and open setting, while the black blowfly (*Phormia regina*) can be found in rural areas and predominates in the cooler months of autumn and winter. Blowflies are found virtually everywhere on earth, having even been found at eighteen thousand feet in the Himalayas. Interestingly, flies are sensitive to light, so dusk brings their activity to a standstill. A cloudy day causes sluggishness, but in hot temperatures the insects can buzz themselves into an absolute feeding frenzy. Indeed, larvae and maggot activity in and on the body can produce its own heat as they mass together to go about their grisly business.

Evidence obtained from maggots first appears to have been used in a prosecution as long ago as the 1930s, when the blowfly larvae on two decomposing bodies discovered in Scotland in 1935 were used to establish the time of death of the victims – the wife and maid of a Dr Ruxton from Lancashire, who was subsequently hanged for murder.

The American Board of Entomology reports five more recent case studies in which maggot activity has allowed investigators to determine times of death for murder victims and, in most cases, secure a conviction. In one case, police were called to a home in the southwestern United States in the middle of November to investigate a foul smell. The decomposed body of a young woman, killed by a gunshot wound, was soon recovered from a shallow grave in the house's dirt basement. Examination of the corpse and the soil in which it was buried yielded the larvae and pupae of *Synthesiomyia nudesita*, a relative of the house fly. Climatic information for the previous month and a study of the soil temperature allowed investigators to estimate that the victim must have died and been colonized by the species of fly twenty-eight days prior to her discovery. A suspect, subsequently identified, confessed to having killed and buried the victim precisely twenty-eight days before her discovery.[101] Maggots, it seems, never lie.

THE BONE MEN

Another type of expert, the forensic anthropologist – the discipline of the Body Farm's Dr Bill Bass – might also be called in to assist the police at a crime scene, especially if a body has lain undiscovered for several years. These experts use physical anthropology – the study of skeletal biology and human adaptation – to identify skeletons or badly decomposed bodies. Human bones, of which there are 206 in an adult, leave behind many clues for a forensic anthropologist. Older people have calcium and other mineral deposits in their bones, so an expert can estimate fairly accurately the age of the corpse. Adult males have narrower pelvises and larger skulls than females, so sexual differentiation is usually a simple matter. It is even possible to determine whether a skeleton is Caucasian, Negroid or Mongoloid based on the shape of the skull and the spacing of the nasal apertures, while height can be estimated by using various formulas: for example, the height of a person is usually five times the length of the humerus. If the humerus is missing, the height can be worked out by means of formulas using the spine, tibia and femur. Even the weight of a person can be estimated by evaluating bone characteristics.

Forensic anthropology was successfully employed to identify one of the twentieth century's greatest villains from what one reporter called 'a pile of bones, six teeth, some clumps of hair and a pair of rotting trousers'.[102] In 1985 the American forensic anthropologist Clyde C. Snow, who specialized in identifying victims of air crashes for the Federal Aviation Administration, travelled to Brazil to help other forensic experts examine the contents of a grave bearing the name of Wolfgang Gerhard. Buried in Embu, twenty miles from São Paolo, Gerhard was suspected of being Josef Mengele, the 'Angel of Death' from Auschwitz, who reportedly died from drowning in 1979. The investigators had little to go on apart from the skeleton, the bones and skull of which had been damaged during the exhumation in May 1985. But as Snow explained: 'It's amazing what a little piece of bone can do.'[103] He soon determined that the remains were those of a right-handed Caucasian male whose estimated height conformed to Mengele's recorded height of 5 feet 8½ inches. Then, using a technique called 'video skull-face superimposition' developed by a German forensic anthropologist named Richard Helmer, the investigators pieced together the broken skull and marked it with pins at thirty anatomic points of comparison to a photograph of Mengele. When the image of the skull was superimposed on the photograph, the points matched up perfectly, confirming Gerhard's true identity. DNA analysis as well as the discovery of Mengele's dental records subsequently served to corroborate this conclusion. Having escaped justice in his lifetime, Mengele testified against himself from beyond the grave.

A skull, a photograph and dental records, the evidence used successfully against Mengele, are becoming crucial in identifying remains and reconstructing the dead. The Mengele case highlights the importance of forensic dentistry. In 1985 Dr Elliot M. Gross, then the Chief Medical Examiner for

New York City, described to the *New York Times* the importance of the forensic dentistry to the Mengele case: 'If the body is skeletalized . . . then the teeth are the only way you can make a positive identification.'[104] Tooth enamel is the most durable part of the human body, more robust even than bones, and so the teeth can survive both long periods and – in the case of, say, air disasters – great conflagrations. X-raying the teeth of a victim and then superimposing the photos on a set taken when he or she was alive will afford evidence about identity. Further testimony is provided by crowns, fillings and other dental work recorded in the victim's dental records. With the help of a forensic anthropologist, the dentist can establish sex and ancestry. Tooth development determines age, and erosion may suggest alcohol or substance abuse, an eating disorder, or even a hiatus hernia, while stained teeth might indicate a smoker. It is even possible to suggest the socio-economic status of an individual or likely country of residence by the quality and quantity of dental treatment. An Italian team of researchers has worked to identify corpses by means of the composition and properties of the alloys used in their dental fillings, which are often specific to the country of origin.[105]

Teeth are revealing in other ways as well. The water we drink helps scientists to pinpoint our geographical origins, since isotopes of oxygen in drinking water get set in our teeth by the time we reach the age of ten or twelve. Incorporated into the body when we drink, these isotopes are used in the formation of our teeth and bones. They vary according to such things as altitude, distance from the equator, distance from the sea, and the mean annual temperature, meaning that our teeth can provide a map of our earliest days, even providing such information as the age at which we were weaned from our mother's breast milk. Using this data, scientists from the University of Durham and the British Geological Survey in 2004 examined the strontium and oxygen in the teeth of twenty-four skeletons exhumed from a sixth-century Anglo-Saxon cemetery in West Heslerton, North Yorkshire. One of these was discovered to have oxygen isotope values that suggested origins in Continental Europe rather than the British Isles.[106]

The skull can likewise provide vital information about the identity of human remains. Forensic sculptors can reconstruct a face with only a skull as the reference point. The first facial reconstruction has been credited to the German anatomist Wilhelm His, who in the late nineteenth century recreated the face of Johann Sebastian Bach after his body was exhumed during renovations to a graveyard in Leipzig.[107] In 1895, Herr His examined twenty-eight cadavers from the Anatomy Department at Leipzig University to find the general depth of the skin and muscles over the skull. In order to do so, he stuck needles into the faces of the corpses at nine predetermined meridian points and six lateral points at the side of the face. Each needle had a cork placed on its tip, and once the needle hit bone the cork rested on the skin's surface. When the needles were removed, His was able to measure them, make drawings based on these measurements, and then use his calculations to successfully to reconstruct Bach's face.

Herr His was not the only scientist to research tissue thickness for facial reconstruction. German scientists also reconstructed the faces of the poet Schiller and the philosopher Immanuel Kant. In recent years, scientists such as J.S. Rhine, H.R. Campbell and C.E. Moore have likewise been instrumental in collecting tissue measurements from the different races and sexes, helping to standardize the reconstruction process by introduc-ing tissue-thickness charts based on their findings, which is essential when reconstructing a face.[108] More recently, skulls to be clothed in flesh have included Philip II of Macedon and Lindow Man, the British Museum's Iron Age bog mummy more jocularly known as 'Pete Marsh'.[109]

The materials traditionally used for facial reconstruction are a combina-tion of Kaolin clay, calcium, sulphate and petrolatum. This modelling clay is non-toxic, non-hardening and odourless, and about 2lbs, or just under a kilo, is usually enough to reconstruct a face. The cranium is mounted on a specially designed stand and the eye orbits and nasal cavity are protected with cotton wool and masking tape in case the skull cracks or chips under pressure. The skull is then ready for the prosthetic eyes to be added to com-plete the process.

Before beginning, the sculptor must choose specific tissue measure-ments corresponding to sex, race and size, which will be listed in the tissue-depth charts. A discussion first with the forensic anthropologist might be necessary to determine details about the skull. Tissue markers are then glued onto the skull at specific points to predetermine tissue thickness, and strips of clay are added and moulded into shape. The whole process calls for great skill and many hours of work.

Facial reconstruction was first applied to forensic work (as opposed to merely satisfying historical curiosity) in the Soviet Union. Mikhail Gerasimov, a palaeontologist working in a museum in Russia, experimented with the facial reconstruction of the skulls in his care, and in 1939 he helped the police solve a murder by recreating the unidentified victim's face, a technique depicted in the 1983 film *Gorky Park*. However, it was a sculptor from Philadelphia named Frank Bender who catapulted facial reconstruction to public prominence. In 1971, a man named John List murdered his mother, wife and three children in New Jersey before fleeing the state. Eighteen years later, Bender was asked to reconstruct the face of List as it might appear in 1989 for the popular American TV show *America's Most Wanted*. With the help of a criminal psychologist, Bender created a three-dimensional face – complete with jowls and crow's feet – that so closely resembled List that a former neighbour of a man in Virginia calling himself Bob Clark rang the police to identify the face. As fingerprints subsequently revealed, Bob Clark, a church-going accountant with a new wife, was indeed John List.

These days facial reconstruction has moved on from modelling clay. The technique pioneered by Richard Helmer has since been refined by a team of Italian researchers who have formulated an algorithm to compare facial photographs with radiographic images of skulls. They claim a success rate of one hundred per cent.[110] It is now more cost effective to use 3D computer graphics programs to recreate the faces of the dead people. Kolija Kähler and Jörg Haber, of the Max Planck Institute of Computer Science in Saarbrücken, Germany, have developed facial reconstruction software that features the added advantage of being able to give personality to a face. The animated head that, like the clay model version, is developed from tissue charts will be able to show subtle facial expressions that people are more likely to recognize.[111]

Likewise, in a project supported by the Home Office, the Research School of Archaeology and Archaeological Science at the University of Sheffield uses a colour laser scanner and computer to take images of a skull as it rotates on a platform. Once the computer produces a 'wireframe' matrix – what looks like a 3D profile of the contours of a head wrapped tightly in chicken-wire – the tissue depth is estimated by using data gained from CT scans as well as any information about age, sex, build and, if known, ethnic group. The team even uses computer software to display the resulting facial image in a range of expressions and in a variety of lighting conditions. But the method is far from foolproof. Facial features such as the shape of the nose and mouth or the location of the hairline – that is, the most distinctive aspects of our appearance – cannot accurately be predicted by the contours of the skull. As one of the Sheffield researchers, Martin Evison, observes: 'The shape of the face bears only a restricted resemblance to the underlying bone structure. Facial reconstructions are inherently inaccurate, therefore, and cannot be used as a positive proof of identification – certainly not in a court of law.'[112]

POLLEN AND POLONIUM

Fortunately, there are other, more reliable ways of determining a body's origins and identity. The air we breathe, the food we eat, even the town we live in, mark our bodies in ways that can be measured by means of high-tech trace element analysis. One of Britain's leading forensic scientists, Patricia Wiltshire, specializes in palynology, or the analysis of pollen. Wiltshire began her career as an archaeologist, studying the vegetation history of peat bogs, lecturing in microbial ecology at the University of London, and working with English Heritage on the palynological analysis of sites such as Hadrian's Wall. Her career veered off in a new direction in the mid-1990s when she was contacted by Hertfordshire police to identify pollen grains found at a crime scene where the victim had been dumped in a ditch and set alight. Since then she has worked on more than eighty criminal investigations, including such high-profile cases as the 2002 murders of Holly Wells and Jessica Chapman in Soham, Cambridgeshire. In that instance, Ian Huntley was convicted after Wiltshire was able to establish that pollen from his shoes and vehicle exactly matched a type in the ditch where the two girls' bodies were discovered.

A new term, 'forensic palynology', has been coined to describe this use of pollen and spore evidence in criminal cases. Pollen evidence can determine, for example, the month, season and location in which a victim may have been murdered, and, as in the case of Huntley, it can place a murderer at the scene of his crime. Forensic palynology also includes information on microscopic organisms such as dinoflagellates, acritarchs and chitinozoans that are found in both fresh and marine environments. The work is painstakingly tedious, as no evidence, no matter how microscopic, can be overlooked. Most pollen is all but invisible to the naked eye, with ten grains fitting on the head of a pin. Wiltshire's particular methodology – she uses a crochet hook to retrieve fragments of pollen clinging to the nasal passages of victims – has earned her a distinctive nickname: she is known as the 'snot lady'.[113]

The value of botany to forensics has long been recognized. Dr Joyce Vickery, a scientist at the Royal Botanic Gardens in Sydney, became famous in Australia for solving the kidnapping and murder in 1961 of eight-year-old Graham Thorne. Graham, the son of the first lottery winner in Australia, was kidnapped for ransom, then found dead a few days later, wrapped in a car rug in bushland near Sydney. A Hungarian immigrant by the name of Stephen Bradley was the chief suspect, but the police had no evidence linking him to the murder until Dr Vickery provided her services. Fragments of plants found on the car rug and in the back of Bradley's car were given to Dr Vickery. She was able to show that the fragments on the rug were of the same cypress bushes that grew in the Bradley residence, and also that the plant fragments found in Bradley's car were identical to the foliage that grew where the body was found. On this evidence, Bradley was sentenced to life in prison – and botany became an important forensic tool.

The first known case of a botanist taking the witness stand was in 1935, during the trial for the kidnapping and murder of the child of the famous aviator Charles Lindbergh and his wife Anne Morrow. This case, known as the 'Crime of the Century', shocked America because, despite Lindbergh paying a $50,000 ransom, the baby, like Graham Thorne, was found murdered in a wood. This high-profile case attracted the attention of Arthur Koehler, a wood anatomist, who offered his services to help solve the case. He employed a new technique called dendrochronology that had been invented in 1928 by the archaeologist Andrew Douglass, who was able to tell the age and origin of a piece of wood by studying its growth pattern by means of its annual rings. Koehler was therefore able to trace the origins of the wood from the homemade ladder that was left behind in the kidnapping. The ladder was linked to both wood and tools in the workshop of the prime suspect, a German illegal immigrant named Bruno Hauptmann. (Nonetheless, the conviction and execution of Hauptmann in 1936 has always been controversial, not least because his fingerprints did not match those on the ransom money found in his garage.)

A British scientist, Professor Stuart Black, who lectures in environmental radioactivity at the University of Reading, works with even more minute and arcane data than pollen and tree rings. Like Patricia Wiltshire, he has pursued his career down avenues that may seem to have little relevance for crime scene investigations, publishing articles on such things as the depleted uranium in unfired British military tank shells. However, he has also found a technique that looks at the amount of the radioactive isotope lead-210 contained in the bones. Lead-210 occurs naturally in the environment, entering the body via food, drink and pollutants, including cigarette smoke. Dr Black is able to measure its content in the bones in order to discover, for example, what food a victim ate: a depletion of certain minerals in the bones might indicate that the victim was a vegetarian, and high rates of both lead-210 and polonium-210 could indicate a heavy smoker (polonium-210 has been identified in tobacco treated with phosphate fertilizers).[114] Moreover, Black can pinpoint the area where the victim lived in the last years of his life by looking at trace elements in the bones. The amounts will depend on the local geology, the kind of petrol used in the area, and the proximity to things such as nuclear power stations. By consulting the database of the Food Standard's Agency he can check how much lead and polonium is found in different foods and thereby determine regional differences in diet.

Dr Black's techniques have produced some impressive results. In 2003 he was called upon by Cambridgeshire police to help identify a body discovered in the village of Upton, near Peterborough, in December 2002. There was little forensic evidence to work with other than a button and a lighter, since the victim had been stabbed repeatedly, shot in the head, and then set alight. Tests on the man's teeth suggested that he came from the Ukraine, but his femur showed non-radioactive isotopes – by-products from the nuclear industry such as lead-208 and lead-207 – that pointed to his having lived in England for the last three to six years of his life, apparently near a nuclear power station: Sizewell in Suffolk or Bradwell in Essex. Tests on his hair and skin, however, indicated that he had not lived in the UK for up to four weeks before his death but rather in Holland or Germany. In due course he was identified as an unsavoury Armenian gangster named Hovhannes Amirian, who had family connections in the Ukraine as well as gangland links in Germany and Holland. In November 2005 an accomplice, Nishan Bakunts, was convicted of his murder.

Dr Black was also involved in the case of 'Adam', the young boy whose torso was found in the River Thames in London in 2001. Analysis of the child's bones by Dr Black revealed traces of a type of pre-Cambrian rock found in West Africa. Detectives from Scotland Yard travelled to Nigeria, taking a hundred samples – from sources including rocks and soil but also elephants, wild game and human post-mortem examinations – from a ten thousand square kilometre area. These samples then allowed them to narrow Adam's birthplace to a location in a narrow corridor of southwestern Nigeria just 160 by 80 km.

LURKING DEATH

A toxicology lab features an alphabet soup of sophisticated instruments and techniques. The contents and composition of the victim's blood, urine, hair and fingernails are scrutinized by (to name but a few) ELISA kits (Enzyme-Linked ImmunoSorbent Assay), GC-MS (gas chromatography-mass spectrometry), AAS (atomic-absorption spectrometry) and HPLC-MS/MS (for the uninitiated, a combination of high-performance liquid chromatography with a tandem mass spectrometer).

With these sorts of techniques at their disposal, toxicologists can usually identify toxins and poisons quickly and easily. However, one day in September 1978 the doctors at the Wandsworth Public Mortuary in South London found themselves confronted with a baffling case. The deceased was a forty-nine-year-old BBC reporter who lived in Clapham but originally came from Eastern Europe. The autopsy revealed a damaged liver, an elevated white blood cell count, and haemorrhages in the internal organs.

There was also a small wound in the upper part of the right thigh and, inside this wound, a pellet the size of a pinhead that proved to be a platinum and iridium bearing used in watchmaking. Close examination of the pellet revealed two small holes that had been drilled with a high-tech laser to create a cavity to hold one-fifth of a milligram of poison. The victim was the Bulgarian dissident Georgi Markov and the poison, it eventually transpired, was ricin. The fatal dose had been administered five days earlier, as Markov waited at a bus stop beside Waterloo Bridge, by an assassin armed with a James Bond-style 'umbrella gun'.

Ricin, extracted from the seeds of the castor bean plant, is the perfect poison, since no trace of it was ever found in Markov's body, and two decades after his murder no vaccine or antidote yet exists. However, his post-mortem condition suggested it had been his enemies' poison of choice, and its use was confirmed when scientists injected a pig with the poison, watched it die, and then observed exactly the same kind of internal damage. It was known that the chemical warfare laboratories of the Soviet Union had been studying ricin as an agent of bio-terror – as indeed had their British equivalents at Porton Down since the Second World War, when the poison was codenamed Compound W and British scientists were hard at work on a weapon of mass destruction called the W-Bomb. Still, if the way in which Markov was dispatched – the rolled umbrella, the 4.50 omnibus from Waterloo Bridge – seems more Agatha Christie than Saddam Hussein, then it's worth remembering that ricin made its first appearance in the public mind in 1929, in Christie's short story 'The House of Lurking Death'. Tommy and Tuppence Beresford managed to solve that particular case without any help at all from ELISA kits or high-performance liquid chromatography.

THE DOUBLE HELIX

In 1985 Dr Elliot M. Gross observed, regarding Josef Mengele, that if the body was skeletalized, then the teeth were the only way to make a positive identification. Sixteen years later, his successor as Chief Medical Examiner in New York, Dr Charles S. Hirsch, was equipped with another means of making positive identifications of human remains. The two hijacked airplanes that struck the World Trade Center in New York on 11 September 2001 caused 2,749 deaths. Nearly twenty thousand body parts – fragments of tissue and bone, some no larger than a fingertip – were ultimately recovered from the site. The task of Dr Hirsch and his team was to identify accurately the deceased and issue death certificates. Since only ten of the victims could be identified by visual means, the vast majority called for various methods of forensic scrutiny. Fingerprinting and dental records were used wherever possible, but many partial remains required a methodology unavailable to forensic scientists only a decade or two earlier: DNA profiling. DNA from the victims was matched to that recovered from their combs, toothbrushes and razorblades, as well as to cheek swabs from their relatives. As of September 2005, Dr Hirsch and his team had identified 1,594 of the victims, of whom 852 were distinguished by DNA analysis.[115]

DNA is perhaps the surest and most durable marker of identity that a body leaves behind. DNA, or deoxyribonucleic acid, is a chemical found in nearly every cell of the body, including in bodily fluids such as in blood, semen and saliva. This chemical carries genetic information from one generation to the next, and with the exception of identical twins, our DNA is unique. Half is inherited from our father, the other half from our mother. Interestingly, our DNA is ninety-nine per cent the same as that of every other human, with the remaining one per cent giving us our individuality – and that is what the DNA experts concentrate on when attempting to identify a victim or his killer.

DNA was discovered in 1869 by a Swiss scientist named Johann Frederick Miescher. He separated the nuclei from the cytoplasm in the cells of fish sperm and the pus from open wounds and then isolated an acidic substance in the nuclei that he named nuclein. The components of DNA were identified in 1909 by the Russian-born scientist Phoebus Levene, and in 1953 Maurice Wilkins, Francis Crick and James Watson proposed the famous double-helical structure after using Rosalind Franklin's X-ray diffraction images of DNA. In the early 1970s came the discovery of recombinant DNA technology – that is, cloning. But not until the 1980s was DNA profiling used in a murder investigation. In 1986 Dr Alec Jeffreys, a scientist in the Department of Genetics at the University of Leicester, was called upon by the Leicestershire Constabulary to help solve the case of two schoolgirls murdered in the village of Narborough, one in November 1983 and the other in July 1986. Dr Jeffreys had been combining genetics with molecular biology to study variation in human DNA. By 1984 these studies had led him to the development of DNA fingerprinting, which he showed could be used to establish identification and kinship. Then, in a momentous development for forensics, in 1985 he co-authored a paper with two scientists from the Forensic Science Service (FSS) demonstrating how DNA could be obtained from blood and semen stains at a crime scene.

Provided with semen samples from the girls' bodies – the only forensic evidence left behind by the killer – Dr Jeffreys showed that the same person had raped and killed both victims. In the world's first mass screening for DNA, blood samples were then taken from five thousand local men, a process that took six months and initially produced no matches. However, suspicion ultimately fell on a twenty-five-year-old baker from a neighbouring village named Colin Pitchfork who, it transpired, had paid a co-worker to present a forged passport and give blood on his behalf. After the co-worker's boast was overheard in a pub, Pitchfork was arrested, and the DNA from his blood sample was matched to the DNA profile from the semen. In 1988 Pitchfork was found guilty and sentenced to fourteen years in prison.

In the decades since, DNA screening has gone worldwide. From 1995 in the United Kingdom, DNA samples have been fed into the National DNA Database (NDNAD), which is funded by the British government and operated by the FSS for the Association of Chief Police Officers. Since 2004, the police have been permitted to take a DNA sample, usually mouth scrapes or rooted hair, from any person arrested for a recordable offence, thus ensuring that the database is getting bigger every year. The FSS website proudly boasts that in 2005 the NDNAD held 2.9 million DNA profiles, and in a typical month, they claim, matching DNA samples solves twenty-six murders, fifty-seven rapes and three thousand motor vehicle, property and drug crimes. In the United States, all fifty states have connected to the FBI's combined DNA Identification System (CODIS), creating a super database called the National DNA Index System (NDIS). These DNA databases can also be useful in exonerating people for crimes they did not commit: in the United States, 201 people have been exonerated since 1989, with some having spent time on death row.[116]

As the example of 9/11 suggests, DNA can be as effective in identifying human remains as it is in fingering the culprits or exonerating the innocent. The mass graves of the eight thousand Muslim victims of the July 1995 massacre by Serbian troops in the Bosnian town of Srebrenica were excavated in 2005, with the Sarajevo-based International Commission of Missing Persons (ICMP) dedicated to returning victims to their families. By 2005, seventy thousand blood samples had been collected from bereaved relatives seeking news of their loved ones, while machines in four laboratories in the former Yugoslavia were busily sanding and grinding the bones of the dead. Skeletons and a few scraps of clothing are all the ICMP has to work with, but fortunately DNA is generally well preserved in bones and teeth: it has been successfully extracted from pre-Columbian Amerindian skeletons that were as much as four thousand years old.[117]

The procedures and software employed in Bosnia were later used at Ground Zero in New York and offer a model for identifying the remains of the victims of other atrocities who lie in mass graves, from Rwanda and East Timor to Kosovo and Argentina. And DNA profiling has other applications and consequences as well. A new discipline called molecular anthropology has recently been developed, using DNA to trace demographic events such as centuries-old migrations across oceans and continents. The Genographic Project, a $40 million (£21 million) privately funded initiative sponsored by *National Geographic* and IBM, plans to collect DNA samples from more than a hundred thousand people worldwide to create a map of how the planet was colonized, and to answer questions such as whether Alexander the Great's armies left a genetic trail and who first colonized the Indian continent. A technique of mass screening first used in 1986 to solve a succession of terrible crimes in a Leicestershire village has truly gone global.

CHAPTER 10

Reinventing Death

The New Technology of Dying

How can we tell when death occurs and a body dies? How, legally and medically, can the moment of death be ascertained? In 1768 the first edition of the *Encyclopedia Britannica* confidently informed its readers that death could be defined as the 'separation of the soul and body'. Medical science has come a long way since 1768, but definitions of death are nonetheless ever more fraught with problems, and the blithe assurances of eighteenth-century dictionary writers have given way to complex arguments. The 2007 edition of the *Encyclopedia Britannica* is more circumspect, defining death as 'the total cessation of life processes that eventually occurs in all living organisms' but noting that the state of human death 'has always been obscured by mystery and superstition, and its precise definition remains controversial, differing according to culture and legal systems'.

One might think that with the advance of new technology it would be a simple matter to diagnose death. No longer is it necessary to apply frightful eighteenth- and nineteenth-century gadgets such as nipple pincers and *Doppelblässers* in order to detect a flicker of life, nor need one wait for the first signs of putrefaction in the *Leichenhaüsser* to confirm the inevitable. Unfortunately, however, in reality we cannot actually express with absolute certainty what constitutes death or when a person has died. Does a human life depend merely on the body's ability to breathe, digest or circulate blood? Or does it include higher cognitive abilities, such as thinking and consciously interacting with the environment? How do we define the precise moment when a human organism expires? Is it when the brain dies, or when every cell and electrical current ceases to function? The age-old problem of confirming death – the problem that lay behind phobias about live burials, and that launched a thousand patents for fail-safe coffins – has become ever more complicated with the advance of new technology and the sophistication of life-support machines. Life-saving techniques such as cardiopulmonary resuscitation and defibrillation have forced a re-evaluation of what constitutes death and when. The stakes in defining death are high, since transplant technology requires organs to be harvested from their donors within minutes of death being declared. Other technologies – genetics, nanomedicine and robotics – are promising to bring about an even more profound redefinition of death, and even a conquest over it.

NOT DEAD YET?

Sarah, a thirty-four-year-old woman, lies motionless on a bed in the Intensive Care Unit (ICU) of a major London hospital. Her eyes are closed, and she looks as if she is sleeping peacefully. Her parents take turns in holding her warm hand, careful not to dislodge any of the tubes that connect her to the machines that force her heart to beat, keep her hydrated, and pump her with antibiotics to suppress infection. Approaching the ICU is a neurology consultant who will break to them the news that their daughter, despite the steady sighing of her mechanical ventilator and the blips of life on her heart monitor, is actually dead. He will recommend that the machines be switched off. Despite the fact that their daughter's brainstem has been irreversibly damaged in a car crash and the likelihood that the machines will be unable to keep her functioning for more than seventy-two hours, Sarah's parents will refuse the doctor's request. They are Jewish and, according to Jewish law, as long as the heart beats – even if artificially – the person is not dead.

Further down the corridor, propped up with pillows on another hospital bed, lies Jonathan, a fifty-one-year-old father of two and the survivor of another car crash. He can breathe and swallow on his own, blink, sleep and sometimes grunt, because, despite the injury, his brainstem, unlike Sarah's, remains intact. However, according to CT scans, his cerebrum, the part of his brain responsible for cognitive abilities, has been damaged beyond repair, as a result of which he is unaware of his surroundings and recognizes no one. Thirty days after his admission to hospital, and following constant observation and tests, he was diagnosed as being in a permanent vegetative state (PVS). He has now been in this condition for two years. The person Jonathan once was no longer exists, and his wife – despite visiting him twice a week – regards him as dead. She believes him to have no quality of life and wishes him to be able to die officially and with dignity. However, she must go to court to argue that ending his life is in her husband's best interests. If the court agrees, his feeding tube will be removed and he will be allowed to die, very slowly, from starvation and dehydration.

The doctors are certain that Sarah is dead even though her heart beats artificially – yet her parents disagree. The legal profession argues that Jonathan is not dead, even though brain-scans show that the part of the brain that gives him his personality and makes him a human being has been destroyed, and even though his wife, who knew him better than anyone else, considers him dead.

As the *Encyclopedia Britannica* notes, the idea of what constitutes death varies according to cultural and legal practices. The diagnosing of death is inevitably influenced by a society's wider philosophical and cultural attitudes. Some Orthodox Jews, fundamentalist Christians, Native Americans and Japanese Buddhists believe that death only occurs after the cessation of the heartbeat, irrespective of whether it beats with or without the aid of machines. From a purely biological perspective, too, the precise moment of death can be difficult to determine. Is it when the heart stops, when the brain dies, either in part or as a whole, or when the organism in its entirety, including its cells, finally expires?

Until the 1960s, death seemed relatively straightforward. It was commonly defined throughout the world as the cessation of both heartbeat and breathing. However, the development of resuscitation techniques and life-support technology challenged this definition, as they enabled the restarting of the heart and the supporting of organs that would otherwise have failed. Reviving patients from the brink of death is, of course, as old as medicine itself. The ancient Egyptians hung patients upside down and applied pressure to the chest in a primitive form of cardiopulmonary resuscitation (CPR), while the Old Testament (2 Kings 4:34–35) describes how the Prophet Elisha revived a dying child by breathing into his mouth. In Holland in the eighteenth century, meanwhile, victims of drowning were given mouth-to-mouth ventilation and – for good measure – an 'insufflation of smoke of burning tobacco into the rectum'.[118] By the early nineteenth century, resuscitation techniques included smelling salts, artificial respiration with a bellows and even electrical stimulation. All of these techniques were performed on Harriet Westbrook, the estranged wife of the poet Percy Bysshe Shelley, after she drowned herself in the Serpentine in Hyde Park in December 1816. The techniques proved to no avail, though no doubt they left a profound impression on Shelley's next wife, Mary, who two years later published *Frankenstein* (in which resuscitation techniques are more effectively deployed).

A century later, better results in reviving the dead were apparently obtained. In the first decade of the twentieth century a chemist named George Poe, a cousin of the writer Edgar Allan Poe, invented a kind of artificial respirator that, in a series of public demonstrations, was said to bring the dead back to life. Poe gassed rabbits and strangled dogs before 'reviving' them with his machine, which operated by suction.[119] Similar experiments in resuscitation were performed on dogs several decades later by Dr S.S. Bryukhonenko at the Institute of Experimental Physiology and Therapy in the Soviet Union. Fortunately, neither Poe nor Dr Bryukhonenko put humans to the test.

Not until the middle of the twentieth century, however, did the technique achieve any real sophistication or success. In 1956 Paul Zoll, a Boston cardiologist, published his account of defibrillation, and two years later an article on chest compression appeared in the *Journal of the American Medical Association*. Buoyed by these advances, in the early 1960s John F. Kennedy declared that over the next decade the new technique of cardiopulmonary resuscitation 'would save thousands of hearts too good to die'.[120]

The age of CPR had arrived, and with it came a strong challenge to the idea that death had inescapably arrived when the heart and lungs stopped. The definition of death as the cessation of the circulatory and respiratory functions caused unease among doctors as patients were regularly brought back from death by means of CPR, thus raising the question as to whether they had actually been dead in the first place. In 1968 the Harvard Medical School, responding to concerns raised by the new life-saving technology, initiated a discussion on redefining death. The 5 August 1968 issue of the *Journal of the American Medical Association* announced the results, a landmark article entitled 'A Definition of Irreversible Coma: Report of the Ad Hoc Committee of the Harvard Medical School to Examine the Definition of Brain Death'. The article defined 'irreversible coma' – a condition (now known as 'brain death') characterized by the complete lack of reflexes, awareness, or response to pain or other external stimuli – as the new criterion for death. The brain rather than the heart and lungs therefore became the focus of attention, and more specifically the brainstem. The death of the brainstem, the stalk that connects the cerebrum to the spinal cord, became known as whole-brain death, as the organism as a whole cannot survive longer than a few days without its support: the brainstem controls the breathing and heartbeat. If, on the other hand, the brainstem survives but the part of the brain responsible for cognition, reasoning and personality – the cerebrum – is damaged, as in the case of Jonathan, the condition known as higher-brain death is diagnosed.

Modern death has thereafter been determined by neurological rather than by cardiopulmonary criteria, and these criteria, with various modifications, have been adopted throughout the world. In the UK, the Conference of Medical Royal Colleges and their Faculties published their definition of brain death in 1976, and in 1981, in the United States, the President's Commission for the Study of Ethical Problems in Medicine and Biomedical and Behavioural Research published its report, *Defining Death*, which agreed that a person should be declared dead once there was total and irreversible cessation of all brain function.

Many neurologists support the view that death should be declared if the brainstem is irreversibly damaged because without a brainstem there is no breathing, no chewing or swallowing, and the organs are incapable of doing their job. If the brainstem is irretrievably damaged, the entire brain will die in, at most, a matter of days. Dr Fred Plum, Professor and Chair of Neurology at Cornell University Medical College, claims never to have

come across an example of a patient diagnosed as brainstem dead who subsequently recovered any vital brainstem function, or who showed any signs
of arousal or consciousness.[121]

Diagnosing brain death is a rigorous multistep process that ranges from
the high-tech to procedures that stop little short of the nipple pincers of
old. Step one entails a positive diagnosis of the cause of the coma, which
must be shown to be irremediable structural brain damage. If a blood clot
is evident, it must be removed; if there is low blood pressure or hypoxia,
both must be treated. Next, certain conditions must be ruled out, such as
hypothermia, drug or alcohol overdose, or metabolic disturbance, all of
which can reversibly impair brainstem functions. Finally, a set of tests is
applied to check that all the senses have failed. These commence with the
shining of a light directly onto the pupils, followed by a test that wouldn't
have been out of place in the eighteenth century: the rubbing of cotton
wool across the eyeball. For a person in a coma but with normal brain function, this action would be extremely uncomfortable and cause involuntary
flinching. Next, 50ml of ice-cold water is syringed into the ear to test the
cranial nerves. This procedure, too, would be so painful that a coma victim
with a functioning brainstem would inevitably react. Pressure is then
applied to areas around the eyes to detect any reaction to pain; and the
cough and gag reflexes are tested by wiggling the ventilator tube attached to
the throat passage: the normal response is to gag. Next, a suction tube
is inserted into the ventilator tube to the lungs, an action which would
produce a cough from someone with brainstem activity.

The final check is the apnoea test. In this procedure, the patient is
pumped full of extra-concentrated oxygen for five minutes, then taken off
the ventilator and observed for no more than ten minutes. A normal person will automatically take a breath unaided, while a blood test confirms
the necessary CO_2 is present in the bloodstream. In some countries, an
ECG is performed to confirm that there is electrocortical silence. In all
countries, the first set of tests is repeated but the time lag can vary from ten
minutes to twenty-four hours. Time of death is recorded after the first set
of tests has been completed.

However rigorous these tests, the development of organ transplant technology has made many people uncomfortable about the implications of

diagnoses of brain death. Transplant technology was developed in the same decades as the life-saving technologies that forced a change in the legal and medical definition of death. The first heart valve was transplanted into a patient in 1955, the first lung transplant took place in 1963, the first heart and the first liver were both successfully transplanted in 1967, and the first heart-lung transplant took place in 1981, the same year, coincidentally, that *Defining Death* was published. The definition of death has obvious repercussions for organ transplants. Since all organs have a better chance of survival in a recipient if they come from a donor who is still circulating blood throughout the body, they are harvested, ideally, from patients who have been declared brain-dead but whose organs are kept viable by means of ventilators and other life-saving technologies.

The scenario of organs being harvested from brain-dead patients who are still connected to life-support equipment has raised a new fear – a kind of modern twist on the old fear of being buried alive. What if the doctor's various tests are wrong? What if a supposedly brain-dead patient can feel the pain of having his organs harvested, yet is unable to cry out in pain? One doctor has warned that a misdiagnosis of brain death is possible in the case of 'locked-in syndrome', which occurs if the base of the pons is impaired, for example, by a stroke.[122] The pons, a 2 cm-long knob, is part of the brain-stem, relaying messages and sensory information between the cerebellum and cerebrum. If it is damaged, the patient will be unable to speak, move his limbs, swallow, or make facial expressions, but consciousness may persist as long as part of the midbrain, the tegmentum, which regulates awareness and attention, is unimpaired. A patient – so the theory goes – could find himself in the horrifying predicament of the hero of Dalton Trumbo's 1939 anti-war novel *Johnny Got His Gun*, aware of his surroundings but unable to communicate with the outside world.

Critics of the brain-death diagnosis argue that, though the tests might be thorough, they are not necessarily foolproof. Worryingly, many who fulfil all of the tests for brain death do not have the 'permanent cessation of function-ing of the entire brain'. For example, some patients who fail the battery of tests nonetheless continue to exhibit intact neurohumoral functions.[123] In one study, twenty per cent of patients who fulfilled the criteria for brain death continued to show electrical activity on their electroencephalograms.[124] It has also been observed that some of those diagnosed as brain-dead respond to surgical incision when organs are being harvested, with a rise in blood pressure and heart rate.[125] If these responses occurred during an operation on a live patient, they would indicate that more anaesthetic was required. Before leaving his post at the Papworth Hospital in Cambridge, the UK's top heart and lung transplant hospital, David Wainwright-Evans argued that the brainstem criterion, a 'reinvention of death', was developed for the justification of organ procurement.[126] Another doctor on a different continent, C.G. Coimbra from the University of São Paulo, claims that the apnoea test may actually induce irreversible brain damage and should be abandoned.[127] As if all this were not bad enough, Dr Stuart Youngner, professor of bioethics at Case Western Reserve University in Cleveland, Ohio, found that only thirty-five per cent of physicians and nurses involved in organ procurement could correctly identify the legal and medical criteria for determining death.[128]

Anxieties about organ transplants going horribly wrong, or being performed for illicit reasons, has long been a Hollywood staple – not surprisingly, perhaps, if one considers that Dr Victor Frankenstein was probably the world's first transplant surgeon. The usual cinematic take on transplantation is ably if gorily demonstrated in the 1991 low-budget horror film *Body Parts*, starring Jeff Fahey as an amputee whose behaviour changes for the worse after he receives the arm of an executed prisoner; or by the Michael Crichton-directed *Coma* (1978), in which comas are induced in healthy hospital patients who are then shipped off to the sinister Jefferson Institute to have their organs harvested.[129] It's doubtful if these films have made anyone hesitate before signing an organ donor card, but a BBC *Panorama* episode in the 1980s, questioning whether transplant donors were truly dead, resulted in a decade-long drop in organ donations in the UK.[130]

THE SLEEPERS

The authors of the 1981 report *Defining Death* stressed that the 'entire brain', including the brainstem, must have ceased to function in order for death to be declared. They thereby clearly distinguished whole-brain death from higher-brain death, in which the brainstem still functions but no cognitive abilities are present. Under this definition, a person like Jonathan is regarded as having neither a legal nor a medical claim to being dead.

The term PVS was coined in 1972 by Scottish neurosurgeon Bryan Jennet and his colleague, the neurologist Fred Plum, to describe a condition that has only been made possible with the aid of modern medicine. PVS sufferers are in a chronic state of wakefulness but have no awareness, as their neo-cortical functioning has been destroyed. The brainstem still works either completely or in part, controlling the respiration, digestion, circulation, reflex response and homeostatic mechanisms, potentially keeping the human organism alive for as long as someone feeds and hydrates it.

PVS patients sometimes become the subject of lengthy legal battles – as in a much-publicized American case that went through the courts for many years. Terri Schiavo entered a PVS following a heart attack at the age of twenty-six. Her husband eventually campaigned through the courts to have her feeding tube disconnected, arguing that she would not have wished to live in such a state. Her parents, who were not her legal guardians, opposed his wishes, and for fifteen years they challenged her husband's rights. Medics were adamant that tests showed no evidence of 'consciousness', but Mrs Schiavo's parents insisted they saw a flicker of recognition in her movements. Several times the feeding tube was disconnected, only to be reinserted following court hearings. The case eventually went as far as the United States Supreme Court, which refused to intervene on the parents' behalf after the Florida State Court agreed, on 18 March 2005, to disconnect the feeding tube for the last time. As a result, Terri Schiavo the 'human organism' was legally starved until she finally died thirteen days later. In the advanced technological age in which we live, with all the machines and gadgets capable of prolonging our lives, it seems a gruesome irony that the only legal way to end the life of PVS patients is to remove their feeding tubes and slowly starve them to death. Treating an animal in such a way is a punishable offence in both Britain and America.

Another case, this time in Britain, also went to the highest court in the land. In August 2003, fifty-three-year-old 'Jessica', the alias by which she became known in the press, collapsed while on holiday in Yorkshire with her husband. Doctors determined that she had suffered a brain haemor-rhage, and she was eventually diagnosed as being in a PVS and moved for care to a hospice. Her husband and family visited her weekly, while insist-ing she would not have wanted to live in such a state. Like Terri Schiavo's husband, they wanted her to be allowed to have her life-sustaining support withdrawn and to die with dignity.

Since the 1993 English case of the Airedale NHS Trust versus Bland, where the House of Lords held that it was lawful not to continue with medical treatment if a patient was permanently unaware of self and environment, all requests to stop treatment must first be approved by the High Court, who will hear both sides of the story. The patient is awarded a solicitor to argue for continued treatment. In 2006, Jessica's husband petitioned the court for treatment to be suspended, but the officially appointed solicitor, Laurence Oates, argued against this procedure on the grounds that an experimental drug should first be administered to the patient as it might bring her round. Even though Professor Keith Andrews from London's Royal Hospital for Neuro-disability told the BBC that he did not think it would work, and that it had shown no results in any of the patients to whom he had administered it, the High Court ruled in favour of keeping Jessica alive and testing the drug.[131] The family were opposed to the treatment from the outset, as evidence had shown that the longer a PVS patient is in his or her state the more severely disabled they become, and by this point Jessica had been in a PVS for three years. It was only when the drug failed to produce any results whatsoever that the family was allowed to suspend treatment. Jessica died twelve days later.

The experimental drug was Zolpidem, a sleeping pill. In 1999 it was acci-dentally discovered to have the opposite effect in some patients. A doctor in South Africa prescribed the drug to a coma patient, Riaan Bolton, in an attempt to control his involuntary spasms, but instead of putting Bolton to sleep, it woke him up – resulting in the theory that it somehow reactivated seemingly dead brain cells in coma patients. After severe trauma, the brain, in order to conserve energy and to help cells survive, is switched off by a chemical called gamma amino butyric acid (Gaba). In a prolonged dor-mant state, the receptors in the brain cells become hypersensitive to Gaba and cause PVS. While a patient is in this state, the receptors respond differently to the sleeping drug.

However, a miracle drug Zolpidem is not, as clearly it does not work on everyone. Medical sceptics argue that it works only if the patients have been wrongly diagnosed with PVS. And according to some doctors, errors in the diagnosis of PVS are not uncommon.[132] Part of the problem lies in the nature of the condition, for there are no clinical tests that can accurately diagnose PVS. A dead brainstem literally turns to mush shortly after it dies, but the diagnosis of PVS is more difficult, as it depends on proving that the patient has a lack of awareness, and such proof is based mainly on observation. 'It is vital, therefore,' explains Derick Wade, consultant in neurological disability, 'that any doctor who assesses a patient is careful in his or her assessment and has appropriate expertise and experience. If there is any doubt about the diagnosis or conflict between different sources of evidence, re-examination at another time or prolonged observation, or both, must be undertaken.'[133]

Perhaps scientists can be forgiven their optimism about Zolpidem. Our culture is replete with stories of people who have fallen 'asleep' for long periods, only to miraculously awaken. Possibly the earliest comes from the Christian tradition, which tells the story of the Seven Sleepers of Ephesus, young Christians from the third century who were shut in a cave on Mount Anchilos by the Roman Emperor Decius. When their tomb is unsealed many decades later, the young men are found asleep and, when they wake up, think only a single day has passed. If the legend of the Seven Sleepers was seen by early Christians as proof of the resurrection of the body, later stories, from Washington Irving's 'Rip Van Winkle' (1819) to Woody Allen's *Sleeper* (in which Miles Monroe, proprietor of the Happy Carrot Health Food Store, goes into hospital for an operation in 1973 and wakes up two hundred years later), usually emphasize the differences between the past life and the strange new world into which the sleeper awakens. After their long slumber, the Seven Sleepers discovered a better world in which Christianity flourished, but later treatments often tend towards the dystopic, as in the case of H.G. Wells's novel *The Sleeper Awakes* (1910): the hero, an ardent socialist, awakens after a sleep of 203 years to witness the horrors and grotesqueries of capitalism. Even Woody Allen's future, despite its 'orgasmatron booths' and the radical discovery that fatty foods are actually good for you, is shown to be an inferior version of the present.

There has never been a case of a PVS sufferer making a recovery or regaining full consciousness. However, in June 2007 Polish television reported the case of Jan Grzebski, who emerged from a nineteen-year-long coma to discover – unlike Wells's protagonist – that capitalism had created a wonderful new world. Struck by a train in 1988, Mr Grzebski went into his coma when the Communist Party ruled Poland, the Berlin Wall stood, meat was rationed, and the only thing in the shops was tea and vinegar. 'Now I see people on the streets with mobile phones and there are so many goods in the shops it makes my head spin,' he was reported to have told Polish television.[134] Perhaps the future won't be quite such a bad place after all.

A GOOD DEATH

While the families of PVS sufferers sometimes campaign for their loved one's right to die, other people have fought to have a painless and dignified death of their own. Euthanasia, which means 'good death', is the practice of killing a person in a painless way in order to end their suffering. The concept of mercy killing has existed for thousands of years. In ancient Greece and Rome, the act was usually performed by a physician. These days, however, euthanizing a patient can land the helper in grave legal difficulties. For example, as the law stands in Britain as of 2007, it is an offence under section 2 (1) of the Suicide Act of 1961 to assist another person to commit suicide. In legal terms, a person administering a lethal injection to end a life is, no matter the circumstances, committing murder. Paradoxically, the withdrawal of life-support treatment or feeding tubes is not regarded as murder, but rather a natural and inevitable cessation of life. This type of passive euthanasia – starving a bedridden patient to death over a period of ten days to two weeks – remains the only type of mercy killing that is legally accepted. This procedure involves disconnecting life-support systems and ceasing all medical treatment. Feeding and hydration are stopped, no CPR is performed, and nature takes its slow but inevitable course. Such treatment is legal when someone is in a PVS or when they are declared brain dead.

Diane Pretty, a forty-three-year-old British woman suffering from Motor Neurone Disease, had nothing to look forward to but dying in pain, possibly choking to death. She felt it was her right to be able to take her own life and, if she was incapable of doing so herself, for her husband to assist her. In 2001 she asked the Director of Public Prosecutions (DPP) to give an undertaking not to prosecute her husband if he assisted in her suicide. The DPP refused, a decision upheld by the House of Lords. Frustrated, Mrs Pretty challenged the decision in the European Court of Human Rights, and although it was agreed that UK legislation on assisted suicide did infringe her human rights, the Strasbourg Court nevertheless refused permission for assisted suicide. It argued that the law existed to protect life, not to take it away.

The first 'Voluntary Euthanasia Bill' was drafted in 1931 by Dr C. Killick Millard, health officer for the city of Leicester. It stipulated that if a dying person secured from two medical officers the opinion that his condition was incurable, he could apply for a euthanasia permit. But despite Dr Millard's well-thought-out rules and careful safeguards, in 1936 it was defeated in the House of Lords by thirty-five votes to fourteen. Since its first hearing it has been resubmitted unsuccessfully to parliament in 1950, 1969, 1985, 1991, 1994, and most recently 2005. In 1969, the House of Lords actually accepted a voluntary euthanasia bill, only to reject it again in the same year. Over thirty years later, the issue refuses to disappear. The last attempt by Lord Joffe, in 2005, aimed to legalize assisted suicide and voluntary euthanasia for those in the last months of a terminal illness, so long as they were mentally competent and suffering unbearably. Although not rejected outright, the House of Lords committee has called for a debate on the bill.

As of 2007, there are only three countries and one American state to offer euthanasia. Assisted suicide has been legal in Switzerland since 1941, and Switzerland is still the only country to allow non-residents to participate. Doctor-assisted suicide and euthanasia, tolerated in The Netherlands since the 1970s, were finally made legal in 2002 under the 'Termination of Life on Request and Assisted Suicide (review Procedures) Act'. Also in 2002, euthanasia was legally permitted in Belgium, with a caveat, rather like the one suggested by Dr Millard, that two doctors be involved. The only state in the United States to permit doctor-assisted suicide is Oregon, where it was ratified in 1997 and, as with Belgium, two doctors must be involved. Assisted suicide is illegal in England, Wales, Ireland, Canada, New Zealand and Australia. Interestingly, in Australia's Northern Territories, where euthanasia was legal for nearly two years, the law was repealed in 1997. In France and Scotland, assisted dying is not illegal, though there is still room for the law to prosecute.

The Prettys were therefore obliged to stand by the court's decision, otherwise Brian Pretty could have been tried for murder and faced a prison sentence of up to fourteen years. In the United States, where similar laws exist, the sentence could have been twenty-five years. Mrs Pretty ultimately died in a hospice in 2002, after which her husband told reporters: 'Diane had to go through the one thing she had foreseen and was afraid of – and there was nothing I could do to help.'[135]

Despite the European Court's legal strictures against euthanasia, a survey by the Voluntary Euthanasia Society found that fifty-six per cent of doctors are in favour of some form of regulated physician-assisted suicide, while forty-five per cent of doctors believed some of their colleagues had helped the terminally ill to die.[136] Another survey in 2003 by the *Nursing Times* found that two thirds of the 2,709 nurses taking part believed voluntary euthanasia should be legalized; however, only one out of three of those responding was actually prepared to help the patient die.

One of the most high-profile cases of physician-assisted euthanasia is that of King George V of Great Britain. On 20 January 1936, the ailing king, a heavy smoker with a history of health problems, began drifting in and out of consciousness in his bedroom at Sandringham before lapsing into a coma. Lord Dawson of Penn, the royal physician, announced that 'the king's life is moving peacefully to its close'. That much was true, but Lord Dawson then proceeded to hasten the pace at which the seventy-year-old monarch's life was peacefully moving. He injected into the royal patient's jugular vein a lethal mixture of cocaine and morphine – nicknamed a 'whizzball' – that enabled him to die swiftly and calmly. His family, who were consulted at every stage, consented to the procedure, in order to ease the dying king's suffering. Also playing something of a part in the process, however, was the desire to have the king's death announced in the morning edition of *The Times* – not in one of the less prestigious evening papers – and Lord Dawson's wish to get back to the patients at his busy private practice in London.[137]

Lord Dawson was not prosecuted or tried for murder. (Details of his actions only came to light many years after his death in 1945, when his private diaries were opened.) There have been many other cases of doctors who have not been so lucky. In 1992 Dr Nigel Cox, a consultant rheumatologist, was found guilty of attempted murder after injecting a seventy-year-old terminally ill patient, Lillian Boyes, with a lethal drug. Mrs Boyes had asked her doctor to help her die, and Dr Cox's action was only discovered from her medical notes, in which he had written up the drug administered: potassium chloride. A nurse alerted the authorities, since this drug is not designed to alleviate pain. Dr Cox was given a suspended sentence and the General Medical Council let him off with a reprimand, as Mrs Boyes had been cremated and it could not be proved that she had actually died from the effects of the lethal injection. Mrs Boyes's family supported the doctor throughout the controversy, claiming that she had requested assistance in ending her life.

On the other side of the Atlantic, one doctor charged with second-degree homicide in administering assisted euthanasia was released from prison in Coldwater, Michigan in June 2007 after serving a ten-year sentence. Jack Kevorkian, known infamously as 'Dr Death', a committed proponent of euthanasia, had been acquitted in several previous criminal trials, demonstrating a flair for showmanship that on occasion witnessed him donning a powdered wig or wearing a placard daring prosecutors to charge him. However, his luck ran out when he allowed a videotape of himself administering a lethal injection to an Amyotrophic Lateral Sclerosis (ALS) sufferer, Thomas Youk, to be shown on the 17 September 1998 edition of the popular CBS current affairs show *60 Minutes*. He was charged with second-degree homicide six months later.

There hasn't always been such a negative reaction to euthanasia. In Ancient Greece and Imperial Rome, patients frequently asked their physicians to provide them with poisons to hasten their demise, and often physicians would oblige.[138] (Greek mythology is full of suicides of every description, some of them quite inventive: Ovid's *Metamorphoses* records that one of the Coronides clubbed herself to death with a shuttle and that Erysichthon, in one of the stranger approaches, committed suicide by eating himself.) The Roman Stoic writer Seneca (4 BCE–65 CE) wrote: 'It makes a great deal of difference whether a man is lengthening his life or his death. But if the body is useless for service, why should one not free the struggling soul? Perhaps one ought to do this a little before the debt is due, lest, when it falls due, he may be unable to perform the act'. Another Roman writer, Libanius (314–394 CE), commented on euthanasia with reference to the city of Athens: 'Whoever no longer wished to live shall state his reasons to the Senate, and after having received permission shall abandon life. If your existence is hateful to you, die; if you are overwhelmed by fate, drink the hemlock. If you are bowed with grief, abandon life. Let the unhappy man recount his misfortune, let the magistrate supply him with the remedy, and his wretchedness will come to an end.'[139] There were objections from the Epicurean and Pythagorean schools of thought, while the words of the Hippocratic Oath, written sometime between the fifth and third centuries BCE, proposed that 'physicians will not give a fatal·drug to anyone if they are asked, nor will they suggest any such thing'.

Yet this opposition was disregarded by the majority of Greek and Roman physicians, and euthanasia and suicide remained unchallenged until the arrival of the early Judeo-Christian doctrine that upheld the sanctity of life and condemned suicide and mercy killings as an affront to God. As Ecclesiastes 8:8 unambiguously states: 'No man has authority . . . over the day of death.' St Augustine (345–430 CE) likewise preached on the wickedness of taking life, an abhorrence which most Christians still uphold today. By the Middle Ages, suicide and euthanasia were seen to be a terrible sin. Abelard, Duns Scotus, John of Salisbury, Jean Buridan and Thomas Aquinas all followed this line of thought, while writers such as Dante (1265–1321), in his *Divine Comedy*, conceived a special place for suicides: they were turned into blackened, twisted trees and confined to the seventh circle of Hell, where their twigs bled when broken.

There are a few notable exceptions in this litany against what Hamlet, contemplating his bodkin, calls 'self-slaughter'. Sir Thomas Moore wrote in his *Utopia* (1516): 'If, besides being incurable, the disease also causes constant excruciating pain, some priests and government officials visit the person concerned and say . . . Since your life's a misery to you, why hesitate to die? You're imprisoned in a torture chamber – why don't you break out and escape to a better world . . . We'll arrange for your release . . . If the patient finds these arguments convincing, he either starves himself to death, or is given a soporific and put painlessly out of his misery. But this is strictly voluntary.' In *The New Atlantis* (1626), Sir Francis Bacon describes doctors assisting a dying patient 'to make a fair and easy passage from life'. Apart from these writers, though, there wasn't much change from the Judeo-Christian stance until the German philosopher Arthur Schopenhauer (1788–1860) put forward in *The World as Will and Representation*, published in 1819, his support for voluntary euthanasia. He argued for individualism and human autonomy, saying that a man should have an 'unassailable title to his own life and person . . . It wilt be generally found that, as soon as the terrors of life reach the point at which they outweigh the terrors of death, a man will put an end to his life.'

Today, those in favour of euthanasia argue that only individuals them-selves can determine the degree and extent of their suffering, and they are therefore the ones who should be able to make a decision when to die. Professor of medical ethics at the University of Virginia and former presi-dent of the Euthanasia Society of America, Joseph Fletcher (1901–91), regarded euthanasia as an expression of love and supported his view with his situational ethics model. In this model, decision-making is based on the circumstances of a particular situation rather than from fixed law. The only absolute is love, and love, he argued, should be the motive behind every decision, including euthanasia. Another proponent of euthanasia is the controversial Australian, Peter Singer, a professor at the Centre for Human Values at Princeton University who looks at euthanasia through utilitarian eyes and argues that all decisions should be made for the greater good – which can also involve alleviating the suffering of distressed relatives. Interestingly, he does not agree to euthanasia for his mother, Cora, who suffers from advanced Alzheimer's disease. When questioned on this apparent inconsistency of application by the journalist Peter J. Colosi, Singer admitted how difficult such decisions are when the patient is one's beloved mother.[140]

Opponents of euthanasia object to the practice on moral grounds, arguing that it is a slippery slope that inevitably leads to decisions on life or
death being made for financial reasons. They support the use of pain med-
ications and palliative care, and argue that these treatments are now so
advanced that euthanasia is unnecessary. However, Michael Irwin, a
retired general practitioner and former chairman of the UK's Voluntary
Euthanasia Society, disagrees, claiming that most strong painkillers have
unpleasant side effects.[141] Morphine, for example, can cause nausea, vomiting, severe constipation and sedation to the point of unconsciousness.

Still, those who argue that euthanasia could be used as a cost-cutting
measure may not be far wrong. In May 2005 British newspapers reported
that a ruling granting a patient the right to request life-prolonging care had
serious implications for the National Health Service. Leslie Burke, then
forty-five and suffering from cerebellar ataxia, a degenerative brain disease,
won a legal battle in July 2004 that prevented doctors from withdrawing
artificial nutrition or hydration treatment until he dies naturally. The
General Medical Council's (GMC) guidelines, which the ruling overturned, state that if the condition of a patient has deteriorated so much that
their prognosis is poor and further treatment may cause suffering, all treatment, including feeding and hydration, may be stopped, causing them to
die. The Department of Health, with the backing of the GMC, then
attempted to have the decision overturned. The GMC's guidelines are
apparently to save the patient further 'suffering', but another more sinister
factor emerged when John Reid, then the Labour Government's Health
Secretary, warned that Mr Burke's court victory would have implications
for the NHS's resources. For reasons of saving money, in other words, the
Department of Health is determined to starve Mr Burke to death, even
though, as he told the *Sunday Times*: 'If I end up in hospital my communication skills will be negligible but my intelligence will be unimpaired. If
food and water were taken away it would take up to two weeks for me to die.
I would be aware of every minute of this and I would be unable to do anything about it. I cannot think of a more horrific process.'[142] So much, it
seems, for the attitude of the government and the medical profession
towards the sanctity of life and the dignity of death. The fact that Mr Burke
will be euthanized against his will while the families of both Diane Pretty

and Jessica were obliged to fight their cases in the High Court to achieve exactly the opposite result illustrates the ambiguities, complexities and plain-old hypocrisies involved in modern death.

DEATH WARMED UP

The only sure things in life, it is said, are death and taxes. But not everyone agrees. New York's 'Queen of Mean', Leona Helmsley, once famously boasted (before going to jail for tax evasion) that paying taxes was for the 'little people'. Likewise, some people believe that death is not inevitable either, and that it can be avoided with the right amount of money, ingenuity and liquid nitrogen.

Cryonics, from the Greek *kryos*, meaning 'cold', is the practice of preserving people for possible future revival by means of freezing temperatures. Supporters of cryonics claim that a cryopreserved body can remain physically viable for at least thirty thousand years, which will allow for science and nanotechnology, in the meantime, to conquer death. The science of cryonics first hit the public's imagination in 1962 when Robert Ettinger, founder of the Cryonics Institute, published *The Prospect of Immortality*. Five years later, Ettinger froze his first client, James Bedford. Bedford, a seventy-three-year-old psychology professor who was suffering from terminal cancer, agreed to undergo the process after his death in the hope that one day – perhaps thirty thousand years hence – he could be resuscitated and cured.

Cryonics is based on the theory that most tissues in the body – everything from the skin to the brain cells – remain alive for a short time after the heartbeat stops and pulmonary activity ceases. Cryonicists believe that if the body is suspended soon after death, preferably within one hour and after no more than six, it will not be irreparably damaged. If the body could be maintained in this state, so the theory goes, then there is a chance it could be fully revived, or 'reanimated', at some point in the future. 'When and if future medical technology allows,' states the website of the Michigan-based Cryonics Institute, 'our member patients hope to be healed, rejuvenated, revived, and awakened to a greatly extended life in youthful good health, free from disease or the aging process.'[143]

The process of cryonizing a body is actually a fairly straightforward one (with the hard part – reanimation – coming hundreds or thousands of years in the future). As soon as the patient is declared dead, he is infused with a substance that prevents the formation of ice, after which he placed in an ice bath and then maintained indefinitely in a state known as cryostasis – that is, he is stored in liquid nitrogen. Time is of the essence in getting the patient in cryostasis and so, for a not inconsiderable extra cost, clients of the Cryonics Institute can have standing by at their deathbeds, armed with organ preservation solutions and a large supply of ice, a team of crack cryonics experts from Suspended Animation, Inc., a cryopreservation research company from Florida. As soon as the death certificate is signed, these professionals cool the body and begin cardiopulmonary support to minimize the chances of brain damage. Their equipment includes such things as a portable ice bath complete with a nylon carrying case and a 'vinyl privacy cover'. A Michigan Instruments 'Thumper' is clamped to the bath to administer chest compressions to the patient as the oxygen levels in his blood are checked by a pulse oximeter. Then the body is suspended in liquid nitrogen (a process that can take more than a week) and the waiting begins.

Critics of cryonics argue that the freezing process is flawed, and that it creates 'freezer burn' similar to that experienced by hamburgers or fish fingers retrieved from the bottom of the freezer, thus rendering future repairs to a defrosted body impossible. To counteract this problem, two cryobiologists, Greg Fahy and Brian Wowk from Twenty-First Century, a Californian cryobiological research company, have developed new cryoprotectant solutions that avoid freezer burn and allow vitrification – preservation in a glassy rather than a frozen state. Unfortunately, vitrification is still in its early days and is presently viable only for freezing the brain, not the whole body.

During the 1980s, before the technique of vitrification was developed, the emphasis was already moving towards neuropreservation, that is, brain-only preservation. Proponents of brain preservation argue that the information contained in the structure of the brain, on which memory and personal identity is stored, is the most important element of the body. The development of DNA cloning and embryonic stem cell technology means, according to neuropreservation's proponents, that a new body could eventually be grown. Any damage caused by freezing, they argue, could be repaired in the future by nanotechnology techniques which would enable the manipulation of matter at a molecular level.

The idea of a head transplant for a cryonics patient might seem like something from the realms of the most far-fetched science fiction; however, in the 1970s Dr Robert J. White, professor of neurosurgery at Case Western Reserve University School of Medicine, transplanted the head of one rhesus monkey onto the trunk of another. Dr White was a pioneer of extracorporeal perfusion, a technique of isolating and cooling the brain in a such a way as to keep it viable, without any circulation, for as long as an hour before bringing it back to life. Using this technique, he surgically attached the head of one monkey to body of another (and thereafter saw his name inextricably coupled in the media with that of Victor Frankenstein). His results were undeniably impressive: when the monkey with the transplanted head opened its eyes, it tried to bite the hand of one of its doctors. Alas, though the operation was a success, the patient died soon afterwards. Dr White retired in 1998, but he has since predicted that the first human head transplant could be only decades hence.[144]

All of this sounds wonderful, but it generates the question of whether it is ethical to remove the head of the host body once it has grown to a suitable size, in order to attach the 'old' one. Cryonics is seldom untouched by controversy or ethical issues. Two early organizations went bankrupt, resulting in the thawing of cryonically preserved bodies. Cellular damage was so bad when the 'patients' (as they were called) thawed out that it became woefully apparent that much more research was needed. Then in 1988 the Alcor Life Extension Foundation, one of the largest cryonic companies, was accused of murdering eighty-three-year-old Dora Kent with barbiturates. The company insisted the barbiturates were administered after death to reduce cerebral metabolic demands during poor tissue perfusion. In the end, no charges were filed, but Alcor was forced to obtain a Temporary Restraining Order to keep the patients from being defrosted while the California police searched the premises.

More recently came the court case regarding the cryonic preservation of Ted Williams, 'The Splendid Splinter', who died at the age of eighty-three in July 2002. One of the greatest baseball players of all time, Williams played nineteen seasons with the Boston Red Sox between 1939 and 1960 (with three years in the United States Marine Corps during the Second World War). John Henry Williams, his son from his third wife, secretly flew Williams's body by private jet to Alcor for preservation; however, his half-sister Bobby-Jo Ferrell took John Henry to court, claiming that her father had wanted to be cremated. She was worried, apparently, that her half-brother was planning to sell Williams's DNA.[145] The case was dropped after the discovery of an informal pact, signed by Williams, John Henry and Williams's other daughter Claudia, stating his wish to be cryonically preserved. In the summer of 2003 *Sports Illustrated* reported the fate of Williams's body at the facilities of the Alcor Life Extension Foundation in Scottsdale, Arizona. His head was shaved, drilled with holes, and then separated from his body (a process euphemistically known as neuroseparation) before being placed in a steel drum that is filled with liquid nitrogen and 'resembles a lobster pot'. His body resides nearby in a nine-foot-tall cylindrical tank likewise filled with liquid nitrogen.[146]

There are at present three other organizations besides Alcor and the Cryonics Institute that will cryonically preserve a dead body, all of them likewise in the United States. Prices vary from $28,000 to $150,000 (Williams's family was given a bill for $136,000) depending on whether the whole body or merely the head is to be suspended. Over one thousand people have been cryonically frozen for future resurrection in the belief that new technology will eventually be so advanced that it will be possible to bring them back to life. Until it is proven that cryonically preserved individuals *can* successfully be brought back from death, this technique will always be dogged by questions and controversy. The thought of being suspended upside-down in liquid nitrogen, waiting thousands of years for technology to catch up, together with the prospect of returning centuries later and being forced to adapt to a world utterly different from our own, makes cryonics appeal only to a minority. It is hard enough for some people to come to grips with using the latest mobile phone or DVD recorder, let alone coping with whatever fiendishly clever technology that our descendants will invent hundreds or thousands of years in the future. On the other hand, if the distant future promises orgasmatrons, a healthy diet of fatty foods and gizmos like the mobile phones that so impressed Mr Grzebski, then perhaps defrosted cryonics patients might manage after all.

THE IMMORTALISTS

Cryonasists are people who want to be brought back to life long after their deaths. But the ultimate alternative ending would be never to die in the first place. The idea of cheating death and living forever is certainly an appealing one. Some people believe that age-related illnesses, and even death itself, might one day become a thing of the past.

In pursuit of this ideal, in 2000 the American entrepreneur John Sperling, then aged seventy-nine, founded the Kronos Longevity Research Institute (KLRI). A billionaire whom Forbes has listed as the 512th richest man in the world, Sperling is no deluded octogenarian Ponce de Léon desperately seeking a fountain of youth. A Cambridge PhD in Economic History, he taught for many years at San Jose State University before making his fortune by founding the University of Phoenix, a for-profit adult education institution. In the 1990s he began providing seed money for life extension and cloning projects (one of his companies was wittily dubbed Genetic Savings & Clone); he made headlines, several years later, over the unsuccessful $19-million attempt of his 'Missyplicity Project' to clone his dog Missy and then the more successful experiment with a feline (named, perhaps inevitably, Copy Cat).

But Sperling's real baby is the Phoenix-based KLRI, a privately funded, non-profit organization that conducts clinical studies into the early detection and prevention of age-related diseases. Studies have examined oestrogen replacement therapy in women, the effectiveness of a cancer-detection test called antimalignin antibody serum, and the effects of testosterone on the progression of atherosclerosis in older men. The goal is to provide what the KLRI calls 'optimal health' while slowing or even reversing the aging process. Sperling does not expect to enjoy the rewards of the studies for which he's signing the cheques. 'It will not help me at eighty-two,' he was quoted as saying in 2004. Nor might it help the rest of us, since he claims it may still take another century of research – and billions of dollars – to conquer death.[147]

Around the time that Sperling founded the KLRI, another entrepreneur was also thinking of ways to vanquish death. Born in 1974, Bruce Klein is more than half a century younger than Sperling but nonetheless shares the same concerns about aging: he claims to be driven by an obsession to 'avoid death and oblivion'. He set up an internet forum to discuss cryonics and life extension, and when the forum rapidly expanded into a network for like-minded 'immortalists' he founded, in 2002, the Immortality Institute. Two years later he edited a book entitled *The Scientific Conquest of Death: Essays on Infinite Lifespans*. Included in the volume are essays by respected scientists and scholars on 'therapeutic cloning', 'cyberimmortality', and 'nanomedicine'. The author of the nanomedicine article, Robert A. Freitas Jr, Senior Research Fellow at the Institute for Molecular Manufacturing in Palo Alto, California, points out that 'natural death' (as opposed to death by accident, war, homicide and suicide) claims tens of millions of people each year. A total of fifty-two million lives worldwide were lost to natural death in the year 2001, underscoring how it is, in Freitas' words, 'the greatest catastrophe that humankind has ever faced'. Deploring the treasure trove of information lost to humanity when these lives are erased, he argues that anything that can prevent these losses, such as nanomedicine – the preservation and improvement of human health by means of molecular knowledge of the human body – should be welcomed. Another of the authors, Dr William Sims Bainbridge, a Harvard University PhD who serves as deputy director for the Division of Information and Intelligent Systems at the National Science Foundation, offers a different means of preserving all of this information. He advocates employing advanced information technology to transfer the contents of a mind 'from an old brain into a freshly cloned one', or even into a robot or an information database.[148]

Klein's Immortality Institute is only one of many such organizations dedicated to increasing lifespans and extending human potentialities through the wonders of genetic engineering, nanotechnology and robotics. Another is the World Transhumanist Association (WTA), co-founded in 1998 by Nick Bostrom, an Oxford University philosopher who is also the Director of Oxford's Future of Humanity Institute. A non-profit organization boasting some fifty chapters and more than four thousand members, the WTA concentrates on ways by which humans can transcend their biological condition through biotechnology and become 'posthuman'. The WTA's 'Transhumanist Declaration', adopted by the membership in 2002, asserts that future technology will radically change humanity such that 'redesigning the human condition' will one day become possible, overcoming 'such parameters as the inevitability of aging, limitations on human and artificial intellects, unchosen psychology, suffering, and our confinement to the planet earth'. Working towards this latter objective, according to a report posted on the WTA's website at the end of 2006, is El Club de los Astronautas, touted as the world's first space agency founded by (perhaps a bit disconcertingly) artists and musicians. A collective based in Barcelona, El Club de los Astronautas promotes the concept of a manned, interstellar flight on a spaceship (yet to be designed) christened *Mare Nostrum*. The members freely admit that they have no training as scientists and engineers but claim to have made 'an effort to understand and digest the complex scientific and technical concepts that may lead to transhumanity'.[149]

These theories are all based on a strong faith in the ability of technology not only to cheat death but also to save and ameliorate humanity by preserving the best in us and jettisoning the worst. But they are also motivated by the age-old fear of death and the longing for eternal life. Eternal life was once offered to a pious humanity by Christianity, which posited a reassembly and resurrection of the body at the Last Judgement. Nowadays extinction and oblivion are to be avoided thanks to exponential increases in technology that will ultimately result, we are told, in software-based humans with fibre-optic spines whose bodies are maintained by nanobots and whose brains are uploaded onto supercomputers.

Even the Christian idea of the Resurrection into Heaven has been given a technological underpinning in Frank J. Tipler's *The Physics of Immortality: Modern Cosmology, God and the Resurrection of the Dead* (1994). Tipler, a professor of mathematical physics, suggests that theology is either nonsense or else a branch of physics. Choosing the latter option, he claims to apply 'the solid results of modern physical science' to the concept of 'an omnipresent, omniscient, omnipotent God who will one day in the far future resurrect every single one of us to live forever in an abode which is in all essentials the Judeo-Christian Heaven'.[150] What follows sounds like the plot of a big-budget science-fiction thriller. In order to avoid extinction

when the sun expands, humans will abandon the earth on spaceships pow-
ered by antimatter engines to colonize other planets with the help of robots
until, 10,000,000,000,000,000,000 (i.e. ten billion billion) years hence, the
entire universe is populated. This interstellar overcrowding will be a good
thing. By the time the universe contracts (the opposite of the Big Bang,
known as the Big Crunch) there will be enough computing power and technical know-how for us to take charge of our own cosmic destiny, and to
bring back to life – albeit inside computers – everyone who has ever lived.
Dr Tipler makes an appealing promise to his readers. If any of them has lost
a loved one, he writes, modern physics tell us: 'Be comforted, you and they
shall live again.'[151] The only catch is that we must wait ten billion billion
years for our reunion in cyberheaven.

   All of this posthuman activity raises the question of whether the war on
death is one worth waging in the first place. Certainly the KLRI's investigation of age-related illnesses and its commitment to 'optimal health' is a
salutary continuation of the medical advances that over the past 150 years
have advanced life expectancies (in the industrialized world, at least) from
the mid-forties to the mid-seventies. But it is a rather bigger leap from
an allotted three-score-years-and-ten to 'superlongevity' and physical
immortality. 'Deathists', as the immortalists label their opponents, argue
that the fear of death and dying actually gives meaning to human life. It is
certainly worthwhile contemplating what might happen if the wish for
bodily immortality was ever fulfilled. If the yearning for life in perpetuity
makes the world go round, would there still be a force within us to impel
love and maintain the life of the world once we achieve it? Or would all
of these things wither away as we assumed our place on the sunlounger of
infinite history?

   Literature provides many examples of the be-careful-what-you-wish-
for variety, none more graphic, perhaps, than that of the Cumaean Sibyl. In
Metamorphoses Ovid tells of how the Sibyl asked Apollo to live as many
years as she could hold grains of sand in her hand: 'He granted me the years,
/And promised me endless youth if he could have me, /But I refused
Apollo' – and so Apollo, in turn, refused to grant her endless youth. The
result of her superlongevity (she is said to have lived a thousand years) was
that she eventually shrivelled away into an ugly and ailing crone. In the

Satyricon of Petronius she is described as hanging in a bottle at Cumae, where she is taunted by the local youths. When they ask her what she desires, her poignant reply is that she wants to die.[152]

Superlongevity has equally unpleasant consequences for Marcus Flaminius Rufus, the protagonist of Jorge Luis Borges's short story 'The Immortal'. Born in the second half of the third century, in the reign of the Emperor Diocletian, Rufus departs on a costly and arduous expedition to discover a mythical river that cleanses men of death and grants them citizenship in the City of Immortals. He ultimately discovers the river, a mere 'rivulet of sandy water', and finds himself in the company of cave-dwelling primitives whom he calls troglodytes, a band of 'naked, grey-skinned, scraggly bearded men' who are seemingly devoid of speech, intellect or compassion. He soon realizes that these abysmal creatures are actually his fellow immortals, and that the City of Immortals, far from being a magical utopia, is a hare-brained architectural confusion of dead-ends, purposeless windows and inverted staircases. Immortality has removed from the troglodytes what Dostoevsky calls the 'living force maintaining the life of the world'. Rufus's only hope is to discover – as he finally does after almost two thousand years – a river that will remove this curse of immortality. By the time he dies in a shipwreck in 1929, he has learned the wisdom of what the Roman philosophers whom he consulted told him at the outset of his journey: that 'to extend man's life is to extend his agony and multiply his deaths'.[153]

Knowledge of our impending death, it could be argued, makes our experiences of life more beautiful and revelatory. A particularly acute insight into how death gives a keen edge to life comes from the British playwright Dennis Potter. In February 1994 Potter was diagnosed with terminal liver and pancreatic cancer. A few weeks later, he was interviewed by Melvyn Bragg for Channel Four's *Without Walls*. His performance was a masterclass in courage, dignity, humour and insight. Puffing on a cigarette and sipping morphine, he began by describing how the sight of the plum tree blossoming outside his window – 'the whitest, frothiest, blossomiest blossom that there ever could be' – was made even more heartbreakingly beautiful by the prospect of his hastening demise (and in fact he died three months later). He claimed that the 'nowness of everything', what he called seeing 'in the present tense', was not only wonderful but also impossible to communicate to anyone who was not facing imminent death.[154] If the transhumanists, like Borges's troglodytes, are blind to such beauties and denied such insights, then the price of immortality, some might argue, will surely be a very steep one.

To conquer death would be to do away with much of what has created our culture and made us who we are. It may well be true, as the immortalists say, that each year natural death robs the world of upwards of fifty million pieces of human treasure. But death has also bestowed much in return. It has shaped religious beliefs, works of art, architectural styles, philosophical systems and scientific advances, as well as given us holidays, customs and superstitions. The land of death has always been the place of our deepest fears and obsessions. To make us exiles from this last great *terra incognita* would surely be to make us, not more, but less human.

Notes

1. Quoted in Richard Sugg, '"Good Physic but Bad Food": Early Modern Attitudes to Medicinal Cannibalism and Its Suppliers', p. 230.
2. Quoted in ibid., p. 228.
3. *Mark Twain's Letters*, vol. 4, p. 472.
4. Richard Colwill, 'Funeral Costs Surge by 61%', *The Times*, 18 January 2006.
5. National Funeral Directors Association, www.nfda.org.
6. Robin Maugham, *Somerset and all the Maughams*, p. 212.
7. www.monochrom.at/experiences/alive.htm.
8. Quoted in William Tebb and Colonel Edward PerryVollum, *Premature Burial and How It Can Be Prevented.* The original source is recorded in the anonymous pamphlet, *News from Basing-stoak* (1674).
9. Stacy V. Jones, *Inventions Necessity is not the Mother of : Patents Ridiculous and Sublime*, pp. 124–7.
10. *La Stampa*, 8 October 2004.
11. Jean-Yves Péron-Autret, *Buried Alive,* pp. 114–15.
12. Ibid., p.13.
13. 'The Number U are Calling Knows Ur Waiting . . .', http://news.bbc.co.uk/go/pr/fr/-2/hi/uk_news/northern_ireland/4417760.stm, 11 September 2005.
14. Personal communication from Peter Mitchell, November 2005.
15. Dr Von Rösser published his findings in *Sach's Medizinische Jahrbücher* of 1858.

16. Jan Bondeson, *Buried Alive: The Terrifying History of Our Most Primal Fear*, pp. 244–5.

17. A. van Hasselt, *Die Lehre vom Tode und Scheintode* (Brunswick, 1862).

18. Ibid., pp. 65–6.

19. David E. Oldach, 'A Mysterious Death', *New England Journal of Medicine*, 338, 1998, pp.1764–9.

20. Anthony J. Carter, 'Narcosis and Nightshade', *British Medical Journal*, 1996, http://bmj.bmjjournals.com/archive/7072ad4.htm.

21. Quoted in Bondeson, *Buried Alive: The Terrifying History of Our Most Primal Fear*, p. 53.

22. Ibid., pp. 138–9.

23. Antoine Louis, *Lettres sur la Certitude des Signes de la Mort* (Paris, 1752), pp. 153–6.

24. Jules Antoine Josat, *De la Mort et de Ses Caractères* (Paris, 1854).

25. Cited in Péron-Autret, *Buried Alive*, p. 16.

26. Rodney Davies, *Buried Alive: Horrors of the Undead*, pp. 201–2.

27. Paul Valley, 'So They Think You Are Dead . . . But Are You?', *Independent*, 9 January 1996.

28. William Tebb *et al.*, *Premature Burial and How It Can Be Prevented*, p. 275.

29. Ruth Gledhill, 'Move House . . . But Thou Shalt Not Take Thy Dead Relatives', *The Times*, 2 December 2006.

30. Charles Dickens, *A Tale of Two Cities* (London: Penguin Popular Classics, 2005), pp. 155–6.

31. For a history of dissection, see Elizabeth Brown, 'Death and the Human Body in the Later Middle Ages', and A.M. Lassek, *Human Dissection: Its Drama and Struggle*.

32. F. Darwin (ed.), *Charles Darwin; His Life Told in an Autobiographical Chapter, and in a Selected Series of his Published Letters* (London: 1892).

33. Cited in H. Cole, *Things for a Surgeon: A History of the Resurrection Men*, p. 83.

34. Ruth Richardson, *Death, Dissection and the Destitute*, p. 247.

35. http://wcco.com/topstories/local_story_248175226.html.

36. www.thestate.com/mld/thestate/news/breaking_news/15907763.htm.

37. Niccolò Machiavelli, *The History of Florence*, Book VIII, Chapter ix.

38. Paul Barber, *Vampires, Burial, and Death: Folklore and Reality*, pp. 3–9.

39. G. Elliot Smith *et al.*, *Egyptian Mummies*, p. 88.

40. See E.O. Gordon, *The Life and Correspondence of William Buckland, D.D., F.R.S.* (London: John Murray, 1894), pp. 94–6.

41. Andrew Bushe, 'Saint's Relics Tour Reaches Fever Pitch', *Sunday Mirror*, 1 July

2001; Manny Fernandez, 'Before the Heart of a Saint, Prayers of Strength and Grace', *New York Times*, 8 October 2006; 'Relics of Spanish Civil War Martyrs Sent to Over Thirty Countries', Catholic News Agency, 13 March 2006: www.catholicnewsagency.com/new.php?n=6216.

42. Chris Ayres, 'Funeral directors "sold corpses for cash"', *The Times*, 6 October 2007.

43. Stephanie Armour, 'Illegal Trade in Bodies Shakes Loved Ones', *USA Today*, 27 April 2006.

44. 'Organs Seized from Inmates for Sale in China', *St Louis Post-Dispatch*, 22 August 2006; 'China's Bloody Harvest', *National Post* (Canada), 23 August 2006; and the website of the CIPFG: http://cipfg.org/en/index.php?news=217.

45. Ian Cobain and Adam Luck, 'The Beauty Products From the Skin of Executed Chinese Prisoners', *Guardian*, 13 September 2005.

46. New Zealand Dermatological Society Incorporated: www.dermnetnz.org/procedures/collagen.html.

47. Peter Cooper, 'Medicinal Properties of Body Parts', *Pharmaceutical Journal*, 273, 18/25 December 2004, pp. 900–1.

48. Ibid., p. 902.

49. Sugg, '"Good Physic but Bad Food"', p. 230.

50. A. Paré, *Works* (London: T. Coles & R. Young, 1634), p. 448.

51. Quoted in Rupert Christiansen, *Tales of the New Babylon* (London: Sinclair-Stevenson,1995), pp.182–3.

52. Personal communication from Sally Woodcock, Department of Art History, University College, London, August 2005.

53. Georgiana Burne-Jones, *Memorials of Edward Burne-Jones*, vol. 2 (London: 1904), p. 114.

54. F. Ferback, *Die Oelmalerei, Lehr- und Handbuch für Künstlerund Kunstfreunde* (1843), p. 145.

55. George Keate, *An Epistle to Angelica Kauffman* (London: 1781), pp. 26–8.

56. Roberta Gilchrist, 'Requiem for a Lost Age', *British Archaeology*, 84, September–October 2005, p. 31.

57. The Musée Fragonard can be found at the École Nationale Veterinaire D'Alfort, 7 Avenue du Général de Gaulle, 94704 Maisons-Alfort, Paris, France.

58. www.bodyworlds.com.

59. Roger Boyes, 'Poles Reject Dr Death's Display Over Nazi Links', *The Times*, 2 March 2005.

60. Michael J. Harner, *The Kivaro: People of the Sacred Waterfalls*.

61. 'Should Shrunken Heads Stay in Museum?' *Oxford Times*, 14 February 2007.

62. 'Artist Pledges to Leave Own Shrunken Head to Museum', *Oxford Times*, 24 May 2007.

63. Luca Landucci, *A Florentine Diary from 1450 to 1516*, ed. Iodoco del Badia, trans. Alice de Rosen Jervis (London: J.M. Dent, 1927), p. 186.

64. Cited in Christine Quigley, *Modern Mummies: The Preservation of the Human Body in the Twentieth Century.*

65. Ibid.

66. Brown, 'Death and the Human Body in the Later Middle Ages', pp. 221–70.

67. *Formaldehyde: A Brief History of Its Contributions to Society and the U.S. Economy* (Arlington, VA: Formaldehyde Council, Inc., 2005), available online at www.formaldehyde.org.

68. Personal communication from Karen Caney, September 2005.

69. Jessica Mitford, *The American Way of Death Revisited*.

70. Personal communication from Peter Mitchell, November 2005.

71. R.C. Turner and R.G. Scaife, *Bog Bodies: New Discoveries and New Perspectives.*

72. *Mystery of the Tibetan Mummy*, 2005, TV documentary produced by Atlantic Productions in association with LA 7.

73. Jean-Antoine Dubois, *Hindu Manners, Customs, and Ceremonies* (Phoenix, AZ: Simon Publications, 2001), p. 353.

74. Jill Neimark, 'Body and Soil', *Science and Spirit*, January–February 2002.

75. Kate Connolly, 'Big Freeze an Alternative to Cremation', *Daily Telegraph*, 30 September 2005.

76. Frank Ahrens, 'Up in Smoke for 24 Dearly Departed, a Rocket Trip Around the World', *Washington Post*, 3 March 1997.

77. Personal communication from Philip Pullman, March 2007.

78. Quoted in 'Pilot Drops Human Ashes on Mariners' Stadium', CNN.com, 24 May 2002, http://archives.cnn.com/2002/US/05/24/seattle.cremains/index.html.

79. Personal communication from Julian Atkinson, April 2007.

80. Guy Trebay, 'For a Price, Final Resting Places That Even Tut Could Appreciate', *New York Times*, 17 April 2006, and www.trulia.com/real_estate/Daytona_Beach-Florida.

81. Claire Davis, 'Downfall of the Devil's Dandy', *Camden New Journal*, 20 February 2003.

82. *Daily Telegraph*, 4 April 2006.

83. James W. Dow, 'Cannibalism', in *Encyclopedia of Latin American History and Culture*, vol. 1, ed. Barbara A. Tenenbaum *et al.* (New York: Charles Scribner's Sons, 1996), pp. 535–7.

84. Quoted in Beth A. Conklin, *Consuming Grief*, p. xv.

85. 'Cannibal Trial Scientist Turns the Ultimate Video Nasty into a Book', *The Times*, 18 September 2007.

86. Interview with Tanith Carey for the official website for the TV show *Dallas*, http://ultimatedallas.com/news/larryhealth.htm.

87. www.theage.com.au.

88. Tom Burke, 'Mae West to Appear Opposite Six Leading Men', *New York Times*, 25 July 1976.

89. Bath & Wells, Birmingham, Chelmsford, Chichester, Ely, Exeter, Gloucester, Hereford, Leicester, Lichfield, London, Norwich, Oxford, Peterborough, Rochester, St Albans, St Edmundsbury & Ipswich, Sheffield, Truro, Wakefield, Winchester and Worcester.

90. Pamphlet published by the Guild of All Saints, St Katharine Cree Church, London.

91. J. Aubrey, *Remaines of Gentilisme and Judaisme (1686–7)*, ed. James Britten (London: The Folklore Society, 1880), p. 35.

92. Wirt Sikes, *British Goblins* (Boston: Osgood, 1881), pp. 322–4.

93. *Jewish Encyclopedia* (vol. 4) article on 'Folklore'.

94. Sydney Oldall Addy, *Household Tales and Other Traditional Remains* (London, 1895), pp. 123–4.

95. www.archeona.arti.beniculturali.it/sanc_en/mann/it11/02.html.

96. Graham Coleman, ed., *The Tibetan Book of the Dead* (London: Penguin Classics, 2005).

97. For a history of the facility, see Bill Bass and Jon Jefferson, *Death's Acre: Inside the Legendary 'Body Farm'*.

98. Ibid., pp.110–11.

99. *Shakespeare's Plutarch: The Lives of Julius Caesar, Brutus, Marcus Antonius, and Coriolanus in the translation of Sir Thomas North*, ed. T.J. B. Spencer (Harmondsworth: Penguin, 1964), chapter 66.

100. Sung Tz'u, *The Washing Away of Wrongs: Forensic Medicine in Thirteenth-Century China*, p. 148.

101. www.forensicentomologist.org/case_studies/case_study_06.html.

102. *Time*, 24 June 1985.

103. Quoted in ibid.

104. John Noble Wilford, 'Identifying Bodies: Using Dental Evidence', *New York Times*, 8 June 1985.

105. Gian Luca Marella *et al.*, 'An Approach to Person Identification by means of Dental Prostheses in a Burnt Corpse', *Journal of Forensic Odontostomatology*, 17(1), June 1999, pp. 16–19.

106. Paul Rincon, 'Teeth Unravel Anglo-Saxon Legacy', BBC News, Science/ Nature, 17 March 2004, www.news.bbc.co.uk/1/low/sci/tech/3514756.stm.

107. W. His, 'Anatomische Forschungen ueber Johann Sebastian Bach's Gebeine und Antilitz nebst Bemerkungen ueber Dessen Bilder', 'Abhandlungen der Mathemtisch Physikalischen Kiasse der Konigi', *Sachsischen Gesellschaft der Wissenschaften*, 22, 1895.   ˙

108. J.S. Rhine, and H.R. Campbell, 'Thickness of Facial Tissue in American Blacks', *Journal of Forensic Sciences*, 25, 4, 1970, pp. 847–58; J.S Rhine and C.E. More, *Facial Reproduction Tables of Facial Tissue Thickness of American Caucasoids in Forensic Anthropology* (Albuquerque: Maxwell Museum Technical Series no. 1, 1970).

109. R.A.H. Neave, 'The Skull from Tomb II at Vergina: King Philip II of Macedon', *Journal of Hellenic Studies*, 104, 1984, pp. 60–78; and idem., 'Reconstruction of the skull and the soft tissues of the head and face of Lindow Man', *Canadian Society of Forensic Science Journal*, 22, 1989, pp. 43–53.

110. Alessio Ricci, Gian Luca Marella, Mario Alexandru Apostol, 'A New Experimental Approach to Computer-Aided Face/Skull Identification in Forensic Anthropology', *American Journal of Forensic Medicine & Pathology*, 27, March 2006, pp. 46–9.

111. 'Forensic Technique Animates Faces of the Dead', *New Scientist*, 29 October–4 November 2003.

112. www.assemblage.group.shef.ac.uk/1/evison.html.

113. Maureen Paton, 'The Crime of Her Life', *Guardian*, 10 January 2005.

114. Gustave F. Kilthau, 'Cancer Risk in Relation to Radioactivity in Tobacco', *Radiologic Technology*, 67, pp. 217–22; and Ashraf E.M. Khater and Hamed A.I. Al-Sewaidan, 'Polonium-210 in Cigarette Tobacco', *International Journal of Low Radiation*, 3, nos. 2/3, 2006, pp. 224–33.

115. James R. Gill, '9/11 and the New York City Office of Chief Medical Examiner', *Forensic Science, Medicine, and Pathology*, 2, March 2006.

116. Tim Reid, '201 Wrongful Convictions Are Tip of the Iceberg, says DNA Charity', *The Times*, 23 May 2007.

117. A. Ribeiro dos Santos *et al.*, 'Heterogeneity of Mitochrondrial DNA Haplotypes in pre-Columbian Natives of the Amazon Region', *American Journal of Physical Anthropology*, 101, 1996, pp. 29–37. On the Srebrenica victims, see Laurie Vollen, 'All That Remains: Identifying the Victims of the Srebrenica Massacre', *Cambridge Quarterly of Healthcare Ethics*, 10, 2001, pp. 336–40.

118. Quoted in Michael Ardagh, 'A Brief History of Resuscitation', *New Zealand Medical Journal*, 117, 7 May 2004.

119. Paul Collins, 'George Poe's Cure for Death', *New Scientist*, 13 January 2007.

120. Quoted in ibid.

121. S.J. Youngner *et al.*, *The Definition of Death: Contemporary Controversies*, p. 53.

122. Eelco F.M. Wijdicks, 'The Diagnosis of Brain Death', *New England Journal of Medicine*, 16, 2001, pp. 1215–21.

123. H.J. Gramm *et al.*, 'Acute Endocrine Failure After Brain Death', *Transplantation*, 54, 1992, pp. 851–7.

124. Madeline J. Grigg *et al.*, 'Electroencephalographic Activity After Brain Death', *Archives of Neurology*, 44, 1987, pp. 948–54; A. Earl Walker, *Cerebral Death*, 2nd edition (Baltimore: Urban & Schwarzenberg, 1981), pp. 89–90; Christopher Pallis, 'ABC of Brain Stem Death: The Arguments about the EEG', *British Medical Journal*, 286, 1983, pp. 284–7.

125. Randall C. Wetzel *et al.*, 'Haemodynamic Responses to Surgery in Brain Dead Organ Donor Patients', *Anaesthesia and Analgesia*, 64, 1985, pp. 125–8; S.H. Pennefather *et al.*, 'Haemodynamic Responses to Surgery in Brain Dead Organ Donors', *Anaesthesia*, 48, 1993, pp. 1034–8; D.J. Hill *et al.*, 'Haemodynamic Responses to Surgery in Brain Dead Organ Donors', *Anaesthesia*, 49, 1994, pp. 835–6.

126. D. Wainwright-Evans, 'The Ethics of Cardiac Transplantation', *British Journal of Hospital Medicine*, July 1986, pp. 68–9.

127. C.G. Coimbra, 'Implications of Ischemic Penumbra for the Diagnosis of Brain Death', *Brazilian Journal of Medical Biological Research*, 32, 1999, pp. 1479–87.

128. Stuart J. Youngner *et al.*, 'Brain Death and Organ Retrieval: A Cross-Sectional Survey of Knowledge and Concepts among Health Professionals', *JAMA*, 261, 1989, pp. 2205–10.

129. For the place of organ transplantation technology in popular culture, see Robert D. O'Neill, '"Frankenstein to Futurism": Representations of Organ Donation and Transplantation in Popular Culture', *Transplantation Reviews*, 20(4), October 2006, pp. 222–30.

130. Carl Grey,'*Twice Dead: Organ Transplants and the Reinvention of Death* by Margaret Lock (review)', *British Medical Journal*, 324, June 2002, p. 1401.

131. http://news.bbc.co.uk/1/hi/health/6164716.stm.

132. K. Andrews *et al.*, 'Misdiagnosis of the Vegetative State: Retrospective Study in a Rehabilitation Unit', *British Medical Journal*, 313, 1996, pp.13–16; N.L

Childs *et al.*, 'Accuracy of Diagnosis of Persistent Vegetative State', *Neurology*, 43, 1993, pp.1465–7.

133. Derick Wade and Claire Johnston, 'The Permanent Vegetative State: Practical Guidance on Diagnosis and Management', *British Medical Journal*, 319, 1999, pp.841–4.

134. 'Pole Wakes up from 19-Year Coma', BBC News, 2 June 2007, http://news.bbc.co.uk/1/hi/world/europe/6715313.stm.

135. 'Diane Pretty Dies', BBC News, 12 May 2002, http://news.bbc.co.uk/1/hi/health/1983457.stm.

136. www.ves.org.uk.

137. Francis Watson, 'The Death of George V', *History Today*, 36, 1986, pp. 21–30; and J.H.R. Ramsay, 'A King, a Doctor, and a Convenient Death', *British Medical Journal*, 308, 28 May 1994, p. 1445.

138. Danielle Gourevitch, 'Suicide Among the Sick in Classical Antiquity', *Bulletin of the History of Medicine*, 43, 1969, pp. 501–18.

139. Quoted in Emile Durkheim, *Suicide: A Study in Sociology*, trans. George Simpson (New York: Free Press, 1997).

140. Peter J. Colosi, 'What's Love Got to Do with It? The Ethical Contradictions of Peter Singer', www.godspy.com/issues/WHATS-LOVE-GOT-TO-DO-WITH-IT-THE-ETHICAL-CONTRADICTIONS-of-Peter-Singer-by-Dr-Peter-J-Colosi.cfm.

141. Laura Spinney, 'Last Rights', *New Scientist*, 23 April 2005, p. 48.

142. Sarah-Kate Templeton, 'Brain Disease Man in Fight for Right to be Fed', *Sunday Times*, 14 May 2005.

143. www.cryonics.org.

144. Malcolm W. Browne, 'From Science Fiction to Science: "The Whole Body Transplant"', *New York Times*, 5 May 1998; and 'Frankenstein Fears after Head Transplant', BBC News, 6 April 2001, http://news.bbc.co.uk/1hi/health/1263758.stm.

145. Matt Donnelly, 'Would Freezing Ted Williams Really Work?', ABC News, 9 July 2003, http://abcnews.go.com/US/story?id=91481&page=1.

146. 'What Happened to Ted?' *Sports Illustrated*, 12 August 2003.

147. Brian Alexander, 'John Sperling Wants You to Live Forever, and He's Promising $3 Billion to Make it So', *Wired*, February 2004. See also S.M. Harman, 'The Kronos Longevity Research Institute', *Experimental Geronotology*, 38, May 2003, pp. 483–7; and the website of the Kronos Longevity Research Institute: www.kronosinstitute.org.

148. Robert A. Freitas, Jr, 'Nanomedicine', in Bruce J. Klein, ed., *The Scientific*

Conquest of Death: Essays on Infinite Lifespans (The Immortality Institute, 2004), pp. 77–92; and William Sims Bainbridge, 'Progress towards Cyberimmortality', in ibid., pp. 107–22. PDF downloadable and HTML online-searchable versions of *The Scientific Conquest of Death* are available from the website of the Immortality Institute: www.imminst.org/book1.

149. www.transhumanism.org/index.php/WTA/more/1254. Probably the most articulate exponent of transhumanism is the renowned engineer and inventor Ray Kurzweil. For his discussions of the subject, see *The Age of Spiritual Machines*; *Fantastic Voyage* (with Terry Grossman); and *The Singularity Is Near*.

150. Tipler, *The Physics of Immortality*, p. 1.

151. Ibid.

152. *Metamorphoses*, trans. Rolfe Humphries (Bloomington: Indiana University Press, 1955), book xiv, lines 140–2; *Satyricon*, trans. Alfred R. Allinson (New York: Panurge Press, 1930), chapter 7, section 48.

153. 'The Immortal', in *Labyrinths: Selected Stories and Other Writings*, ed. Donald A. Yates and James E. Irby (Harmondsworth, Middlesex: Penguin, 1970), pp. 135–49.

154. Dennis Potter, *Seeing the Blossom: Two Interviews and a Lecture* (London: Faber & Faber, 1994), p. 5.

Select Bibliography

Appleyard, Bryan, *How to Live Forever or Die Trying*. Bath: Simon & Schuster, 2007

Ariès, Philippe, *Western Attitudes Toward Death from the Middle Ages to the Present*. London: Marion Boyars Publishers Ltd, 1994

Bailey, James Blake, *The Diary of a Resurrectionist, 1811–1812*. London: Swan Sonnenschein & Co, 1896

Barber, Paul, *Vampires, Burial, and Death: Folklore and Reality*. New York: Vail-Ballou Press, 1988

Barley, Nigel, *Grave Matters: A Lively History of Death Around the World*. New York: Henry Holt & Company, Inc, 1997

Bass, Bill, and Jon Jefferson, *Death's Acre: Inside the Legendary 'Body Farm'*. London: Time Warner, 2003

Berridge, Kate, *Vigor Mortis*. London: Profile Books, 2002

Binski, Paul, *Medieval Death*. London: The British Museum Press, 1996

Bondeson, Jan, *Buried Alive: The Terrifying History of Our Most Primal Fear*. New York: W.W. Norton & Co, 2002

Brown, Elizabeth A.R., 'Death and the Human Body in the Later Middle Ages: The Legislation of Boniface VIII on the Division of the Corpse', *Viator* 12, 1981, pp. 221–70

Bryson, Bill, *A Short History of Nearly Everything*. London: Black Swan, 2004

Cole, H., *Things for a Surgeon: A History of the Resurrection Men*. London: William Heinemann, 1964

Conklin, Beth A., *Consuming Grief: Compassionate Cannibalism in an Amazonian Society*. Austin: University of Texas Press, 2001

Cooper, Diana and Norman Battershill, *Victorian Sentimental Jewellery*. Newton Abbot: David and Charles Publishers, 1972

Cooper, Peter, 'Medicinal Properties of Body Parts', *The Pharmaceutical Journal* 273, December 2004, pp. 900–2

Curl, James Stevens, *The Victorian Celebration of Death*. Gloucestershire: Sutton Publishing Ltd, 2001

Dalai Lama, *Advice on Dying and Living a Better Life*. London: Rider, 2002

Davies, Rodney, *Buried Alive: Horrors of the Undead*. London: Robert Hale, 1999

Dixon Mann, J., *Forensic Medicine and Toxicology*. London: Charles Griffin & Company, Limited, 1893

Dowbiggen, Ian, *A Concise History of Euthanasia: Life, Death, God and Medicine*. Maryland: Rowan & Littlefield Publishers, Inc, 2005

Enright, D.J., *The Oxford Book of Death*. Oxford: Oxford University Press, 1983

Folklore, Myths and Legends of Britain. London: Reader's Digest Association Limited, 1973

Garrett, Geoffrey, and Andrew Nott, *Cause of Death: Memoirs of a Home Office Pathologist*. London: Constable Publishers, 2001

Harding, Vanessa, *The Dead and the Living in Paris and London, 1500–1670*. Cambridge: Cambridge University Press, 2002

Harner, Michael J., *The Kivaro: People of the Sacred Waterfalls*. Berkeley: University of California Press, 1984

Hastier, Richard, *Dead Men Tell Tales: A Survey of Exhumations from Earliest Antiquity to the Present Day*. London: John Long Ltd, 1935

Jallard, Patricia, *Death in the Victorian Family*. Oxford: Oxford University Press, 1999

Jones, Stacy V., *Inventions Necessity is not the Mother of: Patents Ridiculous and Sublime*. New York: Quandrangle/The New York Times Book Co., 1973

Jupp, Peter C. and Glennys Howarth, eds, *The Changing Face of Death: Historical Accounts of Death and Disposal*. London: Macmillan Press Ltd, 1997

Kurzweil, Ray, *The Age of Spiritual Machines: When Computers Exceed Human Intelligence*. New York: Penguin, 2000

—— *The Singularity Is Near: When Humans Transcend Biology*. New York: Penguin, 2006

—— and Terry Grossman, *Fantastic Voyage: Live Long Enough to Live Forever*. New York: Rodale, 2004

Lassek, A.M, *Human Dissection: Its Drama and Struggle*. Springfield: Charles C. Thomas Company, 1958

Lerner, Jeffrey C., 'Changes in Attitudes Towards Death: The Widow in Great Britain in the Early Twentieth Century', in Bernard Schoenberg, ed., *Bereavement: Its Psychosocial Aspects*. New York: Columbia University Press, 1975

Lewis, C.S., *A Grief Observed*. New York: HarperCollins, 2001

Litten, Julian, *The English Way of Death: The Common Funeral Since 1450*. London: Robert Hale, 2002

Lutz, Tom, *Crying: The Natural and Cultural History of Tears*. London: W.W. Norton & Company, 1999

Mackay, Charles, *Extraordinary Popular Delusions and the Madness of Crowds*. Hertfordshire: Wordsworth Editions, 1995

Maugham, Robin, *Somerset and all the Maughams*. London: Longmans, 1966

Mitford, Jessica, *The American Way of Death Revisited*. London: Virago Press, 2000

Moores Ball, James, *The Sack-'Em-Up Men: An Account of the Rise and Fall of the Modern Resurrectionists*. Edinburgh: Oliver and Boyd, 1928

Morely, John, *Death, Heaven and the Victorians*. London: Studio Vista, 1971

Morris, Sir Peter, *Transplants: Ethical Eye*. Germany: Council of Europe Publishing, 2003

Murphy, Edwin, *After the Funeral: The Posthumous Adventures of Famous Corpses*. New York: Barnes & Noble Books, 1995

Nass, Herbert E., *Wills of the Rich & Famous*. New York: Gramercy Books, 2000

Oeh, Karen, 'Putting a Face on Prehistory: The Facial Reconstruction of Two Native American Crania' (http://traumwerk.stanford.edu:3455/31/347)

Palmer, Greg, *Death: The Trip of a Lifetime*. New York: HarperCollins Publishers, 1993

Pan American Health Organization, *Management of Dead Bodies in Disaster Situations: Disaster Manuals and Guidelines Series No. 5*. Washington, DC: PAHO, 2004

Pepper, Ian K., *Crime Scene Investigation: Methods and Procedures*. Berkshire: Open University Press, 2005

Péron-Autret, Jean-Yves, *Buried Alive*. London: Corgi Books, 1983

Poe, Edgar Allan, *Tales of Mystery and Imagination*. London: Orion Publishing Group, 1993

Pringle, Heather, *The Mummy Congress: Science, Obsession and the Everlasting Dead*. London: Fourth Estate, 2002

Quigley, Christine, *Modern Mummies: The Preservation of the Human Body in the Twentieth Century*. Jefferson, North Carolina: McFarland & Co, 1998

Richardson, Ruth, *Death, Dissection and the Destitute*. London: Routledge & Kegan Paul, 1987

Sachs, Jessica Snyder, *Corpse: Nature, Forensics and the Struggle to Pinpoint Time of Death*. Cambridge, MA: Perseus Publishing, 2001

Simpson, Jacqueline, and Steve Roud, *A Dictionary of English Folklore*. Oxford: Oxford University Press, 2000

Smith, G. Elliot *et al.*, *Egyptian Mummies*. London: George Allen & Unwin, 1924

Steinbock, Bonnie, ed., *Killing and Letting Die*. New York: Fordham University Press, 1994

Sugg, Richard, '"Good Physic but Bad Food": Early Modern Attitudes to Medicinal Cannibalism and Its Suppliers', *Social History of Medicine* 19 (2006), pp. 225–40

Tebb, William, and Colonel Edward Perry Vollum, *Premature Burial and How It Can Be Prevented*. London: Swan Sonnenschein & Co, 1897

Timmerans, Stephan, *Post-Mortem: How Medical Examiners Explain Suspicious Deaths*. Chicago: University of Chicago Press, 2006

Tipler, Frank J., *The Physics of Immortality: Modern Cosmology, God and the Resurrection of the Dead*. New York: Doubleday, 1994

Turner, R.C. and R.G. Scaife, *Bog Bodies: New Discoveries and New Perspectives*. London: British Museum Press, 1995

Twain, Mark, *Mark Twain's Letters*, 6 vols., ed. Edgar Marquess Branch *et al.* Berkeley, Calif.: University of California Press, 1988–2002

Tz'u Sung, *The Washing Away of Wrongs: Forensic Medicine in Thirteenth-Century China*, trans. Brian McKnight. Ann Arbor: Center for Chinese Studies, University of Michigan, 1981; reprinted by Southern Material Centre, Inc., Taipei, 1982

Vulliamy, C.E., *Immortality: Funerary Rites & Customs*. London: Senate, 1997

Walker, A. Earl, *Cerebral Death*, 2nd edition. Baltimore: Urban & Schwarzenberg, 1981

Waugh, Evelyn, 'Half in Love with Easeful Death', *Tablet*, 18 October 1947

—— *The Loved One: An Anglo-American Tragedy*. London: Penguin Books, 1951

Wilkinson, Alan, 'Changing English Attitudes to Death in the First World War', in Peter C. Jupp and Glennys Howarth, eds, *The Changing Face of Death: Historical Accounts of Death and Disposal*. London: Macmillan Press, 1997

Woodcock, Sally, 'Body Colour: The Misuse of Mummy', *The Conservator*, 20, September 1996, pp. 1–18

Youngner, Stuart *et al.*, eds, *The Definition of Death: Contemporary Controversies*. Baltimore: John Hopkins University Press, 1999

Useful Information

Algordanza: Making human ashes into diamonds – www.algordanza.com

BODY WORLDS: Official Gunther von Hagens website – www.bodyworlds.com

Capuchin's Catacombs, Piazza Cappuccini 1, Palermo, Sicily, Italy. Opening hours:
9–12 noon, 3.30–5.30pm (7.30pm summer)
– members.tripod.com/~Motomon/index-3.html

Celebrity Morgue: Archive of dead celebrities with lurid photos of crime scenes
and death beds – www.CelebrityMorgue.com

Cremation Jewellery – www.cremationkeepsakes.com

The Cryonics Institute – www.cryonics.org

The Darwin Awards: A salute to the improvement of the human genome by
honouring those who remove themselves from it in really stupid ways
– www.darwinawards.com

Death Mask Gallery: Archive of images of death masks
– www.thanatos.net/deathmasks

Dignity in Dying was previously the Voluntary Euthanasia Society
– www.dignityindying.org.uk

Eternal Reefs: Ashes made into concrete reefs to be submerged in the ocean
– www.eternalreefs.com

Experience the Experience of Being Buried Alive
– www.monochrom.at/experiences/alive.htm

Find a death – www.findadeath.com

The Guild of All Souls: Prayers said for the dead
– www.guildofallsouls.org.uk
– www.orthodoxanglican.org/guild/america.html

Heavens Above Fireworks: Ashes incorporated into fireworks
– www.heavensabovefireworks.com

The Immortality Institute (Imminst): Aims to conquer death with the aid of
artificial intelligence – www.imminst.org

The Innocence Project: Exonerating the innocent using DNA analysis
– www.innocenceproject.org

LifeGem: Making human ashes into diamonds – www.lifegem.com

Memorial space flights: Blasting ashes into space – www.memorialspaceflights.com

Musée Fragonard, Ecole Nationale Vétéinaire d'Alfort, Avenue du Général de
Gaulle, 94704 Maisons-Alfort, Paris, France. Opening hours: Tuesday and
Wednesday 2–5pm, Saturday and Sunday 10–5pm (closed August)
– www.vet-alfort.fr/fr/musee/SiteGB/tx4info.htm

Steady Ed's Memorial discs (discs for sale containing the Frisbee inventor Ed
Headrick's ashes) – www.discgolfassoc.com/index-1yearmem.html

Summun: Modern day mummification Egyptian style – www.summum.org

The World Transhumanist Association – www.transhumanism.org

Index